Institutes
and How To Survive Them

Also by Robin Skynner
One Flesh: Separate Persons: Principles of Family and Marital Psychotherapy

With John Cleese
Families and How To Survive Them

Edited by John Schlapobersky
Explorations With Families: Group Analysis and Family Therapy

Institutes
and How To Survive Them
Mental Health Training
and Consultation

Selected papers by
ROBIN SKYNNER

Edited by John R. Schlapobersky

Methuen · London

To all my teachers,
especially Prue

First published in Great Britain 1989
by Methuen London
Michelin House, 81 Fulham Road, London SW3 6RB
This collection © 1989 Robin Skynner
Editor's introduction and notes © 1989 John R. Schlapobersky

Photoset by Rowland Phototypesetting Ltd
Bury St Edmunds, Suffolk
Printed in Great Britain by
Butler and Tanner Ltd, Frome, Somerset

British Library Cataloguing in Publication Data

Skynner, Robin
  Institutes and how to survive them: mental
  health training and consultation
  1. Great Britain. Residential institutions
  for mentally handicapped persons. Inmates.
  Care
  I. Title   II. Schlapobersky, John R.
  362.3′0941

  ISBN 0 413 42360 3

Contents

Contents

Preface

Most of the papers selected and edited for this collection have been published before and due acknowledgements are made on page ix. Where necessary they have been abridged by the editor to avoid duplication, and the author has re-drafted certain passages in the interests of clarity but without substantive changes.

The author has written an introduction to the book and furnished the editor with historical material and a fresh appraisal of his papers, from which a series of brief introductions has been written to each of the twelve chapters in the book. These set the context in which the papers were originally published and explain the author's purposes in writing each of them.

The editor's introduction outlines the scope of Skynner's work, the structure of this book, the relationship it bears to his three previous books and provides a brief professional biography. Each of the papers is concluded with footnotes, and the book is concluded with an appendix giving the author's published work in historical sequence; a comprehensive bibliography; and a subject and author index.

J.R.S.

Acknowledgements

In compiling this book we are indebted to Christopher Falkus, former Chairman of Methuen and to Ann Mansbridge for their guidance and advice, and to the other editorial staff at Methuen, notably to Alex Bennion whose competence and commitment has seen this book and its companion volume, *Explorations With Families: Group Analysis and Family Therapy*, through different stages of development, and to Sarah Hannigan for her attention to the manuscript. And we are grateful to June Ansell for typing the manuscript.

We are grateful to Dr Pat de Maré for the historical information about S. H. Foulkes at Northfield, included in the author's biography. The author has made his personal acknowledgements in his dedication and introduction. I should here like to express my appreciation to my family and to a number of friends and colleagues, who know my gratitude for their assistance, support and understanding during the time-consuming editorial process.

We are also grateful to the following sources for granting permission to publish or re-publish these papers: for the Author's Introduction, to the Chairman of the Supervisors and Trainers Association of Relate (Marriage Guidance); for Chapter 1, 'Group-Analytic Themes in Training and Case-Discussion Groups', the Editor of *Selected Lectures of VIth International Congress of Psychotherapy*; for Chapter 2, 'A Family of Family Casework Agencies', the Editor of the *International Journal of Group Psychotherapy*; for Chapter 3, 'An Experiment in Group Consultation with the Staff of a Comprehensive School', the Editor of *Group Process*; for Chapter 4, 'Child Guidance from Within: Reactions to New Pressures in 1967', the National Association for Mental Health (Mind); for Chapter 5, 'On the Origins of Family Therapy and Developments in its Practice', the Chairman of the Association for Family Therapy'; for Chapter 6, 'An Open-Systems

Approach to Teaching Family Therapy', the Editor of the *Journal of Marital and Family Therapy*; for Chapter 7, 'The Psychotherapy Teacher: Getting Older – Narrowing Down or Opening Out?', the Editor of the *Bulletin of the Royal College of Psychiatrists*; for Chapter 8, 'Marriage and Personal Change', the Director of the Tavistock Institute of Marital Studies; for Chapter 9, 'The Large Group in Training', Dr Lionel Kreege, Editor of The Large Group: Dynamics and Therapy, and Constable and Co; for Chapter 10, 'Make Sure to Feed the Goose that Lays the Golden Eggs: A Discussion on the Myth of Altruism', the Editor of *The Journal of Psychohistory*; for Chapter 11, 'Psychotherapy and Sacred Tradition', Prof J. Needleman, Editor of *On The Way to Self-Knowledge*, and Alfred Knopf; for Chapter 12, 'Institutes and How To Survive Them', the Editor of *Group Analysis*.

We would like to acknowledge the following sources for permitting the use of extracts from these books: Gower Publishing Group for the extract from Gregory Bateson's *Mind and Nature*; Fritjof Capra for permitting the extract from *The Turning Point: Science, Society and The Rising Culture*; Ursula Le Guin for permitting the extract from *The Wizard of Earthsea*; Mrs E. Foulkes for permitting the extract from *Therapeutic Group Analysis*.

J.R.S.

Editor's Introduction

Robin Skynner is a pioneer whose innovations – as a child psychiatrist, family therapist, group analyst, teacher and writer – have helped introduce change to a number of fields. *Institutes and How To Survive Them* brings together his papers on training, consultation and working relations in the helping services. Together they make a major contribution towards the wider applications of psychotherapy in understanding the choices we make about our work, the problems and benefits of team-work and the role of leadership in change and innovation.

Complementing his recent book on the practice of psychotherapy,[1] *Institutes and How To Survive Them* concentrates on the needs of the therapists – to be understood, resourced and rewarded for their work 'if it is to be of the best and of increasing quality'. The training, supervision and consultation which provide this, rest on the recognition that practitioners often have unacknowledged problems related to those of their clients. If unable to face these difficulties, they are liable to use helping relationships defensively to preserve their own feelings of adult competence whilst the clients carry the problems for both parties. Poor professional development, unsuccessful therapy and reflected organisational problems are some of the consequences. But if professionals can 'include themselves in the equation of change' a process of mutual growth and learning ensues, bringing personal benefits to both sides, steadily enhanced professional skills and corresponding creativity and effectiveness in the organisations.

The approach is a practical one underpinned by a working philosophy that Skynner calls 'the philosophy of plenty'. It is not to be found in formal definitions but, rather, in the anecdotes and conversational style which 'convey best its essential simplicity and directness, its stance of involvement and of sharing in the common human condition, as well as its expectation that both therapist and family will learn from each other'.[2] In a lecture to a group of psychotherapy trainers he approached the philosophy of plenty thus:

> Any attempt to change ourselves, or others, through the use of power rather than through understanding inevitably becomes a form of manipulation that diminishes them and . . . diminishes us as well. . . . We get little aid to make us aware of the importance, if our work is to be of the best and of increasing quality, of ensuring that we get personal benefit from it too. It is not a zero sum equation where the less I gain the more there is for others. The more I gain the more there is for them, and vice versa. Similarly, we are a system, and part of a wider system. The more each of us gains the more there is for everyone, for all of us as a group, and then the more there is for each individual here, including me. Can we together find something valuable for us all in the discussion that follows? (p. 132 below)

This appeal stimulated discussion at the lecture and provides a challenging focus for the collection. It is published at a time when our social institutions are under pressure as never before and will be easily accessible to the interested general reader, as the popular success of *Families and How To Survive Them*, written with John Cleese, confirms. Amongst a professional readership it will be of use to those interested in working relations and the management of change – psychotherapists and counsellors, mental health professionals in medicine, nursing, psychology and social work, as well as those in education, pastoral care, management consultation, occupational psychology and industrial relations.

The book is opened by the author's own introduction, a major new paper that takes his work a long way forward in its application to current training and organisational development. The papers are then organised in three sections. The first contains early papers that introduce the group-analytic approach and develop its basic principles for consultative work. The second section contains papers delivered as public lectures on different occasions which, tracing the development of marital and family therapy in Britain through different institutions, extend the basic principles to the work of larger professional systems. The third section contains Skynner's most original work in this field – a series of papers that explore the complementary relationship between personal growth and professional development.

Section One: Developing the Basic Principles: A Group-Analytic Approach to Consultation

There is a revolution taking place in our understanding of social relations and in our treatment of psychological problems which, in my introduction to *Explorations With Families*, I described as it affects therapeutic practice. In the brief opening chapters of this book the same revolution is seen to be at work from the 1960s onwards, profoundly influencing the training of professionals in a number of fields.

'T-Groups' which had been developed in the US at the National Training Laboratories were being applied to working relations in Britain by the Group Relations Training Association and other organisations.[3] One set of psychoanalytic principles, derived from the work of Klein and Bion, were being applied to the work-place by Eliot Jaques[4] and Menzies Lyth[5] who developed a view of how social systems function as forms of defence. Another set of psychoanalytic principles, derived from Caplan,[6] Bowlby and Irvine,[7] and Turquet and Gosling[8] were being developed at the Tavistock Clinic in what was sometimes called mental health consultation. Balint,[9] also based at the Tavistock Clinic, was introducing group consultation with general practitioners to develop their skills and personal resources. And Abercrombie, influenced by Foulkes's group analysis, was introducing group approaches in the basic training of medical and architecture students.[10]

Many of the influences in this climate of innovation were available to Skynner when he began his early consultative work and there are useful references throughout the papers. To this integration of British work he introduced ideas from American group therapists like Slavson,[11] and added a distinctive contribution of his own – the recognition that mental health practitioners can be hindered in their profession by the very motives that draw them to it; and the discovery that they could 'become especially suited to the work they have unconsciously chosen', once they gain 'insight into their initial motivation'.[12] Like Menzies Lyth he describes work-related difficulties as forms of institutional defence but he draws on this understanding of defences, in the way Caplan and Slavson do, to shed light on practitioners' earlier problems. In the approach that emerges the group consultant's role is governed by the same principles as it is in family therapy and group analysis – the primary task is to foster the self-help resources of the group. The nature of the group's activity, though often just as deep and searching, is subtly different to what would be found in therapy because of the initial focus on members' working relations.

Today there is a wide range of such group applications. They are adapted to a variety of specialist needs and referred to variously as staff and sensitivity groups;[13] consultation groups;[14] case-discussion[15] and supervision groups;[16] awareness and experiential groups.[17] Despite major technical differences between these applications, they rely on the group conductor in a similar way; they have in common a focus on practitioners' working relations; and in many cases they share a basic premise – the essence of Skynner's contribution – that through direct exchange with one another in a group, members can resolve defensive aspects of their professional motivation. Skynner was amongst the first to use groups in this way and these lucid, early papers remain unsurpassed in their clarity, providing cornerstones for the developments described in sections two and three.

Section Two: Applications to Larger Systems Leadership and Consultation

Those with training responsibilities of any kind in the human services will find the papers in this section valuable in many ways. They apply the basic principles described above to the functioning of larger professional systems. They were delivered as public lectures to mark occasions held by different organisations which Skynner had, in some cases, played a vital part in establishing. The papers describe the generative thrust in his work which has helped one institution to grow out of another in a widening cycle of development from the founding of the Group-Analytic Practice in 1960, to the Institute of Group Analysis in 1973, the Association for Family Therapy in 1976 and the Institute of Family Therapy in 1977.

At the heart of these developments are the open-systems principles[18] which, in chapter 6, are fully described by Skynner and his late wife Prudence who worked with him in their development. Through this section these principles are applied to two central themes – the role of the consultant as a leader working from within his own professional system; and secondly, to the place of leadership in organisational change. Skynner's own summary of these issues illustrates how basic psychoanalytic concepts have been recast in the framework of an open-systems approach:

> Innovators in the field of psychotherapy pass on their most positive contribution through their ideas, while the limitations of which they are unaware (and of which their students are unconsciously taught to be unaware) are passed on in their technique. Thus, Freud's greatest contribution was his recognition of the centrality of the oedipal conflict for later development. And his limitation – his actual inability to deal with rivalry and jealousy – was passed on in a technique where those feelings never had to be encountered because the design prevented more than two people from being present at one time. I was attracted to Foulkes' ideas and techniques because he seemed to me to transcend this limitation of Freud's, thereby extending the technique further. And my interest in family therapy developed because it seemed to contain the possibility of carrying this resolution further still.[19] (*Group Analysis* 14/1 April 1981)

Section Three: Personal Growth and Professional Development: Complementary Cycles

The four papers of this section explore how these two cycles of growth, the personal and the professional, relate to and complement one another. They are linked by the concept of generativity which Erik Erikson, quoted on the next page, saw as one of the hallmarks of maturity. Skynner approaches it by posing increasingly focused questions through the papers, about what the therapist actually needs his clients for. The conclusions, worked at in a tentative and searching way, go beyond the therapist-patient relationship and help towards the understanding of all generative relationships – what the teacher takes from a giving relationship with his pupils; the doctor from a healing relationship with his patients; or why it is that parents' care of their children should alter *the parents* in such profound terms.

Each of the papers is illustrated by case examples that convey what he calls the sometimes mythic, universal ideas that groups can generate.[20] The story of Pygmalion, one such mythological character, can be used to describe the answers Skynner works towards. It describes a statue, a lifeless object who was animated by the creative genius of the artist who produced her. What is conveyed in *Institutes and How To Survive Them* is how the growth of the other person – the apparently needy and dependent one – animates the life of the giver. The symbolism of the Pygmalian myth can be inverted to describe the true situation in which life, energy and creativity flow from the development of the one who appears to be taking and the caregiver is animated by the growth of the other person. This understanding throws new light on what it is practitioners are in search of when they make choices about the clients and the problems they work with. In his concluding chapter he says:

> The mental health professional automatically selects the ideal clientele in which to study himself or herself vicariously and discover what the missing, denied aspects are, though the knowledge cannot benefit us . . . until we acknowledge the fact that our work, however useful, has also been an evasion of the truth about ourselves. (p. 233)

In a section of this paper entitled 'I'll look after you if you'll look after the bit of me I can't look after', he considers some of the options 'for helpers to help themselves'. In one option the practitioners use work 'to keep the missing, denied parts (of themselves) projected, in a growth-inhibiting way . . . the therapist remains stuck in an altruistic parental role but never learns . . .' This is what Anna Freud calls *altruism as a form of defence*.[21] In another option 'the professional and the clientele we have chosen can be used to learn more about the (professional's) self, to accept the missing parts, and grow'. This is what Erikson, writing about generative relationships, calls maturity. 'A mature man,' he writes, 'needs to be needed. Maturity is guided by the nature of that which must be cared and catered for'.[22]

These four papers are a map in the search for professional maturity, a means by which people can achieve better-adjusted attitudes towards their work and better relationships with their colleagues and clients. Chapter 9 anchors the search in the context of training courses and staff groups in institutions. Chapter 10 is concerned with the myth of altruism; it explores the needs that caregivers deal with vicariously through their work and discovers these needs to be assets, not liabilities. Chapter 11 introduces spiritual and existential dimensions to the search, and chapter 12 concludes with a summation of Skynner's experience that goes back to his early relationship with Foulkes.[23] The goal of this quest, a sense of self-acceptance, is vividly illustrated by another myth taken from a children's story:

> You thought as a boy, that a mage is one who can do anything. So I thought once. So did we all. And the truth is that as a man's real power grows and his knowledge widens, ever the way he can follow grows narrower; until at last he chooses nothing but does only and wholly what he must do . . . (Ursula Le Guin, *The Wizard of Earthsea*)[24]

As a member of the first generation of group analysts and family therapists, Skynner was a new kind of psychotherapist in the post-war period. His contribution has no better summary than the quotation below in which Foulkes described who this new person might be.

> His interest in his subject must be genuine . . . (but) not overweighted with motives such as 'helping other people' because this is too often based on . . . unresolved conflicts. . . . His interest should be of a more detached, sublimated kind, similar to that of a scientist or artist . . . a poet or writer in the community . . . receptive to the current problems of his time and creative in expressing them in such a way as to bring them nearer to the consciousness of those concerned.[25]

John R. Schlapobersky, 1988

Notes

1 *Explorations With Families: Group Analysis and Family Therapy*, was published by Methuen in 1987.
2 Author's introduction to *Explorations With Families* p. xi.
3 *Sensitivity Training and The Laboratory Approach*, ed. R. Golembiewski and A. Blumberg.
4 E. Jaques, 'Social Systems as a defence against Persecutory and Depressive Anxiety', in *New Directions in Psycho-Analysis*, ed. M. Klein, P. Heimann and R. Money-Kirle.
5 'The functioning of social systems as a defence against anxiety' in *Containing Anxiety In Institutions: Selected Essays*.
6 G. Caplan, *The Theory and Practice of Mental Health Consultation*.
7 E. Irvine 'The Use of Small Group Discussions In The Teaching Of Human Relations And Mental Health', *British Journal of Psychiatric Social Work*, Vol. 5 1959, No. 1.
8 R. Gosling, D. H. Miller, P. Turquet, D. Woodhouse *The Use of Small Groups in Training*.
9 M. Balint, *The Doctor, The Patient and his Illness*.
10 J. Abercrombie, *The Anatomy of Judgement*.
11 S. R. Slavson, *Child-Centred Group Guidance of Parents*.
12 Chapter 1 p. 5 below.
13 Chapter 9 below contains a detailed account of a staff group in a hospital setting.
14 In the courses at the Grubb and Tavistock Institutes on consultation and organisational problems, the groups in which the work is done are referred to as consultation groups. The work of these two Institutes has had a definitive influence on the field through their training courses and through the Leicester Conferences. The most useful introduction to their approach is by E. J. Miller, (ed.) *Task and Organisation*, which provides an overview and comprehensive bibliography.
15 Groups that have cases as their primary focus In the National Marriage Guidance Council, recently renamed Relate, are referred to as case-discussion groups. They are distinguished from awareness groups in which the primary focus is on practitioners' working relations. See note 17 below.
16 On the Qualifying Course at the Institute of Group Analysis, supervision is undertaken almost entirely in groups. They operate much like the case discussion groups referred to in note 15 above, but are known as supervision groups.
17 In Marriage Guidance, groups that have a training purpose but a focus on practitioners' working relations – their personality and interaction with colleagues – are known as awareness groups. On the General Introductory Course at the Institute of Group Analysis, and on the many other such courses that have grown out of this, groups are referred to as experiential groups and run along

almost identical lines to the awareness groups in Marriage Guidance.

18 In their preface to *Family Therapy: Complementary Frameworks of Theory and Practice* which describes the work of members of the Institute of Family Therapy, the editors, Bentovim, Gorrell Barnes and Cooklin, acknowledge the Institute's indebtedness to Skynner's open-systems ideas.

19 A letter to *Group Analysis*, 14/1, April 1981 p. 10.

20 Chapter 12 p. 154 below.

21 See Anna Freud's *The Ego and the Mechanisms of Defence*, chapter 10, 'A Form of Altruism'.

22 See Erik Erikson's *Identity, Youth and Crisis* p. 138.

23 All references to Foulkes's publications are identified by their original publication date and will be found in the bibliography. There the publication date is given for the new edition issued in Maresfield Reprints, London, and currently available from Karnacs Booksellers and from the Institute of Group Analysis, London.

24 Ursula Le Guin, *The Wizard of Earthsea* p. 85.

25 S. H. Foulkes, *Group-Analytic Psychotherapy: Method and Principles* p. 157.

Robin Skynner: Biography

Robin Skynner was born in Charlestown, a sea-port on the south Cornish coast where his father and grandfather maintained a family business mining and shipping china clay. On this side of the family there had been captains in the Royal Navy for several generations and on his mother's side they were also connected with the sea; they lived in a nearby fishing port and his mother was the daughter of a fisherman. Skynner was the oldest of five sons; they attended local schools, he completed his education at Blundell's in 1939 and began training for industrial management.

He volunteered for war service in the RAF at eighteen, was commissioned and qualified as a pilot and in navigation. He spent two and a half years training other pilots in Britain and Canada and then became a pilot in a Mosquito squadron on active service which specialised in low-level attacks. He has written of the trust required between the pilot and navigator who manned these aircraft, and of the total attention and engagement such flying demanded, and attributes to these experiences certain aspects of his therapeutic technique.[1]

After the war he qualified in medicine at University College Hospital and in psychiatry at the Maudsley Hospital. He has written fully of this period himself[2] but there are five associations of note. The earliest was his interest in semantics, epistemology and the philosophy of science stimulated especially by Korzybski's *General Semantics*[3] read whilst he was on war service in Canada. The second, arising out of this early interest, was his membership of the Metalogical Society, a small group initially brought together by A. J. Ayer for dialogue between the philosophers and scientists of whom it was comprised. They met monthly over several years, included Russell, Popper, Medawar and others who were amongst the most advanced and creative thinkers of their time[4] and Skynner attaches great importance to the intellectual confidence fostered by this association. Thirdly, during his psychiatric training, an experience of expanded consciousness under psychedelic drugs led to a lifelong association with others interested in alternative ways towards psychological and spiritual growth described in Christian and Eastern mysticism.[5] Fourthly, he was a pupil of Wilfred Barlow who was developing the principles of the Alexander Technique and he was later to apply to psychotherapy this understanding of how posture and movement relate to emotional states.[6]

And finally he was drawn to the work of S. H. Foulkes whom he met at the Maudsley Hospital. Foulkes was a German psychoanalyst who brought with him to Britain the revised understanding of Freudian theory from the Frankfurt Institute that was to also prove influential in the US in the work of Neo-Freudians like Erich Fromm, Adorno and Marcuse.[7] Foulkes first developed his approach to group therapy in Exeter before the war and was able to apply it successfully on a large scale to the treatment of war neuroses at Northfield military hospital near Birmingham. He developed ideas and practices there amongst a group of colleagues, that were to have a profound impact on the post-war development of mental health services.[8] Bion and Rickman had attempted an earlier and less successful experiment at Northfield in working therapeutically with groups.[9] Foulkes replaced them and, through the changes he introduced, the first therapeutic community was established. One of his associates there, Tom Main, coined this term to describe their work and later extended these developments at the Cassell Hospital.[10] Maxwell Jones[11] and David Clark[12] were also influenced by these developments and, like Main, they played a prominent part in transforming patterns of practice in mental hospitals and therapeutic communities after the war. Foulkes and de Maré took the Northfield perspectives into the concentrated study of small group work, which Skynner then extended to families.[13]

Based at the Maudsley Hospital after the war, Foulkes gathered about him a small group of clinicians and others who explored the small group implications of these ideas and practices, called it group analysis[14] and established the Group-Analytic Society.[15] Skynner joined them, trained with Foulkes and then established with him and others the Group-Analytic Practice. From this base he designed a course on group work, initially to meet the training requirements of some members of the Association of Psychiatric Social Workers, and brought in another member of the practice, de Maré, to run it with him. This was soon opened to other professionals and expanded, and colleagues in the Practice and others from outside it joined its staff. Together they developed this into the Institute of Group Analysis which offers a clinical training and professional qualifications in psychotherapy, and is the main training centre for group therapists in Britain. The original course Skynner designed in 1964 continues to run and now caters annually for some 150 people.[16] The influence on European psychotherapy has also been considerable and there are now Institutes of Group Analysis in Athens, Copenhagen, Heidelberg and Rome and centres in many cities practice and train for group analysis on both sides of Europe, in Israel, the Americas and Australia. There is a journal, *Group Analysis*, regular European Symposia, and increasing representation of and respect for group analysis at international conferences.

Whilst training at the Maudsley Skynner specialised in child psychiatry and became consultant first in Guildford, then Harlow and finally at Woodberry Down Child Guidance Unit and the Queen Elizabeth Hospital for Children serving north-east London and the East End. These developments took place at the same time as those described above, and they came together in the mid-1960s when some of the staff at these latter centres attended the early courses on group work. Then in the early 1970s the increasing demand for seminars in family therapy that Skynner was also leading at the Institute of Group Analysis increased to the point where another large course was needed, similar to that designed earlier but here concerned with family work.

Skynner now brought together a group of family and marital therapists to staff this new project. Some had worked or trained with him earlier, some had been experimenting independently, and others brought experience of work in the US. This course was soon also catering for 150 participants annually and its staff established the separate Institute of Family Therapy which Skynner served as the first Chairman. Since 1976 this Institute has offered a range of long and short courses and a clinical training has been developed which offers a recognised professional qualification. A national organisation, the Association for Family Therapy which corresponds in many respects to the Group-Analytic Society, was established in 1976. At the inaugural address to its first meeting, published as chapter 5 below, Skynner outlined the history of some of these events. It is referenced in the appendix where, as in the introductions to many of the chapters in this book, there is further historical material. There is now a Journal of Family Therapy, training programmes at many major teaching centres and a growing number of books on the subject written by members of the Institute and Association.[17]

Bridging these developments in group analysis and family therapy, Skynner and his late wife Prudence worked together in a partnership until her death in 1987. They provided the early leadership of the family courses which led to the Institute of Family Therapy; they helped to establish the credibility in this country of co-therapy with couples and families; and from 1974 they pioneered the development of therapy groups for couples at the Group-Analytic Practice where Robin continues to work. They taught widely abroad and their international standing was affirmed when they were invited, together with Whitaker and Kaslow, to be the main speakers at the 1978 Annual Conference of the American Association of Marriage and Family Therapy, where they were both honoured with Distinguished Affiliate Membership. More recently they worked together leading groups of bishops of the Church of England and their wives, and have been Advisers in the formation of a Pastoral Work Development Scheme in the London Diocese. There are many references to their partnership in this book, and further references to their writing in the appendix. During the course of her illness Prudence continued working, relinquishing her professional commitments as the illness advanced. She was at home until shortly before her death and passed away at the Marie Curie Hospice, Hampstead, in November 1987. The purpose-built family therapy unit at St George's Hospital, named in her honour, is just one indication of the regard in which she was held.

Skynner was made a Member of the Royal College of Psychiatrists on its formation and was later elected a Fellow. He left child guidance work in 1970 and became Senior Tutor in Psychotherapy at the Institute of Psychiatry and the Bethlem Royal and Maudsley Hospitals where he remained until he retired from University and NHS teaching in 1982. His output as an author has been as prolific as his other areas of endeavour, and the appendix to this collection speaks for itself. He was sixty-four when we began working on these papers and his only reluctance was the time it detracted from windsurfing in the summer and from the sequel to *Families and How To Survive Them* that he is writing with John Cleese, to be entitled *Life and How To Survive It*. He remains active in all three of his primary areas of interest – clinical work, teaching and writing – and with his family spends as much time as possible at their cottage in Wales.

John R. Schlapobersky, 1988

Notes

1 In 'An Open Systems, Group-Analytic Approach to Family Therapy' (appendix reference 36), Skynner writes of how 'the experience of low level bombing . . . high alertness, precise timing and accuracy . . . getting in and out as quickly as possible, profoundly influenced my family work . . . night attacks, including dive-bombing in the dark where a navigator watched the altimeter and slapped the pilot's knee to prevent his diving into the ground, may also have been a good preparation for co-therapy.' This material is not available in the edited form of this paper, published as chapter 13 in *Explorations With Families*, but can be found in *The Handbook of Family Therapy*, A. Gurman and N. Kniskern (eds) p. 41.
2 See note 1 above and chapter 7 below.
3 A. Korzybski, *General Semantics*.
4 In his biography, *Russell Remembered*, Rupert Crawshay-Williams, also a former member of the Metalogical Society, names some of the other distinguished figures in this group, including Ayer who established the group, J. Z. Young the zoologist, F. G. Young the biochemist, Penrose the geneticist; and philosophers including Hampshire, Wollheim, Woodger, Hutten and Tarski. Skynner is named in this group amongst the philosophers and though identified as 'a psychiatrist by profession' (p. 60) he was still a medical student at the time.
5 See Psychotherapy and sacred tradition, chapter 11 below.
6 See W. Barlow, *The Alexander Principle*.
7 For references to and studies of the Frankfurt Institute and the new connections established there between psychology and sociology, see for example, M. Jay, *The Dialectical Imagination*. An overview of the Neo-Freudian's perspectives is provided in E. Fromm, *The Crisis of Psychoanalysis* and *Beyond The Chains of Illusion*.
8 See P. de Maré, 'Michael Foulkes and the Northfield Experiment',

and M. Pines, 'The Contribution of S. H. Foulkes to Group Analysis', both in M. Pines (ed.), *The Evolution of Group Analysis*.

9 See W. Bion, *Experiences in Groups*.

10 See Main's papers, notably 'The Ailment' and 'The Hospital as a Therapeutic Institution', both in E. Barnes (ed.), *Psychosocial Nursing*, based on his work at the Cassell Hospital.

11 For an account of the Henderson Hospital which Maxwell Jones established, see R. N. Rapoport, *Community as Doctor*. For Maxwell Jones's own more recent writing, see his *Maturation Of The Therapeutic Community: An Organic Approach to Health and Mental Health*, and *The Process of Change*. For a recent account of current practice see D. Kennard, *Therapeutic Communities*, and R. D. Hinshelwood and N. Manning (eds), *Therapeutic Communities*.

12 See Clark's account of the history of social therapy in psychiatry and of the relationship between social science and psychiatry in D. H. Clark, *Social Therapy In Psychiatry*.

13 See M. Pines (ed.), *The Evolution of Group Analysis*, and T. Lear (ed.), *Spheres of Group Analysis*, notably the account by Elizabeth Foulkes in the latter, of 'The Origins and Development of Group Analysis'.

14 Foulkes derived the term 'group analysis' from the work of Trigant Burrow, an unusual and original figure who was both an associate of D. H. Lawrence and writers in the Bloomsbury group, and a research psychiatrist who was a founder and later became President of the American Psychoanalytic Association. He was later to leave this organisation over a difference he had in direct dealings with Freud about the differentiation of group analysis from psychoanalysis. See W. Abse, 'Trigant Burrow and the Inauguration of Group Analysis in the USA', in *Group Analysis*, 12, **3** (1979) 218–229; and Abse's book, *Clinical Notes on Group-Analytic Psychotherapy*. Amongst the most useful of brief accounts that differentiates group analysis from psychoanalysis is that of M. Pines, 'Psychoanalysis and Group Analysis', *Group Analysis*, 11, **1** (1978) 8–20.

15 See note 13 above.

16 See chapter nine below.

17 See, for example, R. Whiffen and J. Byng-Hall (eds), *Family Therapy Supervision: Recent Developments in Practice*; A. Bentovim, G. Gorrell Barnes and A. Cooklin (eds), *Family Therapy: Complementary Frameworks of Theory and Practice*, Vols 1 and 2; D. Campbell and R. Draper (eds), *Applications of Systemic Family Therapy: The Milan Approach*; G. Gorrell Barnes, *Working with Families*; D. Will and M. Wrate, *Integrated Family Therapy: A Problem-Centred Psychodynamic Approach*; J. Burnham, *Family Therapy: First Steps Towards a Systemic Approach*; and A. Treacher and J. Carpenter (eds), *Using Family Therapy*.

'We must pass through the threat of that chaos where thought becomes impossible.'

Gregory Bateson, *Mind and Nature*, p. 143.

'The basic strategy of the new experiential psychotherapy requires that, to achieve the best therapeutic results, both therapist and client suspend as much as possible their conceptual frameworks, anticipations, and expectations during the experiential process. Both should be open and adventurous, ready to follow the flow of experience with a deep trust that the organism will find its own way to heal itself and evolve. Experience has shown that if the therapist is willing to encourage and support such a healing journey without fully understanding it, and the client is open to venture into unknown territory, they will be rewarded by extraordinary therapeutic achievements.'

Fritjof Capra, *The Turning Point: Science, Society And The Rising Culture*, p. 429.

Author's Introduction

The Therapist's Present Family as a Source of Help[1]

'I know exactly what you've got to do. That first book of papers was about what you did for all those patients you treated. This second book has to be about what *they* did for *you*.'

This was my son, David, 28, film director. He had been talking over some of his own future plans with me, and I had then told him about the trouble I was having trying to write this introduction to the second volume of my selected papers. I asked him to read the introduction to the first volume, *Explorations with Families*, and then outlined what *Institutes and How To Survive Them* would contain.

Immediately he said it I realised I had fallen into the very same error that the papers themselves were trying to describe. I had come to believe that psychotherapy was most effective when therapists could 'include themselves in the equation' and thereby initiate a powerful mutual learning process in which both therapist and patient changed and grew. I had set out to advocate the idea that therapists should develop the freedom to use the whole of their personalities in their therapeutic work, including the aspects they found most problematic. I had genuinely intended to begin by writing from this position myself; but instead, with each new draft I had chickened out and written at one remove, describing how mental health professionals in general are really studying and trying to solve their own problems in and through their patients. My son's response now showed me that I was using my colleagues in the same way, in order to avoid putting myself on the line. What I had written suggested that we all unwittingly use our patients to contain our own problems, but I had not really talked about how this applied to me.

The Therapist's Family of Origin as a Source of Problems

It made me very happy that the solution should come in this way from one of my children, because I had come to realise that my professional life was really a search for some kind of map or chart with which to make sense of the confusion in which my own family upbringing had left me.

What was the reason for this confusion? I had found it extraordinarily difficult to describe these early difficulties in a way that would both make sense of them to others, and at the same time convey the sense of chaos, isolation and bewilderment I experienced at the time. In my inner world, I had felt in childhood recurrent panic, uncertainty, depression, alarm, fear of others and at times, almost complete depersonalisation. Outwardly this showed itself in terms of bed-wetting, soiling, severe stuttering (together with three younger brothers) that persisted until I began to understand its underlying causes during my psychiatric training, together with social incompetence, timidity, a variety of psychosomatic complaints and awkwardness in physical movement which made me incompetent at sport and physical activity. In adolescence all this began to crystallise into clearer forms which included severe cyclothymic mood swings, hypomanic at one extreme, alternating at the other with despair, accompanied by paranoid feelings and a virtual paralysis of thought.

How the Therapist's Family of Origin Can Become a Source of Help

Yet to others who knew my family, and to me in later years when I began to get my bearings and my vision had become clearer, they were 'normal' and ordinary enough, decent, kindly, honourable people, respected and indeed deeply loved by those who had close dealings with them. Fifteen years ago I had come to understand and accept them through the explorations that my close colleagues and I were then undertaking into our families of origin by genograms, role-play, and family sculpting. I expressed this more positive attitude publicly at the final plenary of the first big conference on family therapy in Britain in which visiting American family therapists led us further into this kind of study of the sources of our beliefs and attitudes.

In this atmosphere, within the safe boundary provided by the leaders from the Ackerman Clinic in New York in which we had all found ourselves able to be more open about our backgrounds, I found myself saying to the 200 colleagues present:

> One of the most valuable things I have got from this conference is to become connected up with my own family. This is something I knew I needed and didn't know how to achieve. But I've realised that all the families I've seen presented here *are* all *my* family – that we've been watching the same family all the time.
>
> Each time, we see an uncertain *mother*, who hasn't had a secure base from which she can venture out. So she still has an ambivalent attachment to *her* mother and is looking for *nurture* from her husband and children but is defending herself against realising this by giving it to others instead, regardless of their needs for autonomy. And she's depressed, naturally, because she hasn't got past that stage.
>
> And each time these families seem to have a *father* who had a bad relationship with *his* father and couldn't escape from the need for *his* mother, and who is angry, impotent, opting-out and excluded.
>
> The couple aren't having a good sexual relationship because they haven't got to that stage yet in their development and they are still looking for parents to look after them instead. Until they get that parenting, which they obviously can't get enough of from each other, they can't go to bed and fully enjoy each other. And the children are all following the same pattern. Because of this, the parents feel very impotent; and because of that, they're trying to be omnipotent and trying too hard to bring up the children properly.
>
> Seeing this same pattern being presented in the role-plays not just of patient families but of families of colleagues, I wonder if I'm like the man who goes outside in the garden, sees the moon, and thinks the moon is shining just for *him*. Maybe everyone here is seeing that same moon, the same family, their *own* family. Maybe there's only one family, the

human family, and there are just different ways in which we get stuck or pushed off course.[2]

Denial of Problems is the Most Serious Problem of All: It Prevents Problems From Being Solved

I had come to see that the difficulties my family had left me with were not so much due to deprivation as to the pervading atmosphere of denial. Denial that anything was wrong with the family at all; or that if it was, it could not be connected with them and must be some meaningless personal fault; or that even if it was connected with them, it would be hurtful, ungrateful and disloyal to comment on it or even to recognise it. So for me, even to understand my difficulties felt like breaking all these family rules.

Since it was forbidden to recognise the deprivation for what it was, it was difficult to gain the missing experience from an alternative source, or at least, difficult to seek it out in any conscious way. Moreover, the deprivation had other consequences, including a strong fear of loss and separation which led to an anxious, demanding, clinging enmeshment of the family as a whole, so that attempts to meet one's needs outside the family system were resisted. Even if they were successful, they were likely to be subjected to intense destructive envy.

The Psychiatrist's Choice of Profession: An Attempt to Remedy or Disown His Own Problems

It is obvious to me now that I entered medicine and psychiatry in search of some understanding that would rescue me from this state of confusion and distress. I was half aware of this at the time, but could not acknowledge it openly even to myself because I was so uncomfortable about admitting my condition, believing it to be a purely personal responsibility. I rationalised the choice in more general terms, as a continuation of studies of semantics, epistemology and the philosophy of science that had begun to interest me during my war service. All the philosophical theories I had encountered appeared to be highly determined by the personality structures or 'psychopathologies' of their creators, and a clear definition of what was 'normal' or 'optimal' in human functioning, though clearly central to every other study of the nature of the world, seemed either to be missing from the theories altogether or, if considered at all, proved to be just another manifestation of the psychopathology of the theorists.

Once embarked on my study of psychiatry, I was helped by three things particularly. The first was a wide-ranging curiosity. I cannot explain why I possessed it, but it meant that the training programme at the Institute of Psychiatry and the Maudsley Hospital, where we were exposed to all types of theories and techniques and left to make up our own minds, suited me perfectly. Although many others complained of the lack of direction and found the rich variety confusing, I eagerly absorbed everything offered and trusted to experience to teach me what to keep and what to discard.

The second factor was the condition of 'deprivation' in which most of my later work took place, where high demand for treatment was matched by great limitations in resources. Indeed, the main centres at which my methods of family therapy were developed in the 1960s were in Hackney and the East End of London, two of the most deprived and disadvantaged parts of Britain.[3] Because of this we had to learn to work fast, and to deal with everyone referred rather than selecting just those in whom we were interested, or who were easy to deal with, or whose problems suited the treatment method in which we had each been trained.

The third factor was my fundamental interest from the start in health rather than in disease, which to my surprise I found to be quite unusual among mental health professionals.[4] The majority of general psychiatrists showed a strange lack of interest – indeed what often looked more like an active avoidance – of any understanding of mental disorder that might link it to ordinary behaviour. It was as if they wanted to keep madness safely outside themselves, though also close by where they could keep a sharp eye on it to make sure it did not take them by surprise and jump back inside their own psyches. Meanwhile, the theories they produced seemed to have as their main object a demonstration that the causes of mental disorder, or severe mental disorder at least, were such that it was unlikely to have any implications for their own mental stability.

The Integration of Personality and Theory

Puzzled and disappointed by the barrenness and impotence of conventional psychiatry, I was attracted by the more psychodynamic orientations, which all shared a common assumption that most mental disorder was a consequence of some kind of fragmentation of consciousness.[5] This quickly made sense of what I was observing in my clinical work, and also began to explain many of my own problems for the first time. Some of these problems even resolved. A severe stutter which had afflicted me since childhood, for example, became understood and ceased from then on to trouble me except when I was fatigued.

At the beginning I found the American 'Neo-Freudians' – Sullivan, Horney, Fromm and Thompson – easier to accept because they were closer to commonsense experience. But as I watched children playing at the sand-tray and saw Freudian themes repeatedly enacted, I was obliged to examine many of his ideas more seriously and ultimately had to accept that most of the conclusions he had drawn from clinical experience had an important core of truth, even if his explanations of them in terms of nineteenth-century mechanics had to be discarded. It took me five years to absorb the main Freudian ideas, against my deep initial scepticism, and another five years after that to accept the principal ideas of Melanie Klein as well.[6] The latter seemed at first too bizarre, too 'mad' to be taken seriously. But gradually I was forced to accept, initially by seeing the mechanisms she described repeatedly enacted in groups, that my resistance to the ideas was a measure of my fear and avoidance of the condition of madness the theory was correctly describing.

Other pioneers seemed to me to complement Freud and Klein, rather than to contradict them. Freud was brilliant in his understanding of the central importance of sexuality in human affairs, but avoided the even more central role of spirituality, condemning such interests as a 'black tide of occultism'. Jung's work therefore complemented his by supplying the spiritual dimension, though he in turn appeared to reject on an equally irrational basis much of Freud's interest in sexuality, as if he felt an equivalent discomfort and saw that as the 'black tide' instead. Alfred Adler complemented both these other pioneers by linking the inner world to its social context, and showed how symptoms could be changed through interaction between the two, often in quite commonsense ways, thereby laying the foundations for the treatment of the family as a unit.

At the time I trained at the Maudsley, the behavioural approach which had recently been developed by Wolpe was being actively developed there by Eysenck and his colleagues. Though they championed these new forms of therapy in a polemical and rivalrous way, as an alternative to methods based on a psychodynamic understanding, the two sets of ideas appeared to me clearly complementary. I therefore set about bringing them together in a way that I could use in my clinical work, initially influenced by Mowrer, Miller and Dollard, Maier and other theorists who took a similar integrative view.

Psychotherapy as Education as well as Re-education

My next interest, in child psychiatry, made this integration more urgent for me. When working with children it was impossible to escape the fact that many of their problems were due to a failure to learn appropriate social behaviour in the first place, rather than a result of conflicts between models which had already been internalised. A little earlier I had also begun to conduct my first psychotherapy group under the guidance of S. H. Foulkes, and here too it was obvious that much of its beneficial effect was the result of mutual learning among group members, whereby they received more adequate feedback about their actual performance together with help in developing more effective social skills through watching the behaviour of others.

Later, when I began experimenting with group therapy for children and adolescents, it became even more obvious that there were two types of problem, requiring two kinds of help. First, there was the initial learning of skills, requiring some form of training. And second, there were learned behaviours that had become conflictual but could not be resolved because they had become dissociated, so that the sufferer was aware only of discomfort or impaired performance, not of the conflict itself.

At first I found it difficult to integrate these two modes of intervention, and wrote in my first attempt to formulate my method of family therapy:

> I have presented the need for communication between parts of the system, and the need for hierarchy within it as if these two principles were separate. But I think this is only a limitation of my own capacity to understand and formulate the problem, for these two considerations are aspects of the same thing, two ways of viewing the concept of *order*. These two simple principles comprise the theoretical justification for the therapist's role in facilitating communication and exercising control. (*Explorations With Families* p. 55)

The Therapist as Part of the System: The Need to Include Oneself on One's Own Map

I continued to feel uncomfortable, nevertheless, about the seeming contradiction between the principle of neutrality that was customary in the psychodynamic therapies, and the authoritative role of the therapist, imposing his own value system, which seemed inevitable in any approach based on a behavioural model, including methods like hypnosis and Minuchin's 'structural family therapy'. Later I came to see that the apparent conflict was due to my leaving the therapist – myself – out of the equation. If treatment was always regarded as a *mutual* interaction which both the therapist and the patient (or the group or family he was 'treating') learned from and changed each other, the contradiction was immediately resolved.

This led to a method of intervention that makes use of both analytic and behavioural ideas, which I have called 'a group-analytic approach' because of what it owes to one of my teachers, S. H. Foulkes. The therapist exposes himself to the dynamics of those he is treating, while remaining attentive to his own spontaneous emotional responses. After a time he will usually notice a strong emotional conflict, between an impulse to say or do something, and a feeling that this impulse is not only personal to him but should be concealed because it would arouse disapproval and rejection by the patient, group or family. When this occurs it usually means that the therapist has internalised, and is suffering from, the very conflict which is the source of the presenting problem.

xxxvi

This 'counter-transference' response in the therapist is then expressed not as a directive, interpretation or other statement about the patient(s), but simply as information about the therapist's own experience, accepting that it may be personal to him, or that it may, on the basis of past experience, be relevant to the problem being studied. Even if the therapist's spontaneous response is a powerful value-judgement which is in conflict with the value-system of the patient(s), it is presented tentatively for examination and discussion, and can be rejected or disqualified if it is wrong, or a premature confrontation, or otherwise inappropriate. In my approach, therefore, the understandings and value-systems of both therapist and patient(s) are constantly open to change and mutual growth and benefit, and decisions are reached by something more like a debate where the final decision takes account of both sides of the argument.

The Therapist in the Equation of Change: Growth of the Therapist, Along with Those Being Treated

Though this 'group-analytic' approach played a central part in the first book of selected papers, *Explorations With Families*, the therapist's role was dealt with there piecemeal, mainly in the case examples, with no study of the process over time. In this collection we see that, if the method is employed in the way I recommend, a developmental process is facilitated in the professionals as well which ensures that they receive as much benefit as the families they are treating. Moreover, the greater the benefit we allow ourselves to receive in this way, the more our skills increase, producing an exponential growth in personal understanding and competence and a similar beneficial chain-reaction in the common knowledge of any group working together and following these principles. I have called this chain-reaction of benefit, deriving from my own version of a systemic approach, a 'philosophy of plenty'.

What is new here? Surely, many readers will say, this growth process is a feature at least of all the psychodynamic schools, even if it is not true of psychiatry as a whole. Though this is true to a considerable extent, I believe there is an important limitation which my method overcomes, and existing schools of psychotherapy do not. Namely, it regards the therapist's reason for doing the work at all as his main pathology, supporting and perpetuating a split between more parental and more childlike aspects of his personality, by projection of the childlike aspects on to patients and clients.

If I am right in suggesting that the mental health professional is unconsciously seeking a substitute experience to compensate for something that was missing in his family of origin, he needs social contacts for this purpose with people who do not share the denial or 'blind spot' typical of his own family. But to the extent that colleagues have chosen the work for a similar covert reason, everyone in the profession will share a tendency to deny similar aspects of their relationships. The institutions they jointly form, at first for mutual support and sharing of experience, and later to train their successors, will be based by default on a collusion to continue hiding the denied deprivation and resultant need, rather than to explore, expose and transcend it. So the family of origin is merely recreated, except that it is now more numerous, more powerful and more inhibiting than ever. It will even be a major source of the professional's friendships and support-system, and will probably have power over the member's livelihood. Our professional has escaped from the frying-pan only to find himself in the fire.

The Professional's Nurture of Others: Serving Denial of Personal Deprivation

What emotions or patterns of relationship is the 'helping profession' trying to avoid? The papers that follow set out my findings about this in detail. It will be seen that the most fundamental issue is a profound need for, and denial of, some form of parental care. The main defence by which the denial is maintained, by the parents in the family of origin, was through projection of their own denied need on to the children or on to a particular child. The care desired by the parent was then given to the child or children instead, often accompanied by such statements as: 'I want my children to have the things I didn't have myself'.

This sounds, and is intended to be, benevolent and altruistic, but unfortunately it leads to a series of unintended negative consequences. The children do not get what they need, when they need it, but instead get what the parents need, when the parents need it. The children are therefore deprived in the real sense of not having their actual needs met, particularly the need to be recognised as separate individuals with identities of their own. Instead, they are not only burdened with the parents' denied needs, but are also expected to behave as if the parents are helping them and to express gratitude for what is, in effect, an invasion of their psychological space.

The parents, in their turn, naturally continue to feel deprived because they are not getting what they need either. Indeed, if the children are (at least in the parents' eyes) receiving what the parents badly need themselves, yet show limited benefit or even react negatively, the parents would be scarcely human if they did not feel some resentment and even envy of their children on this account. The scenario is familiar enough, for it is the interactional pattern of a certain type of deprived family.

Given this background, I believe the motivation which leads the mental health professional to take up this type of work is a compromise between two opposite tendencies. One factor is a normal, biological tendency towards change, growth and optimal health, which seeks an escape from the family double-bind. The other factor is an equally natural clinging to security, to the known, through a reproduction of the original family pattern of deprivation in the form of professional work and the structure of professional organisations.

Three Levels of Professional Functioning

This is all very similar to the compromise on which marital choice is based. At the more positive extreme there is the possibility of a powerful developmental process, where everyone changes and grows in understanding, confidence and skill, as in a healthy marriage and family. A less positive solution is more like the mid-range marriage, where there is a collusion to prevent or limit growth and change, at the cost of one spouse carrying the partner's problems, or the children becoming burdened with some of the unacknowledged problems of both parents: 'Me Tarzan, clever, well-adjusted professional; you Jane, hopeless, crazy patient or client'. And at the most unhealthy extreme we see something more like the paranoid, mutually destructive *Who's Afraid Of Virginia Woolf* marriage. Fortunately, professional ethics and social controls provide safeguards against too obvious an expression of this kind of destructiveness by such professionals towards their patients and clients, and it therefore finds expression mainly in senseless internecine warfare between different schools of thought in psychiatry: between those based on physical versus psychological explanation; or behavioural versus psychodynamic psychotherapy; and different psychodynamic schools among themselves.

Research on exceptionally healthy ('optimally' functioning) families shows that one of their most striking characteristics is an ability to cope with change and loss of all kinds, even including the loss and change resulting from the death of loved ones.[7] This makes it understandable that they can accept events which involve lesser degrees of change and loss, like being open to new ideas which may disturb their current outlook; allowing their spouse and children to grow into separate individuals with minds of their own, and to be independent and have lives of their own; and accepting and enjoying their own developmental changes with a good grace. Their self-image is congruent with reality so that there is no need for collusive concealment of denied aspects of family functioning; this helps to explain why their communication is open and clear, since to the degree that there is no 'cover-up', there need be no fear of accidental revelation of taboo subjects. Communication can also be two-way, with frank feedback and criticism from child to parent as well as from parent to child, and with consultation of all concerned before decisions are taken. Ambivalence is accepted and there is a basic sense of trust, a reaching out to others with warmth, caring, and an attitude of respect and responsibility, arousing similar positive attitudes in return and resulting in an experience of the world which confirms what I have called a 'philosophy of plenty'. Enjoyment, fun, humour and wit are prominent features in such families, and seem not only to be a measure of the freedom and ease of their functioning, but also an important component of their success.

The stability and security necessary for all this to be possible are ensured by three main factors: first, a strong parental coalition and a clear parent-child hierarchy, with power shared between husband and wife; second, a good support-system which includes the marital relationship, the family itself, the extended family, and the wider community; and thirdly, by a sense of connection and meaning provided by a value-system that transcends the present family, whether this takes the form of a religious belief or church membership, or of some more general humanitarian concern giving a sense of connection with the universe at large and extending beyond the lifetime of any one individual.

Three Levels of Health in the Functioning of Institutions

Viewed against the background of this research on family functioning, most institutions which train mental health professionals approximate at best to the mid-range rather than the optimally healthy family.

Occasionally an isolated hospital or clinic will achieve public notoriety because it is exposed as functioning like a really sick family, isolated and at loggerheads with most colleagues and the local community because of its deviant values, and showing such pathological features as splitting, blaming, scapegoating, evasion of responsibility and failure to fulfil its assigned task on many levels. But this is rare and is usually corrected by the removal of a pathological leader from whom the disturbance has stemmed.

However, the majority of institutions show characteristics intermediate between this and mid-range families. They lack the capacity of healthy families to deal with change and loss, so that there is a clinging to past ideas and past structures. The organisation will often have begun when a number of innovators, all dissatisfied with existing ideas and methods, have joined together in a search for a deeper truth.

But as the new ideas are accepted and an organisation gains in prestige, it begins to attract a different membership with a wider range of motivation, such as a desire for status and job opportunities. This wider membership now has a vested interest in maintaining the validity of the knowledge they have gained, because it represents their status and livelihood. In the least healthy institutions, the ideas of the founders are passed on as 'received knowledge', basically beyond question. Revision is possible only by casting it in the form of 'what the founder really meant', or 'what he would have said if he had dealt with this particular subject'. Even where the paralysis is less extreme, individual members will find it increasingly difficult to express views which are widely at variance with the consensus. The power and authority of the leaders is increasingly based on role, politics, wheeling and dealing, and acceptability to others. A compromise, non-threatening figure is more likely to be chosen instead of a leader who acts as a model, who puts himself on the line, sets an example, increases the power of the group process so that everyone gets more. A rigid autocratic regime, or an ineffective committee structure set up to avoid this threatened autocratic regime, takes the place of the original two-way, open-systems communication. The leaders are more cut off than anyone else, grow less than anyone else, because they are hearing only what they want to hear.

Because of this move towards 'closed-system' functioning,[8] the leaders, and the theories they hold, are not subjected to criticism and corrective feedback. The ideas become a doctrine, and the institution becomes a rigid hierarchy. Instead of seeing the learning process by which the knowledge was acquired as something that must continue indefinitely, and being willing to throw existing ideas overboard constantly and start again, the attitude develops that one can have 'enough', can be 'qualified', 'finished', 'fully analysed'.

Those who teach are now supposed to know, and must pretend they do know, to themselves and others, thereby limiting the possibility of opening to further learning. Students are supposed not to know better than teachers, so it becomes more difficult for the teacher to learn from, and with, students. Communication ceases to be open and two-way, and instead becomes one-way. What started as a shared exploration using an open-system group process to draw upon the intelligence of all members of the original institution, now becomes an increasingly dead and empty ritual, transmitting out-of-date information to recipients who learn it by rote or rule of thumb. The whole teacher/trainee/patient relationship is locked into a growth-restricting pattern.

Older members will have difficulty in allowing trainees to grow to their full stature and become independent, and will be reluctant to relinquish control of the organisation themselves. Admission to membership becomes increasingly restricted for fear of reducing the status of those already qualified, and because keeping the skills in short supply will keep the price up. As the numbers of trainees increase, they need patients to treat, so rival schools develop, all competing for 'patients', and for 'students' to train to treat the patients, trying all the time to increase the total supply of patients by convincing as many people as possible – ideally, everyone – that they need 'treatment'.

The Cycle of Deprivation: From the Professionals' Families of Origin to the Institutions They Create

This essentially 'mid-range' pattern is compounded by the problems that led the members to enter the profession in the first place. To the extent that they are suffering from the pattern of deprivation I have described above, and the problem is denied, they will reproduce their family structure in the functioning of the organisation. The professionals will perceive their own denied needs for nurturance as if it is located in the patients or clients. Similarly, within the teaching institute, teachers will perceive their own need as if it is in the students. This leads to infantilisation both of patients, who are burdened with the denied dependency needs of their therapists, and of students, who find themselves in a similar relationship to their teachers. Those on the other side of these relationships – the therapists and teachers – are equally trapped by receiving a projection of impossible adulthood and competence.

With *both* parties locked in rigid parent-child roles in ways that neither understands, the typical duration of analysis and psychotherapy inevitably increases with each decade, and in essence the process is interminable unless the therapist breaks the rules, or the patient decides it is a failure and breaks the contact. Also, in order to maintain the denial of the therapist's original family problem by its reproduction in the therapy, communication across boundary areas has to be severely restricted. There is unhelpful concealment, between therapist and patient often rationalised in professional terms such as 'avoiding contamination of the transference'; between teacher and student; between the therapist's marital and family life and his life in the institute and work with patients; between the life of the institute and the outside world. By concentrating only on the patient whom the professional is 'helping', change in the therapist, and the painful insight accompanying it, is avoided and this avoidance is exported down the line to others.

The avoidance of a two-way flow of information prevents a

necessary developmental progression in the therapist's/teacher's role and relationship, from an initially idealised parental figure, through the stage of a teacher with whom it is possible to struggle and argue, to a more equal human interaction as 'brother' or 'sister', and colleague, friend or fellow human being. Not only is the patient's progress impeded; the professional is locked ever more deeply into his family pathology and is prevented from growing up.

Applying the Principles of Healthy Families: Towards the Creation of 'Healthier' Institutions and Training Programmes

As I gradually became more aware of these factors which interfere with effective therapy, and as I have, at the same time, searched for a better understanding of healthy family functioning, I have taken every opportunity to explore how our increasing knowledge of healthy families could be applied both to my own practice of psychotherapy, and to the training programmes and institutions for which I have had responsibility. Exactly how it was applied is the story of this book, but I will mention a few of the more central conclusions.

Open, two-way communication

The main key of the 'open-systems' principle is open communication.[9] Within the context of secure containment and a good support-system which provides adequate security, communication is encouraged to be as free and open as possible. It is open not just to all interpersonal levels, but also to intrapersonal levels as well so that the resources of each person's inner world, including what is unconscious, can be drawn upon. Information flows freely up and down the hierarchy as well as laterally on each level of it, ensuring mutual learning so that the intelligence of the whole network is fully utilised. In trying to follow this principle, I have experimented with increasing levels of self-disclosure, and explored the stages at which this is helpful and appropriate. I have noted how developmental processes in therapy groups, institutional dynamics, and one's own marital and family interaction show striking parallels, and I often deliberately pass this kind of information across the usual therapist/patient and home/institutional boundaries when it appears that events in these different realms may facilitate each other. I invited my late wife, Prudence, to train and work with me as co-therapist to maximise this kind of interaction, and on occasion she would join me in dealing with professional groups and institutions as well.

Physician, heal thyself

It is also a central, explicit assumption that mental health professionals have taken up their work because of a problem in their family of origin of the kind described above, so that their first responsibility, if they are to do really good work, is to understand and help themselves.[10] With more healthy colleagues this can be expressed more openly, but even with those who want to avoid facing these truths, much can be done to help them towards a better understanding and acceptance of themselves in more indirect ways, through case supervision where they can learn by identification with people they are treating, or through identification with the teacher who is open in revealing similar problems in his own family. Role-plays, 'family sculpting' and 'simulated families' are other less direct and confrontative ways towards the same goal.

The open acceptance of diversity

It is very striking how facilitating it is to the growth and autonomy of children or of trainees, when their parents or teachers clearly express differences in their views, provided they put the common task first (the education of children or students) and seek acceptable compromises to that end. A rich diversity of views among the teachers, and their tolerance or even enjoyment of these differences, gives maximum permission for, and help towards, the development of a strong and independent identity. It seems to bring awareness of, and acceptance of, differences among individuals. Needless to say, the exposure of such disagreements needs to be tailored to the level of security of the students, and the age of children.

Jealousy as a growth-enhancing force

The main obstacle I have met in encouraging this open expression of difference, by the teachers in front of the students, is the way it exposes the teachers to experiencing jealousy among themselves in a public arena. When this is publicly owned it is merely amusing for the students and even reassures them that the teachers show ordinary human frailties like themselves. But I have found it to be the main reason why 'open-systems' functioning is avoided among the staff in large group situations, and there is instead usually a strong tendency to maintain a 'united front' and conceal differences, presenting the students with a 'monolithic bloc'. This has the effect of keeping all the jealousy in the students, thereby restricting growth and the development of confidence, as in families where parents try too hard to avoid being divided.

Group Analysis: A Direct Experience of How Systems Function, from Within

Finally, I should acknowledge how immensely helpful I have found the group-analytic method of S. H. Foulkes in exploring these difficult questions. Group analysis was an early example of a systems approach. But it differed from other systems approaches used in family therapy in that it embodied a practical form of training (a personal group analysis) which brought about an automatic tendency to be aware of, and remember, the various levels of any system in which the individual later became involved. Lacking this knowledge of other systems theories, or practice and supervision in applying systems principles to one level – for example, to the family system – seemed always to leave the person blind to the systemic aspects of other levels – the individual, for example, or the mental health profession as a whole, or society generally.

By contrast, a constant awareness of the larger systems in which one's own work, institution or profession is embedded, helps one to be more intelligent in following one's aims. Awareness of the professional system, from within, makes the professional's contribution to it more adaptive and effective. It helps to create an institution that is learning and growing, and has increasing power in the sense of an ability to achieve and influence others, because it influences through *understanding*. It fits in, adapts, sees itself as part of something bigger in which it tries to find its most useful place and relationship. So it helps others to help themselves and provides knowledge where it is required, in a form that can be accepted, within the limits of the possible.

The way that family therapy was readily accepted in Britain and rapidly established itself in the main teaching institutions, as compared with the United States where it remained more peripheral was, I am sure, related to the influence of Foulkes in helping us to consider our work in the context of the total system of the helping services, and of dealing with it as with any other system or group situation.

Robin Skynner, 24 November 1988

Notes

1 This introduction was given as a paper at the 1987 Annual Meeting of the Supervisors and Trainers Association, Relate Marriage Guidance, Birkbeck College, London.

2 *Families and How To Survive Them*, pp. 172–3.

3 Skynner was the Director of the Woodberry Down Child Guidance Unit, and Consultant Child Psychiatrist, Queen Elizabeth Hospital for Children, in Hackney. An account of how family therapy in Britain was pioneered at these centres is to be found in *Explorations With Families*, chapters 1 and 3, (appendix references 5 and 6) and in the editorial introductions to these chapters. (Ed.)

4 For an account of psychological problems rooted in the study of 'normal' family experience, see *Explorations With Families*, chapter 12 (appendix reference 40) and its editorial introduction. (Ed.)

5 See *Explorations With Families* chapter 12, p. 283 ff.

6 Skynner gives an account of the psychoanalytic perspectives he has assimilated and applied in *One Flesh: Separate Persons: Principles of Family and Marital Psychotherapy*, Appendix A, pp. 363–384, and pp. 34–40. (Ed.)

7 Skynner's use of the terms 'optimal', 'mid-range' and 'dysfunctional' to categorise family relationships is derived from the Timberlawn Research Project on healthy families. See J. Lewis et al., *No Single Thread: Psychological Health in Family Systems*, 1976; J. Lewis, *How's Your Family*, 1979; and W. R. Beavers, *Psychotherapy and Growth: A Family Systems Perspective*, 1977. There was a good deal of interchange between Skynner and these researchers, and their findings corroborated the conclusions he drew from his clinical work. See *Explorations With Families* chapters 5 and 13, and their editorial introductions. (Ed.)

8 The distinction between 'open-' and 'closed-system' functioning is set out in Schermer V. 'Interactive Concepts in Psychoanalytic Developmental Psychology', in Pines, M. and Rafaelson, L. *The Individual and The Group: Boundaries and Interrelations*, Vol. 1. (Ed.)

9 ibid.

10 Skynner's view that mental health practitioners seek resolution to
    personal problems through their professional activities, has close
    parallels with Jung's idea of the therapist as 'wounded helper' (Jung
    1954). This idea has been applied to the study of psychiatrists by
    C. J. Groesbeck and B. Taylor, 'The Psychiatrist as Wounded
    Physician', *American Journal of Psychiatry*, 37 (1977), pp. 131–139.
    In Section Three below, particularly in chapters 10 and 12, Skynner
    examines how the therapist can draw upon his own past experience,
    including experience that may have been troubled, and make an
    asset of this in his work. See, for example, p. 232 below. There is a
    further discussion of these ideas in *Explorations With Families*
    chapter 13 pp. 357–361, where Skynner considers some of the
    therapist's most essential personal requirements and compares him
    with the healer or shaman in traditional societies. An excellent
    introduction to this subject is J. Halifax, *Shaman: The Wounded
    Healer*, which draws especially on the work of M. Eliade's
    Shamanism.

One

DEVELOPING THE BASIC PRINCIPLES: A Group-Analytic Approach to Consultation

1 Group-Analytic Themes in Training and Case-Discussion Groups

The opening section of the book illustrates the use of groups to develop skill and awareness amongst mental health and other professionals. The simplicity of this approach to group consultation makes the profound and sometimes discomforting conclusions easily accessible. The key idea – that to understand others you have to understand yourself – is applied to working relations amongst mental health practitioners studied at three different levels.

Each level is emphasised by a different paper in this section. As we move from the dynamics of individuals in the first chapter to group dynamics in the second and institutional dynamics in the third, a recurring feature becomes evident: the power exercised over people's professional motives and career choices, by an unconscious search for solutions to problems brought with them from their early lives.

In this first chapter, themes in the consultation groups indicate how practitioners are attracted to agencies where they can study themselves at one remove. As Skynner shows this to be true of the professionals with whom he works, he also finds it to be true of himself. This use of self-discovery is fundamental in group analysis where the examination of one's own process is a touchstone for working with others. The paper thus initiates the book's study of professional motivation and its dynamics, and is at the same time a personal account of the group-analytic method at work.

Learning on the job through a constant examination of one's own experience is a progressive theme running through this collection of papers. Therapists are – through others – dealing with themselves at every stage in their work. But where the vicarious nature of this pursuit is most frequently seen as a liability, the shift in perspective here discovers in it 'the goose that lays the golden eggs'. This is the subject of chapter 10, where the myth of altruism is explored.

J.R.S.

Introduction

During the first eight years of my practice as a children's psychiatrist in company with my colleagues in a child guidance clinic, I acted as leader of several training and case-discussion groups for members of other services and agencies, with the object of disseminating skills.[1] Although in these groups case-discussion is a constant point of departure and the participants do not reveal details of their personal life or history, experience has suggested that such groups can sometimes function with benefit, and without danger, at a deeper level than that often recommended and closer to the level of group-analysis as developed by S. H. Foulkes.[2]

As in other training groups, each person bringing a case is helped to see, by focusing on his own responses, how he duplicates the patient's problem by the way he presents it to the group and how the group in turn perhaps takes up his usual pattern as therapist. But in addition the leader's attention is constantly directed to the group theme as it unfolds and develops from session to session and at opportune moments this overall pattern is interpreted. A homogeneous training group will usually reveal that the members are attempting to solve vicariously problems similar to those most commonly found in the type of client with which their agency deals. If the interaction is allowed to reach the level favoured, the group as a whole will act out in the group transference successive themes similar to those which would need to be dealt with in successful treatment of their clients.

If these group situations are successfully recognised, interpreted and to some extent resolved, the members may become especially suited to the type of work they have chosen since they have not only personally experienced, but also to some degree worked through and integrated, difficulties most typical of the clients referred to their agency. On the other hand, it is likely that some training groups founder or become blocked if the group theme is acted out but not understood.

Consultation in Marital Casework

This possibility was first forced upon my attention through a recurrent difficulty which occurred in a training group of eight female voluntary workers with several years' experience of working for an organisation providing counselling help in cases of marital difficulty. During the first year the group operated fruitfully except that one more articulate member was constantly paired off with me as an outwardly admired co-therapist, but she was subtly attacked until she became so disturbed that I had to transfer her to a treatment group. This member's intense competitiveness, which invited the response she received, led me to overlook the contribution of the group to this crisis until the new member who filled her place was immediately cast in a similar role. The group felt puzzled by what was now experienced as a strange, irrational compulsion to repeat this process of pairing and rivalry, the creation and destruction of a 'marriage'. Once this was made conscious it did no further damage and in fact provided the most illuminating aspect of the group interaction. The theme of the cases presented moved from a focus on fears of destructiveness and jealousy to a shared dislike of a type of female client who needed to dominate and resist involvement. As they gradually saw that these clients represented their mothers, then that they stood for unaccepted aspects of themselves, I was still kept as an idealised figure. But in the last phase, as they perceived more objectively the faults of husbands and fathers in the cases discussed, I was pushed off my pedestal and allowed to be more of an equal.

At the end of the group's two-year course they repeatedly used symbolism suggesting that they stood outside the door of the parental bedroom and, after attributing their hesitation at opening the door to fear of a mother's jealousy or a father's exciting but alarming assault, they settled for a more prosaic fear that they might not be sexually preferred after all. It thus seemed that these people had been attracted to marital casework through a need to solve some childhood problem they had experienced in relation to their parent's marriage, a problem which was presumably felt as a threat to their own as well. While this remained unconscious, it was a handicap, both personally and in their counselling. But the very fact that they had suffered this type of experience made them unusually well able to understand and help their clients once the unresolved conflict was made conscious and worked through in the 'here and now' of the group situation.

Consultation with Child-Care Workers

The behaviour of the group above suggested a common predominant fixation at the level of the oedipal conflict. As a contrast, I will briefly outline the course of another case-discussion group where the themes were mainly at a pregenital level. This group, which met fortnightly for five years, consisted of about a dozen houseparents of children's homes, the members being mixed as regards sex and marital status. For the first two years discussion centred around two main themes: first, their feelings of inadequacy when dealing with those severely deprived and demanding children without the capacity to trust, who frustrated the efforts of staff to help them; and second, their conviction that their lack of qualifications and status, and consequent lack of self-esteem, denied them the respect of professional colleagues and led the administrative hierarchy to exploit them.

Both themes appeared to represent displacements of their own unaccepted infantile demands and the transference behaviour corresponded closely. There was idealisation of the leader and impossible demands for magical help, but they had such fears of revealing emptiness, greed and envy that they could not form a group, expose themselves or accept the real help available. I felt, in relation to them, as frustrated as they did with their problem children, but attempts to interpret the pattern were met with heavy silences, emotional withdrawal and themes suggesting wishes to break the relationship.

Though we came close to foundering many times, some more insightful members kept the group together and finally, in the third year, some began to admit to personal problems over negative feelings stirred up by the children's behaviour. After this there was a steady and increasing capacity to trust each other till the group eventually became the most positive and supporting situation I have witnessed in this type of work. As with the children, it seemed that the houseparents could only begin to trust after a long period of testing out and working through their ambivalence. Rather than through interpretive interventions, the crucial changes seemed to follow clearer perceptions of me as a real figure subject to weakness and failure like themselves yet prepared to work through our differences together. When this occurred the ambivalence, previously solved by projection on to those they regarded as more powerful, who then appeared as saviours or persecutors, appeared to become less intense and more bearable as an inner conflict.

At one group session, for example, when the removal of a mentally ill housemother (not in the group) from her post had led to a state of near-panic and perception of the administration as a terrifying arbitrary power, they were able to see how they felt they had damaged this difficult woman themselves and how the administration lost its threatening nightmare quality when they accepted their share in the guilt at what had happened. Later still, when I gave warning of my departure (in the sixth year), an unusually pitiful case was brought of a boy with multiple handicaps. His self-destructiveness and refusal to allow his housemother to form a relationship were quickly perceived by the group as caused by his fear that his hatred had damaged his mother, who had recently died of cancer. Yet the group behaved as if they could not bear the boy's pain and alternated between ideas for cheering him up and heavy, depressed silences.

Finally, when they saw the connection between the case and my departure, the talk jumped from one to the other so rapidly that we all became confused. Then they were able, in the remaining few sessions, to express their fear that their anger would destroy the good experience we had shared, some speaking as if I had been literally introjected and was being protected from their attack. Depression was seen as a necessary price if they were to keep what they had gained and make it their own, a lesson fundamental to their dealings with their children.

Consultation with Probation and Child-Care Workers

It is difficult, of course, to know how much this kind of observation is a product of the group leader's own attitudes and theories, or how much the group is acting out his expectations. Two further examples suggest that these patterns are not altogether of my own making. In another case-discussion group, consisting of more or less equal numbers of probation officers and child-care officers, there was a complete turnover in membership during the five years the group met. Yet the group themes and transference behaviour of two sub-groups remained typical and distinct from each other throughout. The probation officer themes were typified by a case, repeatedly discussed, of indecent exposure. The man concerned had failed to resolve his oedipal conflict by a satisfactory identification with his father and in casework was outwardly compliant but subtly resisted the probation officer's efforts to be accepted as a benign authority, successfully manipulating him instead into accepting the probationer's own guilt and impotence. At one point this probationer was reported as amusing himself by fashioning a series of clay heads, each smaller than the last, though it was difficult to decide who, out of all of us, was the head-shrinker and who was being shrunk since the *probation officers typically repeated this type of conflict with authority themselves, both with their colleagues and with me, as if creating an admired father-figure to identify with, then subtly challenging him but avoiding a real confrontation.*

The child-care officers, by contrast, avoided conflict and disagreement at all costs. Not unnaturally, the themes repeatedly presented involved attempts to keep together families threatened with disruption. *Characteristically, they denied the destructive forces in the relationships and often lost the chance of dealing with these before it was too late.* Similarly in the group, the ambivalent transference so characteristic of the probation officers never appeared openly among the child-care officers and friction was avoided by denial and a strong reaction formation which made them reluctant to question their basic principles at all.

Consultation with Health Visitors

The other example concerns a group of health visitors which, after meeting with me for ten sessions, was subsequently led by two

9

psychiatric social workers, a man and a woman, who had till then sat in as observers. Apart from occasional themes suggesting curiosity about sexual impulses in children, such as the motives for stealing knives and playing with fire, this group repeatedly presented cases of impossibly good women married to impossibly bad men (so bad indeed that the health visitors never troubled to meet them!), while the members divulged little information about the cases, complained that they got nothing back, and arrived increasingly late. When I finally remarked that I felt like a bad man married to a group of good women, and that we seemed as little able to get together as the married couples they described, the lateness ceased but they produced, next time, a case of an impossibly bad woman married to an impossibly good man.

This pattern of themes and transference has persisted more or less unchanged since I left the group a few months ago and, as might be expected, my colleagues soon found themselves not only frustrated and angry with the group, but divided against each other as the group listened attentively to the woman and ignored the man. When my colleagues recognised their counter-transference problem and sat side by side in unconscious expression of their solidarity, the indignant group response gave support to the earlier hints that vocational choice for these workers might be determined by an early siding with one parent against the other as a solution to the oedipal conflict, a solution perhaps encouraged by a real parental problem *which later led them to seek experience of motherhood without the need for sex or men.*

Conclusion: Giving up a Privileged Position

Common to all these groups was an even more general theme, which time permits me only to mention briefly. This was concisely expressed by one marital counsellor in a report written about her group experience:

> We returned frequently to the question of why we had become counsellors. Dr S. would not let us get away with any 'high'-minded notions of being helpful nor with any 'low'-minded generalities about sexual curiosity or maternal instincts. Our questioning somehow was tied up with our desire to be safe.

We tried to persuade ourselves that counselling was a safe professional relationship, that love was conditional and that we could always withdraw. If someone in the group brought a case and we could show her the problem in herself so that she became a client and we became the counsellors, it gave us a marvellous feeling of being able to abandon our own problems and concentrate on hers without any danger to ourselves.

Of course, I shared with the members of these groups, as I presumably do with the readers of this chapter, these general problems presented by work which offers both the pleasures and dangers of vicarious experience, contact without commitment and involvement without risk of self-exposure. When this theme appeared *I sometimes found my own role fluctuating in a bewildering way if I relinquished my right to a privileged position and, for example, toward the end of the caseworkers' group found myself working through their depression as well as my own until I realised this and felt a heavy burden lifted as soon as I pointed it out.* One valuable experience for me, which seemed important for the others as well, was the realisation that a correct detachment would lie not so much in maintaining a constant emotional distance or barrier, as in finding a degree of inner freedom that would enable one to move back and forth, as the situation demanded, between a position of human equality and the parental authority and distance which was a responsibility imposed by the therapist's or group leader's role.[3]

The idea that people are initially attracted to what have been called 'the helping professions' by the need to solve their own problems is certainly not new. But the experiences reported lend encouraging support to another very positive idea, that people may become especially suited to the work they have unconsciously chosen, once they gain insight into their motivation.

Notes

1 This paper was presented to the Sixth International Congress of Psychotherapy, London 1964, and was first published in *Selected Lectures: VIth International Congress of Psychotherapy*, S. Karger, Basel New York.

2 See the Editorial Introduction note 23 page xix for references to Foulkes's publications.

3 The search for 'a degree of inner freedom (in therapeutic work) . . . that would enable one to move back and forth, as the situation demanded . . .' was to exercise Skynner throughout his professional life. Twenty years later when the search had matured to what he called the open-systems, group-analytic approach, he described it thus: 'to use my approach the therapist must simultaneously or at least in rapidly alternating fashion both maintain a parental "holding" role, keeping the situation constant and safe and provide a model of "play", explore, open up, risk and venture out into the unknown.' 'The therapist both joins the family and remains outside, oscillating between one and the other position, in order to pick up the projections and to reflect on and analyse or act from them.' (*Explorations With Families* chapter 13, pp. 360 and 364).

2 A Family of Family Casework Agencies

In this paper we can follow how Skynner establishes a distinctive way of working with a group as its consultant. As practitioners discuss anxieties about their work, they tend to mirror their clients' behaviour, unwittingly re-enacting some of the working difficulties reported. Exploring the dynamics of the group-as-a-whole, Skynner follows this reflection process, enabling the group to provide members with a direct, vivid experience, in the here-and-now of the group process, of the difficulties they are trying to resolve outside.

In the homogeneous groups described in chapter 1, themes were seen to reflect the shared defensive systems of their members. The focus in such groups can thus be on peoples' shared sources of motivation arising in their early or other formative experience. However, in this group Skynner is dealing with a heterogeneous membership drawn from different local agencies which are brought into communication through shared responsibility for clients. Obstacles to good practice in relations between the agencies include the same envy, rivalry and destructive competition found in family relations. The purpose of group consultation in this case is:

- to help individuals discover how inter-agency dynamics constrain and affect their work
- to equip them to use group discussion to promote movement, as they would in other family situations, in the direction of support and collaboration.

The distinction between 'haves' and 'have nots', which becomes a central concern in the concluding section of the book, emerges here for the first time. Skynner describes the risk run by agencies dealing with deprivation, that they will reproduce a cycle of deprivation amongst themselves. There are the rudiments here of his *philosophy of plenty*, to be worked out in the chapters that follow, which encourages agencies that seek to reverse this cycle to do so first in their own staffing and management policies. These principles are incorporated in the open-systems approach when it is extended to the training of family therapists in chapter 6 and of group therapists in chapter 9.

J.R.S.

Introduction

In the previous chapter based on work with training and case-discussion groups, I presented some evidence for the thesis that people working in what have been termed 'the helping services', are attracted to their choice of agency by a need to solve problems of their own related to those most commonly found in the agency's clients.[1]

This paper presents some further conclusions on this topic, based on a year's experience with an inter-agency case-discussion group which included probation officers, child-care officers, psychiatric social workers, a school medical officer, senior health visitors, a mental welfare officer, a member of a Family Service Unit, and a member of a combined agency casework unit, as well as occasional visitors such as a general practitioner. The group met fortnightly for an hour in the health centre which housed four of the agencies represented. There was no programme other than an expressed interest in agency co-operation, which we all agreed could best be studied by discussing actual cases. My own aim was to learn something of what actually happened when agencies met together. I had no intention of being either a teacher or an administrative coordinator. If anything was to be learned, it was to be learned by all of us through experiencing the way in which we operated.

The Cases Presented

The first case discussed, that of a boy attending the Enuresis Clinic who was failing to show any improvement and whose family had previously shown minimal response to four years of casework at the Child Guidance Clinic, set a pattern which was to appear again and again. Repeatedly, we found ourselves dealing with families who made intense demands for help, either in their own right or for difficulties they had with their children, but who resisted real involvement and never formed an honest therapeutic contract. They seemed to try to get without giving, to seek advice without revealing frankly the inner difficulties upon which advice could be based; they sought guidance and management while subtly holding on to control of the situation themselves. The ambivalence of family members towards each other and towards the caseworkers involved with them was always intense but concealed and denied, and a crucial discovery of the group was the way in which this denial was colluded with by all the agencies who dealt with them.

Because of this collusion, therapeutic movement had become blocked and instead of perceiving the cause in the subtle hostility and rejection by the family, the caseworker's frustration and denied counter-hostility had taken the form of feelings of failure, helplessness and self-blame, leading to a vicious cycle of increased but fruitless effort. When a second agency became involved, the feelings the family generated in those dealing with them usually led to inter-agency conflict which sometimes took the form of overt criticism and annoyance but more often appeared in such subtle forms as overt self-criticism with covert failures of cooperation and communication. Various defences would be used against this threat of conflict such as withdrawal of one agency altogether, a rigid structuring of roles, a banding together to make a scapegoat out of some third agency, or a joint collusion of all the agencies in displacement of the problem. An example of the latter occurred in a family with which the senior health visitor, a mental welfare officer, and a general practitioner had all been involved; everyone had seemed to join with the family in displacing all the intrafamilial hostility and feelings of 'badness' on to the daughters' ugly noses. On this false basis some cooperation was possible between the agencies, which eventually included arrangements for plastic surgery, but the family was left with their real problem unresolved and the agencies were left with natural feelings of failure.

The cases discussed seemed to become more overwhelming and hopeless at each group session, reaching a climax with one family which had succeeded in playing off agencies so brilliantly and rapidly that a member of the group declared that even if one hired the town hall and got all the agencies together to prepare a combined operation, the family would have involved a completely different set of agencies within a week.

The Pattern in the Group as a Whole

Just as the families appeared to pass their own feelings of worthlessness and failure on to the agencies, and to bring about a threat of conflict between them together with defensive measures against this danger, so in general did each case presentation seem to weigh our own group down with an increased sense of hopelessness and uselessness. This took the outward form of self-blame with each at first finding fault with his own agency. In the third session I was puzzled to find myself feeling ashamed and critical of all the doctors in the case described, only to find that others were having the same negative feelings toward their own counterparts. The frequently stilted discussions, lateness, unexplained absence, and forgetfulness indicated hostilities and tensions. These would briefly flash across the room, but more usually they were denied and safely displaced on to unrepresented agencies.

As the group members became aware of the hostility and manipulation in the families discussed, a fearful and punitive response was at first evident in us, expressed by themes of shutting up all this madness and badness in approved schools, prisons and mental hospitals. Gradually, as more detachment was reached and we began to see that these families were not so utterly different from ourselves, we began to find in our own previously denied responses ways of dealing with the situation more effectively. We became less compelled to see ourselves as kind, permissive and giving, and we realised that it could be equally valuable, at proper times, for us to say no, to control, to withhold, to delay, to meet a challenge with a display of our own power. We seemed to have been living at one pole of the parental function and failing to include the other; we liked being motherly but we hesitated to be fatherly.

This was expressed in many ways. In an early session, a Family Service Unit worker presented the case of an immature married couple in which her casework provided an example of superb mothering and filled a gap in the early experience of her two clients. In the group the caseworker's problem quickly became clarified; the need she experienced from the couple, but which she felt she was

17

not meeting, was that they were ready for a father. They were ready to grow through some of the demands, frustrations and stimulations of the wider world. Here it was the probation officers, the closest in agency function to the fathering role, who had the most valuable contributions to make.

Later this theme was exemplified even more clearly in a case I took part in presenting (while another member took over leadership of the group). When my clinic was asked to present a case, I felt that my position as leader would make this difficult and hoped my clinic colleagues in the group would solve the problem for me. I then forgot all about the matter until the day before the group met. Since this made it apparent that I, like everyone else, was resisting the real issue the group involved, I decided to present a case about which both I and a social worker colleague in the group had received strong criticism from another agency, as well as from each other. Arriving at the clinic on the morning the group met, I found that the social worker had also completely forgotten our commitment, while our other colleague had gone on leave. These facts were, of course, included in our presentation.

The case itself concerned an adolescent boy who had been in treatment with me while seeing the probation officer as well. From the start there had been an unusual feeling of conflict and a lack of proper communication between the two departments. I forgot to send him my report, a copy of his did not reach me, and so on, all by 'accident'. Following another offence, the boy was sent to an approved school against my strongest recommendations, an event which disturbed me.

In the group, it became immediately apparent that the clinic and the probation officer had adopted and been cast in opposite roles, and that our perceptions of the problem had been completely split. The probation officer had focused on the delinquent behaviour and was highly critical of the excessively controlling mother in the family who had bound the children even more tightly to her after the tragic death of another of her children. The probation officer seemed to be trying to take the place of the inadequate and impotent father in order to rescue the children from what he saw as crippling domination. The family had been as hostile and resentful to him as they were open and apparently cooperative at the clinic, and we began to realise that they had successfully appealed to us, like a child hiding from the father's authority behind the mother's skirts. At the clinic we had been impressed by the depression in this family, following the disaster of the death, and by the way the patient's self-punitive behaviour followed this incident and seemed to be carried out on behalf of them all.

In the group this conflict emerged when the probation officer criticised us for ignoring the delinquent aspect. It had been present in other children in the family long before the tragedy. He also criticised us for protecting the family against authority, just as in the family the mother kept the father powerless. The social worker, on the other hand, saw the probation officer as heartless and punitive, indifferent to the tragedy and the subsequent depression, and so she felt protective. I had been aware in myself, from the beginning of this case, of a curious oscillation between these two aspects which I was unable to experience simultaneously or to integrate. The probation officer and the social worker had been angry with each other, while I had been annoyed with both of them and they with me. Expression of these feelings in the group was quite intense, but three sessions of discussion led to a more combined and balanced view by all of us as well as to a considerable change in our relationships.

In this and subsequent cases, it seemed possible to formulate a therapeutic response which would encompass both the family's need for nourishment and their sense of helplessness, while also challenging and controlling their manipulation and resistance. It was the integration of these two fundamental parenting roles, or, at an individual level, the integration of the masculine and feminine aspects or principles, which was the most obvious general result of the year of group discussion.

Relations Between the Agencies

There were two striking results of these meetings. Firstly, in the course of our discussions the members became divided into two groups, the 'haves' and the 'have nots'.[2] The 'have nots' referred to their agencies as though they were stern autocratic homes in which there was little trust or encouragement of initiative; they felt neither protected against the overwhelming demands of their clients nor adequately fed in the sense of being provided with time for further training and development of skill. The 'haves', in contrast, came from democratic agencies in which there was greater freedom regarding communication and initiative. They felt cared for through being protected against giving too much time and energy to their clients, and they were helped to grow professionally through opportunities for further education and training, both within and outside their own agency, including the sometimes tremendous efforts made by some agencies to enable their members to attend this group. Later, the 'have nots' were able to express their difficulties in attending the group (earlier explained, if at all, by pressure of work) in terms of their fears of professional inadequacy due to lack of knowledge or training, and especially their fear of their envy of the 'haves' as typified by me esconced in my comfortable office protected by my secretaries and my long waiting list.

In contrast to this prominent role of envy in the 'have nots', the 'haves' repeatedly expressed deep gratitude for what their agencies had given them. Similarly, in the group, it was the 'haves' who came most regularly and who could most easily express need and accept help from others. The 'have nots' were more often late or absent and found it difficult in the early stages to admit needs or to use the group situation to satisfy them. The tendency of the 'have nots' to overwork and feel overwhelmed by the demands of their clients seemed due to a need to placate their clients' real or projected envy. The 'haves', for their part, seemed much more able to resist demands and to give something to themselves as well.

This pattern, however, was only present at the beginning. For those who stayed the course the second most striking result of our meetings was a change in all the members in the direction of being able to attend to their own needs, accept help, and express gratitude for the experience itself. Everyone moved from the 'have not' to the 'have' direction.

Only later, while preparing this paper, did I become aware of the possibility of another pattern in this relationship between the two sub-groups; because this conclusion was only partially tested and confirmed by interpretation in the last session it must remain more speculative. The 'haves' were understandably irritated by the 'have nots' when they were defensive and fearful of criticism and so obstructed progress, but they were also strangely impatient and unsympathetic whenever the 'have nots' faced their difficulties more frankly. The 'haves' complained that such sessions had been 'boring', though their boredom seemed caused by their own withdrawal and failure to bring their feelings into the situation. At the time I felt surprise that the more experienced people did not share my pleasure when the less sophisticated ones made what was, for them, a big advance, for they would certainly have enjoyed similar moments of growth in patients or clients. I realise now that I did not wish to face the fact that this hostility, which appeared to be directed towards the 'have nots', was plainly aimed at me. Once this was apparent, I perceived the close analogy to a family where the younger siblings are envious of the powers and privileges of the older ones and the latter express their jealousy of the baby's greater claim to the parents' patience and tolerance by condescending ridicule and denial of their wish to be in the same position.

The Leader's Role

Although my understanding of group dynamics put me in a special position regarding the group structure, we were all in the same boat as regards the fundamental problems we were solving through helping others and the difficulties this caused in actually doing the job. I found I wanted, and at the same time did not want, to be a mother, a father, a demanding baby, and to share the comradeship of the older siblings. I experienced all these roles in turn. I see in retrospect that I experienced, in relation to the group, exactly what the agency members felt with their problem families, and made exactly the same mistakes. I often felt I was dealing with the group badly, failing to give them enough, being too weak or too controlling, while also experiencing a feeling that I was being taken advantage of and that information that could have enabled me to be useful was being withheld. The group was blocked as long as some members succeeded in getting me to feel their problems as my own, and it moved as soon as this process became more conscious and I was able both to accept my share in the common difficulties and to refuse to accept more than that.

In the life of this group, it seemed particularly important that these difficulties were openly shared with the group as a whole and that I, as leader, became a group member when it was my turn to present a case. Each of us thus had the opportunity, at different

21

times, to be both caseworker and client and to see the problem reproducing itself at each level.

Conclusion: Four Working Principles

1. The experience of this group's operation provides further evidence for the thesis previously presented that *workers in what have been called the 'helping services' are attracted to the agency they choose by a psychological kinship with their clients, who are struggling to resolve similar types of problems to those the workers have faced themselves*. It also further confirms a previous conclusion that people who are self-selected in this way can become particularly skilled at the work they have chosen if they can accept insight into their deeper motivations for taking it up.[3]

2. *Where two or more agencies are involved with a person or a family, there is a danger that the agencies will reproduce between themselves the psychopathology with which their clients or patients confront them*. The examples given here have stressed the reproduction of marital conflict, with two agencies representing the male and female partners, as well as the other side of the coin in which the integration of a marriage and of each individual in it seemed facilitated through the integration of complementary viewpoints in the case-discussion group. The type of conflict to which each agency was most vulnerable seemed related, as might be expected, to the typical 'blind spots' of its caseworkers which led them to identify and collude with a particular family member or personality feature.

3. *These typical inter-agency conflicts may be expected to be reproduced in any group made up of members of a number of different agencies*, the overt form depending on the degree to which feelings are permitted expression. *Their recognition and understanding appears to be not only a precondition of real agency cooperation but a singularly broadening experience for all those who undergo it*, leading as it does to an exchange and sharing of understanding at an experiential rather than intellectual level. Each worker takes away with him some part of the experience and viewpoint of all the others, each of whom possesses something he lacks.

4. *If these conclusions are valid, their importance for the development of an integrated family service requires no emphasis. Unless the assets and liabilities peculiar to each agency or profession are clearly*

recognised and combined to form a balanced whole, and unless the difficulties and conflicts which must accompany any truly organic growth are anticipated and provided for, improvement in service to families cannot be expected. A truly effective family service is subject to the same laws of growth and development as a healthy family, and the necessary conditions for its evolution require an understanding and application of those laws.

Notes

1 This paper was first published in the *International Journal of Group Psychotherapy*, 18 (1968), pp. 352–360.
2 For a more extended discussion of 'haves' and 'have nots', see below chapter 10 pp. 164 ff.
3 Providing trainees with insight into their deeper motivations for taking up work, with particular reference to the clients they work with, was to become a feature of the group-analytic approach towards training. For the application of this principle to the training of group therapists see chapter 9; and to the training of family therapists see chapter 6.

3 An Experiment in Group Consultation with the Staff of a Comprehensive School

As it is extended to institutional settings like the school to which it is applied here, the group-analytic model becomes well-defined in a number of respects, notably:

- the role of the consultant
- the nature and quality of group communication to be encouraged and focused upon
- the way in which group transference is worked with
- the combination of small and large group principles, including the use of a consultative team to meet different requirements
- the composition of consultation groups with membership varied to meet different requirements, some catered for by homogenous groups and others by heterogeneous groups
- the location of consultation groups which can be varied to meet different needs, some established outside the work setting – on courses or for supervision – and others made a part of the work setting as staff groups.

Indications and contra-indications are provided for different methods of application, including those described in the two preceding chapters. And then the method chosen for this application – in which a team offers consultation to a staff group in a school – is described in detail.

At the time it was written Turquet was developing the use of consultation groups at the Tavistock Institute which emphasised the development of transference fantasies centred mainly on the consultant. Without excluding this from consideration, Skynner focuses instead on group interaction and exchange. When transference is considered, it is seen to concern members' relationships and identifications with their clients, agencies and professions no less than with himself. In such work Skynner recommends the avoidance of 'plunging' interpretations likely to evoke regressive and defensive reactions amongst staff and instead construes group behaviour in here-and-now terms. When interpretations are used they are articulated from a counter-transference position with a high level of self-disclosure by the consultant to facilitate staff identification with him and to encourage a group process emphasising the shared professional concerns of the consultant(s) and consultees.

Skynner attaches much importance to the use of structure and authority not only in terms of transferential meaning but, as in family work, in terms of reality-based role relationships. Current interest in managers' authority and responsibility as critical institutional factors adds to the salience of this chapter. When the consultative team enters the staff room two 'natural' systems are brought into contact with one another and it is in their communication that some of the institutionally specific problems of the organisation undergo change. The leadership role in this process, defined in group-analytic terms, has much to do with boundary maintenance and the protection of a structure within which problems can be shared and better understood.

J.R.S.

Introduction

A model derived from group-analytic family therapy[1] is described in its application to another type of 'natural' group.[2] Principles developed for time-limited interventions with families are applied by a psychiatric team to the entire staff of a large comprehensive school. Besides the surprising positive potential of this type of intervention, the special difficulties of such a situation are illustrated, including the need for adequate structure and control and for techniques which maintain relationships of mutual professional respect.

Working with Institutions as a Whole

In the two previous chapters, I described the use of group situations for facilitating the growth of professional skills and the development of personal insight. These followed a group-analytic model where the focus was on the developing group themes and transference behaviour, the latter usually demonstrating that the psychodynamics of group members resembled the typical problems of clients served by the agency to which they (the group members) belonged.

External groups for staff training: advantages and limitations

Such groups resemble the artificially-constituted 'stranger' groups utilised in conventional small group psychotherapy, in that members are drawn from different agencies and efforts are usually made to avoid including people who are working together or likely to come into frequent contact outside. This method facilitates a free exchange between members by diminishing anxieties they may have that revelation of professional or personal problems may have adverse effects on relationships with working colleagues, or on their reputation and standing with superiors. But the approach also

27

creates other difficulties. There is often a 're-entry problem' in that the members of the training group work through their own resistances to new knowledge and skills in the group, but when they return to their own agencies they encounter strong resistances in others which prevents the knowledge gained from being generally utilised. Indeed, those undergoing the training can often exacerbate such reactions by developing a rather precious, superior attitude which fails to allow for the natural caution of colleagues. Furthermore, even if care is taken by the leader of the training group to secure sanction for the process from those in positions of authority, and to ensure that this sanction is repeatedly renewed, it is impossible to avoid arousing anxieties amongst those in authoritative positions that the new knowledge may cause some problems. For example, they may worry that their juniors will acquire skills they do not possess themselves, or that the situation may create divided loyalties which will undermine their own position. All those who have run such groups will be familiar with these hazards and with the readiness of some trainees, because of unresolved personal problems, to exploit them in their work situations.

Internal groups for staff training

These considerations, as well as an increasing awareness of the power and potentiality of working with 'natural' groups – families, or married couples – led me to believe that it might be preferable to find ways of working with agencies or institutions as a whole. Using a group-analytic model, with a focus on facilitating interaction and exchange between group members rather than on encouraging the development of transference fantasies centred largely on the therapist, I had discovered that the main therapeutic work was carried out between sessions. This made possible profound and lasting changes, both in family functioning and in the well-being of its members, in what seemed an impossibly short time if one considered only the few hours the family met with the therapist and neglected the time, perhaps a hundred-fold greater, during which the problems continued to be worked out at home.

I hoped that agencies, institutions and other organisations in which individuals worked together as a group on a common task might be able to use group-analytic interventions in a similar way, or perhaps even more effectively since the working group would be less likely than families to function by means of a collusive system of defence. Also, as in families, resistance to new understanding would be faced and worked through simultaneously by the whole group, ensuring that such changes as were achieved could be expected to survive over time.

Agencies and work organisations seem to resemble families in possessing collusive defensive systems to avoid insight and change to a much greater degree than I anticipated, not only because of emotional pressures on new members to share the agency's ways of perceiving themselves and others, but even more because of the unconscious mutual selection process – akin to that occurring in marriage – which brings together people of similar personality type or with similar psychopathology. For this reason, organisations tend to become manifestations of the personality structure of the leader, overtly mirroring his conscious beliefs but covertly demonstrating his unconscious attitudes. At least children and parents are spared the disadvantage of being able to choose each other![3]

An invitation from the Islington Family Service Unit to meet regularly with the staff as a psychiatric consultant, and later from the East London Family Service Unit, gave me an opportunity to put these ideas into practice. I met with each unit every two months over several years, and became convinced that the possibility of setting in train a process of growth and development in the organis- ation as a whole, and so in the individual members, did indeed exist to a point where the intervention could become part of the culture of the institution.

The Pastoral Work of a School and the Need for Consultation

By 1967 I felt I had discovered an ideal method of assisting schools with children who presented problems to them, a task which could clearly never be met by any imaginable increase in conventional child guidance provision, at least in the localities with which I was concerned. At the clinic and hospital I served, we had become increasingly aware of the need to make some of our knowledge and skill available to teachers, since so many of the cases referred to us were unresponsive not only to child psychotherapy but also to work with the whole family, separately or conjointly.[4] These families

29

were often hostile to all social agencies, including clinic and school, or were so inadequate and preoccupied with simple issues of material survival that little energy was left for other tasks.

In either case, clinic attendance was difficult to secure and cooperation was rarely prolonged even when they did come to the diagnostic interview. Such families never came to us of their own volition but were pressured to attend because of complaints that their children showed anti-social behaviour in school. We began to see that a better approach might lie in helping schools directly. Our aim was to develop more psychological understanding of these children amongst school staff who could more effectively counteract the negative influence of an anti-social home, or compensate for some of the inadequacies of parents unable to fulfil ordinary responsibilities towards their children. It was at this point, when we were wondering how we might best approach a school with an experiment of this kind, that a request for this kind of cooperation came through the educational psychologist of a local school.

The Social Environment of the School and its Pupils

The comprehensive school concerned was in fact ideal for such a study. It had been formed a few years earlier from a number of neighbouring schools; all were in old, dismal buildings in an area of North East London with bad housing, marked social mobility, breakdown of traditional cultural groupings and high rates of delinquency and psychosis. Immigrant children from the West Indies, often suffering the effects of two separations (the first when their parents left them behind with relatives, the second when they left these relatives a few years later to re-join their parents), formed two-thirds of the population of the school we visited. Even in the past, before immigrants made up such a large proportion, one of the component schools was already known as a 'sink' school in which all the most difficult problems were likely to end.

The Professional Standards and Motivation of the Staff

Nevertheless, by the time the staff contacted us, vast efforts had been made to improve the situation. We were greatly impressed by the understanding of the headmaster and his senior colleagues, and during our visits we developed a profound respect for the high morale, patience, devotion and sheer knowledge of the children's personalities and homes that the staff demonstrated. Thus, although this was a good test case for our experiment, because of the high incidence of problem children and families, we had the advantage of collaborating with teachers who were unusually cooperative, frank and willing to learn with us. In this as in other matters, those most in need of help are usually the least prepared to accept it, but it remains to be seen whether the interesting results of this experiment can be generalised to other schools and amongst other teachers.[5]

Making a Beginning: Establishing the Ground Rules

At a preliminary meeting with the head and his deputies held at the clinic, a basic structure for our collaboration was agreed. As it was an experiment from which we hoped to learn as much as the school, all the specialities represented in the clinic team – psychiatrist, psychologist, psychiatric social worker, and child psychotherapist – were to be represented. We would meet regularly on the school premises, with as many members of the school staff as possible, so that there might be an opportunity to facilitate a learning or growth process in the school staff as a whole.

We tried hard to secure an hour and a half, or at least an hour and a quarter, for these meetings but this was not possible. We had only an hour to play with, which was already dangerously short if clear conclusions were to be reached, and it put us in greater peril of an inconclusive and unsatisfactory discussion if, for any reason, we started late. As to frequency, the head and his deputies had been thinking in terms of meeting once a term. This was too infrequent in my experience for any real group interaction to develop. My colleagues felt strongly that we should meet not less than fortnightly, while my own intuitive choice was for monthly meetings which were frequent enough to permit the group development I hoped for, but were also sufficiently spaced out to avoid arousing fears of dependency or of a 'takeover' by the clinic, with all the resistance which this would arouse. In fact, when asked at our first meeting the school staff spontaneously chose monthly meetings and this remained the rule, modified by holidays and other expediencies, to about six to eight meetings a year.

The First Three Meetings: Establishing Some Boundaries

The first meeting: the wish for magic solutions

At our first meeting there was a large attendance, perhaps about thirty teachers in all. The four members of the clinic team scattered themselves around a large central table in the library where we met. Most of the teachers also gathered around this table, but some sat more peripherally at tables near the walls and this possibility of choice regarding the degree of involvement and so of a gradual approach to the situation seemed valuable. Some teachers would come in and pretend at first to read a book at a distant table, later allowing themselves to be drawn into discussion. We were not at any time introduced to the staff, and there was no preamble. A deputy head, who acted as the main representative of the school on these occasions, at once took out notes and asked for advice on a child whom he proceeded to describe.

As might be expected, this first case was one in which failure had already occurred. It concerned a child already committed to an approved school so that neither they nor we could help him further in this setting. We showed them our own limitations and acknowledged that we found ourselves similarly helpless in the face of many problems of this kind. This led on to other feelings of discouragement and hopelessness in the staff about the difficulties of influencing some children through the healthy environment the school strove to provide, when the teachers were working against the influence of a whole neighbourhood with anti-social or delinquent values. They seemed to be showing us the size of the burden they had to carry, hoping that we could help yet fearing that they would feel even more inadequate by comparison if we were able to do so. We therefore sought to assist by sharing their difficulties, rather than by taking the role of experts. We recognised that this would lead at first to feelings of disappointment or anger that we were withholding our 'magical' solutions and such responses were indeed frequent and were pointed out as they appeared.

The second and third meetings: establishing authority

Senior staff altered arrangements for our second visit without prior agreement or warning, perhaps because they felt the large group situation had been too chaotic. Only four teachers were present, and it was explained to us that these were the only ones concerned with the case. The meeting was inevitably more formal and the case itself centred around anxieties about control. A twelve-year old West Indian boy had aroused anxieties in the school staff by his violent rages, particularly as he had, during one episode, injured another child with a milk bottle. This boy lived alone with his grandfather, and in the course of our discussion the lack of a mother figure appeared increasingly relevant. Although the staff gradually perceived that the boy's rages were related to his deprivation and realised that he was therefore calmed by a nurturing, maternal attitude on the part of the staff, there was a constant demand that the clinic team should relieve the staff's anxiety through taking action or responsibility rather than by the more gradual and uncomfortable process of offering understanding and insight. Should the boy not be referred to the clinic, they asked? Should he be sent away to a boarding school? What would happen if he were more accurate with the next milk bottle? These insistent demands for a practical and immediate solution made real discussion difficult, and interfered with the help we could offer through our knowledge.

We emphasised the need to stick to our original plan of working with as many of the school staff as possible, but the third visit brought a crisis. We arrived on time to find the library locked, while the teachers were still eating and paid little attention to our presence in the dining hall through which the library was approached (my colleagues began to understand why I insisted on meticulous time-keeping on our part). A teacher finally saw us and fetched the key, but the deputy head was five minutes late and made inadequate excuses for his colleagues who drifted in without apology over the next fifteen minutes.

The case presented was another West Indian boy who avoided effort and difficulty, and was supported in this by an over-protective mother. She sent notes claiming that he was delicate and asking that he be excused games and exercises. The staff appeared sympathetic about the inadequacies and fears of both boy and mother and this seem to inhibit them from acknowledging or expressing the frustration and anger they also felt. They wondered whether they should listen to his excuses. Was he really unfit for physical exercise? They appeared to seek an external authority, in the form of medical sanction, to enable them to apply the firmness which they sensed was necessary without running the risk of damaging him. The clinic team sought to help the staff see that the two needs of the child to which they were responding – to challenge the manipulation and firmly demand effort, while at the same time providing nurturance and support – were not incompatible but were in fact complementary. Throughout the discussion a difficulty in integrating these two aspects of parental care, perhaps representing a union of paternal and maternal stereotypes, appeared again and again.

Exactly as the session was due to end, a second case was raised which took us ten minutes over our time and shortened our own brief lunch period. It was no doubt significant that the problem was one of stealing! But I perceived too late the significance of this, and my colleagues were annoyed, I thought, at my allowing the school staff to steal from us. Two of them confirmed this by arriving exactly ten minutes late to the staff conference which followed at the clinic, saying they had needed extra time to finish their lunch; but they refused to accept any suggestion on my part that their lateness had any connection with their feelings over events at the school.

This refusal of my colleagues to accept an interpretation of their behaviour which seemed blatantly obvious led me to question the whole basis on which communication over such issues between professional colleagues needed to rest. I realized that the use of interpretation was really inappropriate, both between my colleagues and myself as their leader, and between ourselves and the school, because it placed those to whom the interpretation was made in a childlike, dependent role and turned them into patients, when we sought above all to share in the solution of problems from our different but complementary professional position. At this point I also perceived that, while *interpretations about* attitudes to authority based on a parent/child model made this impossible, the *use* of actual authority within the professional structure was in no way incompatible with the maintenance of adult professional relationships based on mutual respect.

In fact, the reverse was true; I had not only a right but a duty, as head of the clinic, to demand proper time-keeping at clinic conferences if everyone was to benefit from them; and our team had a similar duty to ensure that the school fulfilled their responsibilities in a situation where they looked to us for guidance. It was clear that my management of the situation, at clinic and school, was permitting anxiety to rise to excessively high levels, thereby threatening the project with breakdown and leading individuals to set up their own boundaries because those I was providing were inadequate.

It was at this point, therefore, that I became convinced that more structure was needed, and that we should accept and work within the hierarchical pattern on which ordinary schools are traditionally based, seeking to modify this temporarily only enough for our purposes. I saw that the headmaster's authority was in fact passed to us by his sanction during the session, and that I, as leader of our group, must be prepared to take his role to some extent. Accordingly I telephoned the head and 'carpeted' him for his staff's lateness and the disrespect this implied. At the next session the rebuke had clearly not only been registered but also passed on down the line. The turn-out was large, everyone was on time and the previous demoralised atmosphere was replaced by a much more keen, alert and cooperative response. I took a more active role to start with in relation to the school and my colleagues, summarising the development of the discussions until then, and linked the problems of authority in their form and content. From this point on the discussions went well, and although the difficulties were repeated later in various forms, we appeared to deal with them more adequately.

Developmental Themes in Case-Discussions

The themes underlying our discussions resembled the progress of a patient in psychotherapy, or the phases through which a training group passes.

Regressive Themes

First, as already described, there was a general regression as the staff brought cases where the presenting problem indicated increasingly primitive and infantile functioning in the children concerned, while the anxiety over the fantasies these cases aroused in the staff was gradually faced. This regression reached its greatest depth, I think, with the discussion of another deprived boy whose uncontrollable screaming obviously aroused panic and rejection in

others. As it happened, this boy gave a blood-curdling demonstration outside the library door at a critical point in our discussion, at
which I reported my own spontaneous fantasy of wishing to strangle
him. This led to the expression of similarly violent but previously
denied feelings in the staff, and enabled us all to accept such
alarming emotions more easily and so also to accept the boy himself.
Other cases discussed were usually not mentioned again for some
time, presumably indicating improvements or at least increased
staff tolerance. After some months we would often be told how
much improved they were. However, they felt this case was beyond
them and the headmaster said firmly that the boy should be seen at
the clinic. I had no alternative but to agree, but I let him wait for two
months.

As I hoped, he was no longer a serious problem by the time I saw
him, and no further action was needed. I found him an open, warm
and friendly boy who agreed he used to get into trouble but said he
had improved because 'the teachers are different this term'. He
found it hard to explain the difference but made such comments as,
'if I'm asked a question and I don't know it, they will tell me now so
the work is easier for me'. A school report stated that he was less
aggressive, was working harder, was helpful to the staff, and appeared happy. There was no mention of the screaming attacks and
the tone of the report was strikingly sympathetic and positive. Two
months later, both mother and boy reported further improvement
at home.

Themes of control and sharing

After this nadir was reached we appeared to undergo a maturational
process as the cases presented demonstrated successive stages of
child development. The staff group, and indeed our own team,
steadily became able to function with greater freedom, confidence
and spontaneity. The need for the initial hierarchical structure
diminished, and all members began to share responsibility more
readily. Teachers seemed less threatened by the group, more
confident of the value of their individual opinions and increasingly
aware that honest expression of differences would lead most quickly
to the truth we searched for. The developmental process in our own
team paralleled or perhaps preceded that of the school. In our
own team hierarchy was more pronounced and I usually took the

lead; at the first session, when I suggested we should all distribute ourselves among the staff around the central table, my colleagues compromised by sitting opposite me but next to each other!

Later, we functioned increasingly as a group, and if I did not feel I had a useful response to a comment by the school I could be sure that someone else from the clinic would rise to the occasion. I think our own capacity to discuss and disagree openly was a crucial example for the school staff with which they gradually identified, and they did indeed confirm this later. The development of the group is clearly seen in the following session, where sexual associations of adolescence were manifested for the first time both in the case presented and in the interaction of the staff.

My report of the meeting states:

> This must have been the largest gathering we ever had in the school, between fifty and sixty including ourselves. The room was full, the central table crowded and all the surrounding tables occupied as well, though it was noticeable that many people could have sat centrally but preferred not to do so. People were mostly on time. They seemed keen and involved, and the impression was of a very positive and interested attitude. The main feature of the case-discussion was the way in which the group became split down the middle, as far as the school staff were concerned, on sexual lines. The case presented was of an adolescent boy who seemed, from many elements of his story, to be unsure of himself as a male. He lacked confidence with all the girls in his class and though he tried to win approval, they did not respect him. The staff were particularly concerned that he was known to have interfered sexually with a much younger girl on more than one occasion.
>
> In the discussion it emerged that he caused little problem to two of the male teachers, who managed him in a way which increased his confidence, and he also seemed to be amenable with three female teachers whose relationship with him was mainly motherly and based on their perception of his feelings of inadequacy, so that they encouraged and supported him. The main difficulties arose with those teachers, both men and women, who responded to his sexual challenge as a kind of

37

threat to themselves, and who could not see it as indicating a need for help and support.

An active, lively discussion ensued throughout the session with much giggling and laughter and with undertones of sexual excitement which clearly indicated that the staff were resonating to the same sexual issues with which the boy was struggling. One of the main complainers about this boy was a young and attractive female teacher who demonstrated a marked 'masculine protest'; she seemed to feel challenged and threatened by this boy's behaviour, needing to control him and in effect castrate him. Most of the staff seemed to feel helped and satisfied by a focus on the boy's feelings of sexual inadequacy and the way in which it was revealing itself in all the symptoms; they gradually began to understand, where they had not done so already, that the boy needed help in finding a satisfactory masculine identity. We suggested the male teachers might facilitate this by offering themselves as stable, reliable and strong paternal figures who would demand cooperation from the boy and help him to control himself, while the women could also build his confidence through helping him to feel more sexually adequate in his relationship to them, making him feel more of a man. Most people agreed with this but the pretty teacher who found such difficulty with him continued to protest. However, the school staff as a whole were obviously beginning to operate in relationship to us and each other as adolescents, talking for the first time as if they were aware of sexual differences and able to find some pleasure in them. Their amused response to their still dissatisfied colleague made us confident that they would continue to assist her maturation!

It would be misleading to leave the impression that progress in understanding and in group development was continuous. As in therapy or in a training group, a marked advance would often be followed by a partial regression, a well attended and lively session by lateness, absence and seemingly unrewarding interchange. The session reported above, for example, was followed by another in which many of the events of the difficult third session repeated themselves. We found ourselves once again locked out and the teachers eating; almost everyone was late and they made no excuses. The discussions of cases seemed inconclusive and marked by indifference and fragmentation with people often talking together in twos or threes. The children discussed all showed similar characteristics, living in grandiose, wish-fulfilling fantasy, lying, stealing and challenging the teachers' authority in subtle ways. Our psychotherapist member pointed out the denial of adolescent challenge to adult authority in these cases, and though I did not grasp it at the time, I perceived later through my colleagues' comments that the staff were saying to us, like the children to them, 'we can do without you', but doing so in a way that 'stole' from us by denying the value of the help we had given to make it possible. Nevertheless the situation in the group as a whole was by now very different and such challenges to us were dealt with by interchange among the staff members, as if part of this group had internalised our function.

Termination

These two sessions occurred towards the end of the second year of our meetings, when we discussed with the staff whether to continue or terminate. There was much enthusiasm for the meetings and a firm decision to continue, which our team shared, but the discussions in the following term seemed to have lost their former liveliness and vigour and attendance was less reliable. It took us some time to realise that we had all decided to continue because we had come to like and respect each other and to look forward with enjoyment to the meetings, but that our work was already done. We perceived that we had prevented the school from taking the next step of separating from us and making what they had learned their own. When we suggested this, they agreed with our assessment. During a few more meetings which focused on working through the termination, there were feelings of strong ambivalence and evidence that the school was already making such group discussions an integral part of their work.

Discussion

Though what we learned will be apparent from the description of the experience, it may be helpful to set out the main conclusions in more compact form.

Basic Principles

1. The visits of our team seemed without doubt a highly effective and economical way of dealing successfully with the wide range of problem children who would otherwise have been referred to the clinic, probably with limited cooperation and poor results despite a large expenditure of professional time. *The whole culture of the school was changed towards a 'therapeutic community' function.* This enhanced the existing positive factors by additional psychological understanding so that clinic involvement was necessary only for a limited time, apart of course from the on-going support through traditional clinic functions in cases they could not cope with.

2. Meeting with the whole staff avoided many problems encountered when a part of the teaching staff attends a conventional training group elsewhere. Instead of conflicts of values being stimulated between those receiving the training and those who do not, with anxieties aroused in senior staff that their authority may be undermined, *everyone shared in this experience and, as with a family in conjoint treatment, such resistances and conflicts were clearly faced and resolved at each step.*

3. *In working with an institution in this way, it proved desirable to accept the existing structure and relationships and to work within these*, rather than attempt to impose a different frame of reference from the beginning as may be desirable in a training situation conducted away from the setting in which the actual work is carried out. *Thus in visiting schools one should be prepared at first to fall to some extent into the traditional teacher/pupil pattern. The new ethos can be communicated gradually, in the course of the discussions.*

4. To preserve relationships of mutual professional respect and avoid placing the staff of the institution in a 'child' or 'patient' role, interpretations should be avoided in general and insights communicated by other means.

Some of these are:

    a: Focusing on the dynamics of the case, recognising that this always reflects the current pre-occupation of the group at the time it is presented, but leaving it to the group to understand this for themselves through identification. Caplan (1964), has of course done much to clarify this technique.[6]

b: Demonstrating the value of freer communication through the actual functioning of the clinic team. The fact that much learning of new skills takes place through identification with the clinic team helps to justify the greater professional time involved when several clinic members participate.

c: Many issues which could, under other circumstances, be worked out in treatment by interpretation can be dealt with equally well by exchanges within the bounds of ordinary professional relationships. This is clearly illustrated by my criticising the staff's behaviour towards us in session 3 instead of interpreting this behaviour in terms of infantile conflict.

d: Interpretation can nevertheless be safely used if one applies it also to oneself, thus sharing the experience and understanding rather than 'talking down'. My expression of my impulse to strangle the screaming boy was an example of this, allowing the staff to accept their own primitive emotions and in turn to accept the boy who had provoked them.

5. It was most important that we did not see the children discussed, though the staff often asked us to do so. By working as we did we were obliged to see the children through the eyes of the staff, and they to some extent through ours. *Thus the very difficulties of communicating about the problems, provided we struggled honestly to understand, ensured that what emerged contained the psychological insight of the school as well as the clinic team and brought the two closer together to form a new and more comprehensive understanding.*

6. The beneficial effects of these meetings seemed to come from this understanding, which in its turn brought acceptance and more appropriate handling. The children presented had been rejected in the sense that they had not been understood. They could not be contained psychologically in the minds of those dealing with them. It was clear that these children responded dramatically to the feeling

41

of acceptance and contact they received when the staff could look at them squarely and simply without fear or puzzlement.

7. Needless to say, some knowledge of the laws of group interaction, and of large groups in particular, is vital if one is to cope with such a complex situation. Fortunately, such training is becoming more widely available and the Institute of Group Analysis, for example, now includes a large group experience as part of its Introductory Course in Group Work.[7] Those who have worked with large groups have often preferred to do so in company with a team of colleagues, and this experience certainly emphasised the value of such an approach. A situation of this complexity is a heavy burden for a single-handed conductor and a team is undoubtedly able to offer more adequate and flexible leadership. It was also of great importance to have the different disciplines represented. Time and again the child analyst made the child's behaviour meaningful to the staff when I had no adequate answer. The psychiatric social worker was able to represent the parents' point of view, or that of other agencies involved, while the educational psychologist who visited the school in other capacities was known and trusted by the staff. She had teaching experience as part of her background and frequently played a vital role in helping us perceive where difficulties of communication might lie, and in clarifying the difficulties of each side to the other.

Conclusion: Three-Year Follow Up

Just over three years after the experiment ended, the educational psychologist and I returned to take lunch with some of the staff in order to assess the long-term effects of our meetings. There was evident pleasure on both sides at renewing our acquaintance, but there was a comment by one teacher that they wished they could still have our help with problems, which sounded more like an expression of politeness than of need. This was confirmed when, after the initial exchange of courtesies, we enquired about current difficulties. The teachers looked at one another, increasingly perplexed, and one said, 'Whatever became of all those problems we used to meet?' The children discussed at our meetings had, with one exception, all improved, and even this exception had been contained and coped with until the normal leaving age. They found it

difficult to think of any children currently presenting serious problems, and even the one they finally remembered was clearly not
occasioning much anxiety.

This change had occurred in a context, according to the educational psychologist who still works in the area, of a continuing
increase in maladjustment in most other schools in the locality. It
was, however, impossible to decide how much our meetings had
contributed to this improvement. The school had moved from its
previous Victorian buildings to spacious new premises; there had
been more time for the old schools combined in this comprehensive
to integrate; and a new system of year-masters had been instituted
to provide pastoral care.[8] Nevertheless, other schools which had
possessed similar advantages over a longer period were suffering
more acute problems. The staff here spoke of the ability they now
had to share problems and communicate about them, as well as the
confidence they now possessed that they could cope. If they had
derived some of these new strengths from their meetings with us,
they had clearly forgotten their origin, so much had they made this
new knowledge their own. And that, I believe, is as it should be.

Notes

1 This chapter was first published as a paper in *Group Process*, 6
  (1974) 99.
2 Skynner's model of group-analytic family therapy is developed in
  One Flesh: Separate Persons and *Explorations With Families*
  chapter 4 and the five chapters in Section 3 of that collection. (Ed.)
3 For further references to this idea see, for example, *The Neurotic
  Organisation*, M. F. R. Kets de Vries and D. Miller 1984.
4 Skynner is referring here to Queen Elizabeth Hospital for Children
  and Woodberry Down Child Gudance Unit, both referred to in the
  Author's Introduction, note 3.
5 For a description of further work along these lines see, for example,
  E. Dowling and E. Osborne, (eds), *The Family and the School: a
  Joint Systems Approach To Problems With Children*, 1985.
6 Readers interested in following this reference to Caplan's early
  work should also be aware of his major text, *The Theory And
  Practice of Mental Health Consultation*, which was to appear in 1970
  shortly before this paper of Skynner's. Despite its importance as the
  single most useful publication on consultation, Caplan's major text

is, remarkably, out of print. Skynner's acknowledged use of this work here and elsewhere in the book gives ready access to Caplan's ideas on the subject.

7 See The Large Group In Training, chapter 9 below.

8 A major research project directed by Michael Rutter at the Institute of Psychiatry, arrived at the conclusion that certain school characteristics – institutionally specific factors – play a vital part in determining the outlook and quality of a school's provisions. See M. Rutter, et al., *Fifteen Thousand Hours: Secondary Schools and Their Effects on Children*. Skynner is here offering a method for influencing these school characteristics towards 'open-systems' functioning.

Two

APPLICATIONS TO LARGER SYSTEMS: Leadership and Consultation

4 Child Guidance from Within: Reactions to New Pressures

(Paper Given to the 23rd Inter-Clinic Conference, London 1967)

Spanning a period of twenty-one years, the five papers in this section were each delivered as a formal address to occasions held by different organisations. They provide a history of Skynner's development and, in extending the principles developed in the first section to the development of larger institutions, they also provide a history of family and marital therapy in Britain.

Skynner's central concern with training is conveyed in a conversational style to which anecdotes – from both case histories and his personal life – give a distinctive openness. The level of self-disclosure increases as he and the group-analytic approach mature and he takes the reader increasingly into his confidence about what might appear to be stresses and failures which, when explored, can lead to success and achievement. The use of modelling, as important in Skynner's teaching as in his clinical work, requires an informality and openness which comes through in these presentations. They were not intended to be academic documents but, rather, to facilitate and gain wider acceptance for the changes in professional work that he is presenting. They therefore have a commemorative sense and convey in descriptive terms 'the state of the art' at the time they were delivered.

The first paper was given to an Inter-Clinic Conference in the Child Guidance Movement in 1967. These were major events in Children's Services and Skynner used the occasion to give one of the first clinical presentations in this country on family therapy. The paper's importance is not only historical. Those currently concerned with the protection of services for children will find much here to guide them as Skynner defines the need for change at a

47

critical point and gives direction to developments that were to have lasting influence.

The most revolutionary of the developments described here include:

- the wide focus recommended on the total social network involved in each referral to define the key combination of people – the minimum sufficient network – with whom intervention is likely to be most economical and effective.
- a corresponding broad definition of the clinical team to undertake this work, drawing on a range of skills and experience within which multi-disciplinary differences are used as a resource.

Though it is not always used explicitly, the concept of the minimum sufficient network now underlies much of family therapy practice in Britain, and multi-professional or multi-disciplinary teams also play an essential part. The case study here is reproduced in full because, whilst it is currently available in *Explorations with Families*, where it illustrates the opening chapter, readers of this volume will not necessarily have access to it.

Many of the personal references in these chapters are to Skynner's own marriage and to his late wife, with whom he worked as co-therapist and co-trainer until her death in 1987. Their partnership is at the centre of a number of these papers and chapter 6 is, in fact, written jointly by the two of them. Prudence died whilst this book was in preparation and the papers stand together as the most eloquent account of her contribution to the field. Skynner pays tribute to it in chapters 5 to 8.

J.R.S.

Introduction

In reviewing the practical and psychological pressures to which Child Guidance Clinics are currently exposed,[1] it is suggested that the structures of clinics and the roles of the team, established when knowledge of group theory and therapy was minimal, have crystallised our thinking in individual concepts and delayed the acceptance and use of true group and family approaches. The development of ideas regarding groups are briefly reviewed and a case is presented to illustrate the limitations of individual-centred thinking with certain types of problem. Finally, some concepts are presented that lead towards a more unified way of thinking about interpersonal and intrapersonal events.

Over the past few years we have, in these conferences,[2] left our clinics to examine our links with adult psychiatry, with the social services generally, and with the community. Though this discovery of new viewpoints and approaches has been stimulating, it has perhaps left us in a certain temporary confusion as we try to integrate our discoveries within our existing framework of knowledge. We need now to withdraw temporarily to digest what we have been given, to re-establish our limits and boundaries and find ourselves again. Speakers were therefore charged with the task of returning to the work of our clinics as the central theme of our contributions, focusing especially on ways in which we are trying to respond to the new pressures we face in a changing world.

This theme interested me especially because, for two years, I have been engaged, in company with my colleagues at the Woodberry Down Child Guidance Clinic, in just this type of enquiry. We have felt the need to set aside time when we could examine and criticise our current approaches as well as the ideas of others, in the hope that new and clearer principles would emerge. Today I shall try to summarise and share with you some of the conclusions we have reached together, and I shall try to place them in the larger context of the development of our fundamental concepts.

Sources of Pressure in Clinics

1. The mounting demand for treatment

What are these pressures? They come, I think, from four main directions. To begin with, the very success of those who pioneered our disciplines has led to a demand for treatment far beyond the resources we have to provide it, even in those areas where psychiatric services are best developed. We have come of age, and despite our comparative youth, the limitations of our work and the harm often done by excessive claims, nevertheless the value and usefulness of our knowledge and techniques is now so firmly established that, far from needing to advertise our wares, we are increasingly preoccupied with mounting referrals and waiting lists. Even the recent controversy over the value of psychotherapy is an indirect tribute to our success, for the opposition becomes more emotional and vocal, though retaining the guise of scientific argument, as the truths we have long recognised and stood for become impossible to evade.

2. Consultative services to other professionals

Secondly, our disciplines have become steadily more respected and valued by other professionals, so that we are increasingly called upon to provide consultative services where others can draw upon the body of knowledge our clinics and departments have accumulated, in order to illuminate the social, psychological and psychiatric aspects of problems they meet in the course of their own work. The beneficial implications of such diagnostic and consultative services to other professionals are in some ways even greater than those possible through the provision of treatment since – through consultation – we increase the capacity of others to carry a share of the treatment load. Nevertheless, the initial investment of time and energy is heavy and to start with we can expect little return, so that for some time this work simply makes mounting demands on our resources.

50

3. The development of social services

A third set of pressures is coming from the social services generally, and from the community as a whole, in a different way. The various social and medical services, voluntary and statutory, set up piecemeal to provide for different types of human need, have developed to a point where a more rational integration is inescapable. The findings of the Seebohm Committee are now awaited hopefully – or apprehensively – by us all and the conclusions of this and similar investigations are bound to alter our roles and relationships and to demand that we find our place within a larger whole if we are to play our full part in the future.[3]

4. New concepts and treatments

Fourthly, more subtle pressures have come from within our own discipline, in the form of new concepts and theories[4] which are requiring us to rethink our whole approach to our work, and putting us into the kind of potentially productive confusion which Erikson has called Identity Crisis. These more subtle pressures demanding our adaptation take many forms, but they all result from a growing integration of our existing knowledge, providing unified theories where rival and apparently incompatible viewpoints existed before. For example, the influence of genetic and environmental factors, both physical and psychological, over which warring schools once took sides, are beginning to find their true place in a balanced whole. Psychoanalytic ideas and learning theory, still seen by some as rival claimants to the task of explaining human behaviour, are becoming viewed as two facets of one truth which can eventually complement each other, provided we are not so naive or possessive as to claim either as exclusive truth in its present form.

An Historical Overview of Child Guidance: Its Concepts and Contexts

One reason, perhaps, why such integrations provoke our resistance at first is that they *stretch us, they demand that we admit the imperfections of our existing ideas, and force us to begin again to construct something more subtle and difficult.* This applies equally to another integration, between the worlds of psychology and sociology. This has resulted in the understanding we now possess of group

51

dynamics and the variety of methods available for securing the benefit of individuals referred to us by treating them in group situations, whether natural groups of married couples, families and so on, or artificial ones especially brought together for a therapeutic purpose, such as therapeutic communities. In reflecting on the subject of this meeting today, I found that our expanding ability to view the individual within the context of the group proved to have more relevance than I had previously realised, to all the other problems I have just mentioned. I would like to make a brief survey of the development of our work in order to indicate how some of our present problems of adaptation have their roots in the time when the concepts then current were crystalised into the structure of Child Guidance Clinics. This basic form has remained relatively unchanged ever since and has, in my view, automatically restricted the development of our theory and practice.

We are faced, it seems, with a curious paradox. From the establishment of the first clinics forty years ago, child psychiatry has been more ready to see those referred to them against a social context, and to direct attention and therapeutic effort towards other family members. At the same time we are in some ways more rigidly set in the patient-centred, individual-centred, two-person relationship-centred viewpoint than much of adult psychiatry or social work generally. Our discipline began with a most remarkable stride in the direction of a more comprehensive, rational and enlightened approach to human suffering. The focus of interest moved beyond the individual child to his family and all the social influences playing upon him, while members of related disciplines – psychiatrists, social workers, psychologists, psychotherapists and others – began to work together in a partnership that was decades in advance of its time. But we have done this despite our theoretical concepts which have remained rooted in the psychology of the individual and have prevented us from recognising the implications of our own experience, which could educate us towards a broader approach.

This has come about, I believe, because the structure of our clinics, and our clinical roles, were laid down around 1920 when the main findings of Freud and Jung were still being worked out in terms of the individual. The processes discovered within the individual psyche proved to be so subtle and complex, and so difficult to view without subjective bias, that nearly half a century was needed to map out the main features with any certainty. During this time it might well have been harmful to this primary task if too much attention had been given to the still greater complexities of individuals in group interaction.

But within psychiatry, a number of factors combined to increase interest in psychological processes extending beyond the individual, round about the time of the Second World War. Cultural anthropologists were revealing information about child development in other cultures, which called into question the biological orientation underlying Freud's ideas and demonstrated that the role of cultural and social factors was far greater than had been thought. In the United States neo-Freudians such as Fromm, Horney and Sullivan were modifying analytic theory to take account of these findings. In this country Melanie Klein and her followers were extending our psychological understanding back into earliest infancy and into the psychotic stages corresponding to this period of life. Investigation of these early months of human development necessitated a radical change in our view of what constitutes a human personality, for at this stage the boundaries between mother and infant scarcely exist, and the two, if all is going well, interpenetrate and face with each other to a point that makes it impossible to consider them apart. The War was splitting up families, and on both sides of the Atlantic the consequences of early mother-child relationships received increasing experimental study. Spitz, Goldfarb, Bender, Bowlby, and others, encouraged a view of mother and child as a couple, not understandable in isolation from one another. Schilder and Wender had already made their first tentative experiments in bringing psychiatric patients together for treatment when, during the war, psychiatrists and psychoanalysts found themselves in large group situations within the armed services, and were called upon to play a part in selection, training and treatment procedures. Psychiatrists began to experiment with the possibilities of the group, and began to see it as an added dimension which gave new therapeutic potentials rather than just hindrances to intimate contact. At the Northfield Military Hospital, S. H. Foulkes had begun to develop his group-analytic technique which now forms the basis of group work at many leading centres. Bion and Rickman were simultaneously experimenting there along similar lines which later led to the group approaches of the Tavistock Clinic and Institute, and all the work which has flowed from this. In England Maxwell Jones, Main and others extended these developments to mental hospitals, transforming the whole environment to a therapeutic community, a concept now fundamental to the in-patient treatment of adults. Balint had been stimulated by his earlier experience in Hungary, where the fact that training cases were supervised by the trainee's own analyst led to more focus on the counter-transference than was usual here. His consequent perception of analyst and analysand as a couple led him to use the group situation for training purposes, focusing on the trainee's own responses to the patient (often reproduced in the group's response to the trainee) as keys to understanding. In the United States, roughly similar developments in group therapy of adults were taking place in parallel. In the United States, too, comparable developments took place within the field of child psychiatry. Slavson, Durkin, Axline and Ginnott, to mention only a few, recognised these new possibilities and applied them with considerable success to the therapy of children and parents. Though at first they followed established adult techniques by placing children and their mothers in separate homogeneous groups, there soon developed an increased awareness of the importance of fathers (who were discovered about 1955!) and this led in turn to the inclusion of siblings and the emergence, especially in this decade, of techniques and theoretical concepts applicable to the psychotherapy of the family together, notably by such American authorities as Ackerman, Bell, Jackson, Fleck and Grotjahn. For reasons which are still unclear to me, but which perhaps have to do with the very richness of the knowledge produced in this country through individual analysis and psychotherapy with children, *we have been slower to enrich ourselves with these new treatment modalities based on the group, and our discipline remains individual and patient-centred to a degree not now generally found in other fields.* Certainly it is partly due to the fact that the structure of our clinics, and the form of our training were laid down at a time when it was assumed to be better to split the family and talk with members in separate individual interviews. *The contemporary challenge to this way of thinking and working is one of the major theoretical pressures we face, but if we can meet it I believe it can help us more than anything else to deal with the practical pressures for more and more adequate treatment and consultation, and for our integration within the larger group situation of the social services as a whole.*

An illustration of family therapy at work

What follows is an example I have chosen because it illustrates the possibilities of family therapy with unusual brevity and clarity, as well as some charm. Other colleagues from our clinic here today could tell you that this intensity of interaction and speed of change is by no means unusual. I have presented it to show how we can easily collude in a family splitting process, and make things more difficult for ourselves, by our conventional focus on the referred patient. Family therapy has some merits in dealing with this.

Sandra, then aged twelve, was referred to a child guidance clinic for persistent stealing and jealous, provocative behaviour at home and school. Several months of separate treatment led to symptomatic improvement in the child but complete deadlock in interviews with the mother, who rejected any connection between Sandra's problems and her own personality, despite the fact that she recalled she had been very similar in her own childhood.

Six months later the problem recurred. This time the whole family were seen as a group: Sandra, her sister Susan, one year older, her brother Philip, one year younger, and two younger children, four and five, who played near the father and mother but took no active part.

The first interview

Everyone began by blaming Sandra, who at first appeared to seek acceptance, then became stubborn and defensive and eventually wept. Doing in the group what she was always said to do at home, she excluded herself and drew her brother into mischievous whispering. Mother then spoke of her own closeness to the elder sister Susan. Sandra said, 'But I have got Dad.' Father, looking uncomfortable, denied this. The interview was otherwise unproductive. My co-therapist, a psychiatric social worker, was confirmed in his belief that Sandra's difficulties were not explicable in terms of family dynamics, and I partially agreed. On reflection though, I recalled how hard Sandra had tried to establish a good relationship in the earlier part of the interview, and how she had been driven relentlessly into opposition.

The second interview

At the next consultation two months later everyone again accused and reproached Sandra, and treated her as the family problem. This time she did not attempt to defend herself and refused to take part even when I invited her to do so. The other children said Sandra was carrying out her threat to keep silent and possibly to leave.

I pointed out how everyone was again focusing on Sandra as the problem and suggested that she was in some way functioning as a scapegoat. I acknowledged that I had colluded in this at the previous session. At this mother put up a good deal of resistance, pressuring me to alter my assessment, but I reaffirmed it. The parents then began to talk about their own feelings of failure. Father said that Sandra made him feel frustrated, mother that she made her feel helpless and inadequate. Sandra still refused to join in even when I invited her. The other two children said she feared she would be picked on if she spoke, and at this point Sandra said she had been picked on by the whole family after the previous interview. The parents denied this, claiming the children had freedom to speak their minds, and Sandra began to sulk once more.

At this point an unexpected intervention came from the elder sister, Susan. (Unexpected in that such interventions are always a surprise, even though in family therapy the siblings often play this crucial role.) She hesitated, then plucked up her courage and said: 'It will all have to come out now, it will all come in a rush, and everything will have to be said, even if people get upset.' She then began to attack her father, saying he was always picking on the children because he was so grumpy. Father, passive and withdrawn until this point, became animated and defended himself, while Susan's criticisms became more vehement. Sandra entered the discussion again, giving up her role of the naughty child and defending her father fiercely against the criticism. From this point on she remained a member of the group and only once fell briefly back into her previous, excluded position. Mother joined Susan in criticising father. Eventually all three children including Sandra were criticising him, saying he was always complaining but never really firm; they said he would keep on at them about doing the washing up, but would eventually do it himself. The three children all agreed that he should be more definite and *make* them do it. As all the children attacked father in this way, mother moved to his defence, though she seemed to agree with their criticisms, saying among other things that the children were not as helpful as they should be.

It was at this point that the attack seemed to move to mother, and it came first from the boy Philip. He complained that even when they tried to help, the parents would not accept it. He instanced an occasion when he had offered to go and make the tea but mother had stopped him, saying that he would only make a mess. The other children began to agree that the mother had no right to grumble, since she would not accept their help when they offered it. A sudden change now occurred in the group pattern. It seemed only a few seconds before the whole family were once again attacking Sandra in the way they had done in the beginning, blaming her for being stubborn and unhelpful.

I interrupted to point out how Sandra had been an active and constructive member of the discussion, accepted by everyone, until everyone had suddenly begun to blame her and drive her outside the family circle. This had followed immediately on some criticism of the mother, the only one who had avoided it till this point. The mother began to argue stubbornly with me, saying that it was Sandra who had been sent to the clinic as the problem; they had all come to have something done about *her*. I said we had now clearly seen that the problem lay in the family as a whole; they could all be united against Sandra when Sandra was bad but when Sandra was not in this position as scapegoat, other family conflicts immediately began to emerge. Susan said, 'Yes, the real problem might not be Sandra at all, but someone else.' Mother still seemed angry with me. She was determined to keep the problem in the children, and to disagree with my formulation. After a short time the parents and I noticed that the girls were pulling faces and whispering. We asked what this was about. Susan once again took the role of family spokesman, this time criticising the mother. Apprehensive but firm and definite, she said that the mother was not the same since the babies had arrived. 'She is different, she has changed completely.' All three older children gradually joined in the unanimous criticism of mother, saying she gave all her love to the two smaller ones and had little left for them. They felt the mother did not realise they still had needs, just as the babies did.

After these criticisms of mother had continued for some time, she began to attack Susan, usually her ally. One of the most interesting and moving moments in the interview came when Sandra then suddenly leapt to Susan's defence, saying, 'Now we are all doing to Susan what everyone was doing to me when we came in.' The time allotted to the interview was nearing its end. I suggested that just as the older children still needed something they had had as babies, mother might have her needs too. The mother said she wanted to give them all the affection she could but that they would have to help her more so that she could in turn give more time. Susan seemed to be less forgiving and to be dictating terms to mother, while it was Sandra who now defended and supported mother. Strong feelings of affection and need appeared to be released at this point, after the earlier feelings of resentment and rebellion. The older children seemed to be trying to come to terms with the fact that the babies now needed to have what they had had before. Susan said, 'We had all the love before they came. At first I was alone, and I had everything, then Sandra came and she had it, and now the little ones have to have it instead.'

The third interview

At the third family consultation a month later, the situation had changed dramatically. Sandra had been integrated into the family and remained a member throughout the session. She seemed to have little need to speak, she was warm and relaxed and, significantly, looked after the two younger children throughout. Susan, by contrast, was now revealing a full-blown adolescent conflict with the mother which at times would include all the children and both parents, over the usual adolescent strivings for independence. The father for the first time took a leading role and both parents felt that all this was a natural stage they had to pass through. They did not wish for further help but wanted access if necessary.[4]

Who Should Do This Work? Family Therapy and Multi-Disciplinary Teams

One question I would like to ask is this: who should do this work? The emergence of these techniques poses new problems regarding our roles and relationships. Should it be the prerogative of the psychiatrist? I should be sorry to think so, for this would gravely limit the aid such methods could give us in dealing with mounting demands for help. It would also fail to draw upon the special skills and experience of other members of the team – the PSW's (Psychiatric Social Worker's) long experience of dealing with families, the educational psychologist's expertise in the educational use of group situations, the psychotherapist's special knowledge of individual psychopathology and treatment, with all the light this could throw on group approaches as well. But if the PSW's work is to be widened in this way, surely more experience of child therapy is needed. If the psychotherapist is to do the work it will require far more attention to group dynamics and techniques than is at present given in training programmes. If it is to be part of the psychologist's role, a clearer therapeutic role must be assigned and prepared for.

It seems to me that the training of all members of the team should include a wider common basis, as well as the more particular skills specific to each function. Certainly all should share some training and experience in the therapy of adults, adolescents and children, by individual and group methods. Ideally this common foundation should be laid before qualification, but it may be possible to accomplish a good deal by in-service training alone. Fortunately, conjoint family therapy is something conducted with multiple

59

therapists, and one partial solution to the training problem, ready to hand, is the use of periodic joint sessions, attended by all members of the family and all the members of the clinic team involved in the case. This is a regular event at our clinic, as well as many others, and if all who take part learn as much as I do from these meetings their time is well spent.

There is a further reason why such an expansion of our techniques is desirable. Treatment of individuals in a group context not only offers economies in time and effort; it also extends the range of our therapeutic powers because certain types of problem, comprising a large proportion of those referred to us, are more accessible in a group situation. Some are treatable *only* in a group, and are relatively untreatable individually.

The Minimum Sufficient Network

Why is this so? To explain this, it will help if I introduce the idea of the 'minimum sufficient network'. This is a cumbersome phrase and I should be delighted if someone can suggest an alternative. By it I mean the minimum assembly of psychological structures which can function autonomously. These structures may all be within one person, or they may involve a number of people. In the kind of neurotic patient on whom psychoanalysis was first practised and developed, these necessary psychological structures were more or less all within the individual, and treatment directed to that person alone, without involving relatives or other people in contact with him, was more or less adequate. However, even when confined within one person the 'minimum sufficient network' may involve a greater or lesser part of the personality. In traumatic neurosis, for example, a large part of the personality may remain intact, so that our effort can be directed to a limited aspect of the person's functioning and treatment may be relatively swift. With character neurosis, on the other hand, the problem may involve most of the personality and here we may expect treatment to be more prolonged.

Though these are the cases we prefer and feel most at home with, many of the cases referred to us in child guidance practice do not fall within this category. With many referrals, particularly among those who are less intelligent, educationally deprived or who come from limited or chaotic backgrounds, there is often confusion over identities and roles, extensive employment of projection and introjection, use of different family members as externalised good objects or bad objects; and, in general, a splitting and sharing of psychological functions between individuals to a point where it is meaningless to try to consider one person in isolation. One child may act out a parent's denied impulses; this parent may then act as a superego figure, blaming and punishing the child to control the projection, but their own capacities may be so limited that they use the other parent as a repository of ego strength to achieve this control. Another child, the 'good one', may be used to keep the parent's good qualities safe against the destructive feelings which are kept in or directed at the 'bad' child. In such a case, no individual is able to make use of the full range of psychological functions that a mature adult recognises in order to operate. Only in combination do the members of the family have available an 'ego', 'superego' and 'id'. Only in combination can they operate adequately or be treated. Here the 'minimum sufficient network' represents the minimum number of individuals which must be involved in therapy if therapeutic change is to be possible.

The 'minimum sufficient network' may, however, reach beyond the nuclear or even the extended family, to include some part of the wider community. Families which function in a primitive way will often involve others in their psychopathology, projecting personality functions on to community agencies. One of the commonest patterns we meet is referred to us as a child who presents a behaviour problem at school but is said to be normal enough at home. It frequently transpires that the mother is herself seriously immature, unable to tolerate frustration or rejection. In an attempt to avoid conflict with the child and maintain a close relationship, she projects all controlling functions on to the father, from whom she then shields the child. The parents would then find themselves in conflict (in a more open or more subtle way), but they can avoid this if they both identify with the indulgent, nurturing role (essentially 'motherly') and combine to project all controlling and frustrating functions (essentially 'fatherly') on to the school. The school then becomes the target of the parent's hostility and the child too is encouraged to displace his own hostility away from the home and on to teachers. The whole procedure has the purpose of maintaining some unity within the family, and the situation is not easily changed by work with the parents alone, if we omit consideration of the school within the network. In such cases, we have usually found that facilitating communication between the school and the family, as well as between the two parents (both communications really representing marital interactions) is the most effective approach. In being confronted by, and accepting, the school's authority, the father then has the strength to use his authority within the family, and the mother in turn can accept her authority over the child. But first, of course, the clinic must accept its authority in this situation, to confront the various contestants with their true positions in the conflict.

One principle we have discovered is that it is vital not to restrict communication in any way within the minimum sufficient network. To do so is, almost by definition, a guarantee of failure, for we then disconnect elements of a structure which must remain connected if it is to be capable of intelligent response and change. Our conventional notions about confidentiality often get in the way here. For example, we may find ourselves hamstrung if, in a dispute within a family, or between a family and a school, we allow ourselves to receive information from either side with an implicit understanding that it remain secret. We should agree to receive it on these terms only if we make it clear that we cannot help if our hands are tied in this way, and that we can only be useful provided we are trusted to act as honest brokers, assisting the two sides to communicate better. Dealing with such a network throughout as a group is, of course, the simplest solution, for then all communications are automatically shared and the therapist can receive no secrets. Where people are seen separately, we can still avoid the difficulty by *thinking of them as a group, a network which must remain in contact, directly or through our mediation. This is not to question the importance of confidentiality and respect when we receive personal information, but only to emphasise the importance of a clear, open and honest contract at the beginning in cases where our function will be mainly to serve as communicative links.*

This is perhaps a good place to say that I am mainly advocating a different way of thinking rather than a change away from individual towards group methods. At the Woodberry Down Clinic there was a swing towards use of joint marital interviews by the PSW's after I became Director there. Now we have found a balance, and use separate or joint interviews in a more discriminating way, but the individual sessions themselves are in some way changed. One PSW put it that *The father is always present in her mind, even when seeing the mother alone. In speaking of him, therapist or patient may gesture towards his usual chair. The intactness of the network, then, is maintained first in the mind of the therapist, and only secondly through actual procedures.*

The Typical Range of Clients

If we begin to think of a network of functions each time a case is referred to us, other questions at once arise. Who is disturbed? Who is disturbing? Who has the motivation to alter the situation? And who has the capacity to alter it? Four different people may be involved here, or one. If the former, we are in for trouble and disappointment if we follow our usual procedure. Within each network we must locate the main need or motivation, or we will waste time concentrating on the wrong part of the network or ignoring some crucial part of it.

Psychoneurotic problems

A certain proportion of cases come to us because the main need seems to lie in themselves. They knock on the door and complain of depression, of feelings of conflict between conscience and desires, of inability to achieve their aims and find satisfaction in relationships or work. Some parents come in this way for themselves, almost consciously using the child as an admission ticket, seeking help for their own personal distress, their marital difficulties, or their failures as parents. Even when patients of this kind are referred by others, the person referring them may be acting as no more than a signpost, and we may not need to consider them in the network. These are the patients for whom psychoanalysts and analytic psychotherapy, particularly on an individual basis, was first designed, and as long as giving this type of treatment for this type of patient is the best main use of our available resources (which I am, of course, questioning), no particular problem arises.

Applications to Larger Systems

Chaotic families

Next, there is a group of cases, large in child guidance practice, if it is based on the education service rather than a hospital, in which the need for intervention lies in people doing the referring, or in other sections of society who are able to put pressure on the referrers. The families who come in this way tend to include conduct disorders occurring outside the home, especially at school, but which are either absent or within limits of tolerance in the home situation. This group will comprise delinquency, anti-social behaviour, promiscuity, and all the feckless problem families which disturb law-abiding citizens and harass officialdom. In all these the motivation for treatment is in the referrer or in society generally, rather than in the people referred.

There are three types of motivation here:

1. To express impulses and gain instinctual satisfaction
2. To control the impulses because of their harmful consequences, actual or supposed
3. To find a compromise and resolve a conflict between instinctual drives and social controls.

The third category, those with motivation to find a better solution to a conflict between 'superego' and 'id', includes the cases for which our usual techniques are well suited. The first category, people who are seeking instinctual satisfaction without personal conflict, never come to us except under pressure from the second category, who are suffering from them and wish to see them controlled. If we can keep the first two categories in contact (the anti-social family and the socialising forces of society, equivalent to 'id' and 'supergo') and help them to communicate by acting ourselves, in effect, as ego-components, we are then dealing with something like the third situation, a conflict situation with which our techniques are designed to deal, and where we can hope to facilitate a better compromise of more pleasure with less suffering all round.

The Network as the Patient

However, all too often we make the mistake of accepting, explicitly or implicitly, the responsibility for changing this situation. When we do so we automatically become the part of the network which carries the motivation. The referring agency sits back, relieved of its anxiety, leaving everything to us – and so does the family referred, if it had any anxiety in the first place. The anxiety and concern is experienced instead by the clinic staff who, in most cases, lack the facilities either to supply what the family needs or the authority or social sanctions necessary to control them. Much of the disappointment and frustration that other people experience in their dealings with child guidance clinics stems, I believe, from this fundamental mistake. In such situations our functions should always be to act as a communicative link between the people expressing the impulse and those wishing to see it controlled, without seeking to change matters ourselves. For example, one often finds situations where a family is in constant conflict with authority as if seeking to provoke it into some positive action they really need, but where the authority, be it court, school or probation service, hesitates to act because the family are at the same time arousing feelings of concern and sympathy. Where this is the case the clinic can often bring the two sides to a more fruitful awareness of their relationship, helping the family to see that what they are really demanding, yet resisting, is benevolent control, and helping the authority to provide this without oscillating between attitudes of punitiveness or indulgence.

The Dynamics of Referral Systems

Sometimes we accept more responsibility than we should because the pressure is coming indirectly from the patient referred, through a referrer. Insistent demands from referrers that a case should be seen or treated often arise when the referrer is unconsciously frightened of the rage which threatens if a patient's demands are frustrated. One way to avoid this is to identify with the patient, and incorporate the demand, which is then passed on to the clinic. If this is not recognised, the clinic becomes wrongly involved in an interminable therapy with the family, as if feeling obliged endlessly to feed an insatiable child, located in both patient and referrer. Discussion with the referrer, so that psychologically the demands can be put back in the family where they belong, and where they could perhaps provide motivation, is of course the right action.

Networks of this kind can be quite complex. In one family which functions in many ways at a psychotic level, treatment of the mother by a PSW led her to stop accepting the whole family's depressions, which she had previously done partly to shield father from an awareness of his own inadequacy. As the mother became more aggressive and faced him with increasing awareness of his own impotence the father, frightened of hitting back at her, wanted to punish the daughter instead. But lacking the capacity even to do this, he repeatedly aroused the anxiety of the child's physician in a hospital where the older sister had died of a kidney infection. This history lay behind the physician's repetitive demand for psycho- therapy for the younger sister, despite the fact that treatment was repeatedly offered by the psychotherapist and sabotaged by the family.

In the children's hospital at which I work I find a fair proportion of patients are sent because the paediatricians feel they have done some harm in a way they cannot understand. Most often the mothers are schizoid, and the paediatricians have unwittingly accepted a hostile projection, acting upon it by becoming angry and blaming, and feeling subsequently that they made matters worse by their intervention. This usually proves to be a fantasy in the physician's mind, for they have in fact been used as part of a defensive splitting manoeuvre, but it will interfere with their future handling of the family and my procedure is to clarify what has happened and relieve the guilt associated with it, by showing how and why I have had an exactly similar experience in my own interview. I recall a rather similar case referred by the children's department, where I was unable to understand their insistent demand for psychotherapy which I thought inappropriate, until it emerged that this was a 'second generation' deprivation case, where the children's officer felt doubly responsible for not having averted this present problem through their handling of mother when she was in care during her own childhood.

These are problems which could happen to any referrer lacking sophistication in psychiatric processes. There are other referrals which have more to do with the psychopathology of the referrer, or perhaps of society itself. One school I know sends us a succession of cases of behaviour problems in children who have suffered depri- vation, even where this is clearly being remedied very effectively, if gradually, by the foster home and school, because the headmistress has suffered deprivation herself. Another school shows exceptional intolerance to being made into a bad object as a solution to a family's difficulties, and reacts to this by simultaneously excluding children and referring them to our clinic, which they use as a bad object in turn. A general practitioner I knew referred a large series of patients for psychotherapy who were often unsuitable because they lacked motivation and came at his persuasion. The referrals ceased when he began his own analysis, no doubt because he was at last able to refer himself directly instead of vicariously.

We can carry this further, of course, and see that many cases are referred because of values in our particular society with which we would not all necessarily agree. It is perhaps just as well that there is not sufficient time to venture into this controversial ground today, but I am sure we have all had experience of demands that children should not be aggressive, or sexual, that they should value academic achievement over living experience, or put social conformity above the search for their own identity.

Conclusion: The Clinic in the Network

Finally, we must consider ways in which the clinic becomes part of the network. Since we are always supplying some psychological functions the patients cannot provide for themselves, we necessarily become part of the minimum sufficient network until such time as these functions can be internalised. As far as possible, we try to remain detached from and conscious of our responses in this way, but we will inevitably fall short of this ideal and find ourselves motivated by unconscious personal factors such as enjoyment of the protected intimacy of the therapeutic situation, a desire to solve problems vicariously, to engage in false reparation, and so on.

At least, we *may* find ourselves again, and resume a more valid therapeutic role, if the organisation and atmosphere of our clinics can contain such difficulties, regarding them as inevitable and natural, and provide the mechanisms for recovering and indeed learning from them. I am sure that one essential element here is that the Director and senior members should share in this process and be prepared to learn from and be corrected by the clinic group as a whole.

In preparing this paper, I have realised how much of what I have to say is only one contribution to an on-going group process taking part in the whole field of child psychology and psychiatry. Looking back over the previous conference records, I found again many ideas which have influenced me and which I have taken, I hope, a little further. At this conference, too, the papers appear to complement each other in a remarkable way. We are all part of a living process in which each individual contribution has its real value when seen against and within this larger background. Our conference too is an organism, a group situation, and if under the leadership of our chairman we can begin to tap the possibilities of this we may, in the small group and plenary discussions, be able to take part together in a further step towards the development and integration of our disciplines.

Notes

1 This paper was first presented at the 23rd Child Guidance Inter-Clinic Conference, London 1967, and published in N.A.M.H. Publications, London.

2 The Inter-Clinic Conferences of the Child Guidance Movement were, until the 1980s, well-attended and influential events providing an important opportunity for the exchange of views and approaches. (Ed.)

3 This paper is dated by the optimism with which Skynner anticipates the findings of the Seebohm Committee. Its recommendations were the basis on which generic social services were introduced. The unintended but serious consequence of this move, in the loss of competence in specialist areas, was to lead to critical questions about the way these changes were introduced. However, the change in roles and relationships envisaged by Skynner led to the extensive use of family therapy in social work agencies. Their staff were amongst the most numerous and active recruits to this new way of working. (Ed.)

4 This case illustration is reproduced from *Explorations With Families*, pp. 8–12.

5 On the Origins of Family Therapy and Developments in Its Practice

(Opening Address to the Inaugural Meeting of the Association of Family Therapy, London 1976)

Standing on the threshold of major developments, Skynner addresses the inaugural meeting of the Association for Family Therapy with the view that this is not merely a new technique in treatment but a revolution in practice and understanding. Subsequent developments confirmed his view that they were living through change on a scale they could not grasp at the time: 'with implications,' as he writes here, 'we have only begun to work out'. The three succeeding chapters in this section explore some of these implications, giving an account of how rapid and far-reaching the changes were to be. As they make clear, the frontiers are still being extended.

Until the Association for Family Therapy was established in 1976 there were no organisations to represent the work of practitioners in this field. Those (referred to in the paper) who helped establish the Association were working at the Institute of Group Analysis on the first family therapy training course in the country. They were soon to establish the Institute of Family Therapy as a separate training body and the field has seen a burgeoning of organisations and orientations. Today a family approach is an integral part of the training of all the professions and institutions in the field; the Association for Family Therapy has a membership of some 1,200; and the sense of promise to be had from 'cross-fertilisation between disciplines that had previously been separate' has been borne out.

Amongst 'the good things that grew out of that first coming together of family therapy teachers' in the group Skynner brought together, was the climate of their working relationships. The same qualities described in this paper are discernible in a number of organisations spawned by these early developments. The Institute of

Applications to Larger Systems

Family Therapy and Association of Sexual and Marital Therapists, for example, are distinguished by a respect for diversity and the recognition of how professional excellence can be enhanced by the sharing and exchange of varied orientations and methods. Now that they are established as autonomous bodies a number of these organisations have taken collaboration one step further by linking up with one another through inter-organisational associations of different kinds, notably the Rugby Conference on Psychotherapy, and the Standing Committee for Couples in Trouble.

J.R.S.

Introduction

Since we are gathered together to consider marriage and family, and ways of improving its function and diminishing its dis-ease, it seems appropriate to begin by acknowledging my debt to my own wife, not just personally and professionally as regards our joint therapeutic work, and for the part this has played towards the development of family concepts and techniques, but also in the growth of the Family and Marital Group Work Course at the Institute of Group Analysis, whose staff initiated this Association, which in turn has organised this conference. Discussion with her prior to this presentation led me to see that my opening address would need to reflect, in its structure and content, something of the viewpoints that family work has brought in its train.[1]

For me this inevitably involves, first, a developmental approach whereby we try to understand current needs in terms of a particular position within a developmental sequence. I have therefore tried to understand what was required of me today in terms of the origin of family therapy and its precursors, and its growth in this country. Moreover, I was led to remember that the systems concepts which have so richly contributed to family theory apply at all levels, and that some of the more fundamental organisational and developmental laws which apply to families are operative also in social systems generally, including the relationships between professional disciplines, in the formation of a new professional association like this, and in the problems any such organisation introducing new ideas must encounter from the wider world. I also realised that what I said would have to be personal as well as general, just as family work strangely challenges us to reveal and use ourselves as real persons, if we are to be most effective in our work and to grow in skill and stature.

71

And so, as you see, I have started in this way, where all families must start, with a marriage and with the sharing, mutual help and acceptance of each other's authority which, despite the fights and frictions, must form the keystone for the satisfactory development of children. In the wider social sphere we are concerned with in the formation of this Association, the capacity of the founder members to share, exchange and work together, pooling strength and re-sources while respecting each others' orientations and individuality, indeed welcoming and encouraging these, has been a very great pleasure to experience. It will, I hope, provide a rich and supportive matrix within which individuals from different disciplines and with different theories and styles, as well as sub-groups from different geographical regions, will flourish, grow in confidence and auton-omy, and engage in increasingly productive mutual exchanges from which we will all benefit.

Family Therapy as a New Paradigm

I have spoken so far of the origins of family therapy, at least in so far as I have been involved in it, in this country. But as we know, apart from John Bowlby's early experiments of combining conventional individual therapy for family members with occasional joint inter-views with both parents and the referred child (but not the siblings), reported in 1949, the first decade of development of family therapy took place almost exclusively in the United States.[2] There, too, it has from the start been not just a new technique of treatment in addition to existing methods, but rather a remarkable meeting ground permitting fruitful cross-fertilisation between disciplines that had previously been relatively separate including psychiatry, psychoanalysis, sociology and social work, anthropology, com-munication theory, mathematics, systems theory, and so on, which resulted in new concepts and viewpoints that have implications for all existing therapies and techniques. I believe it represents a revolution in our ways of thinking about what 'helping' means, with implications we have only begun to work out. To use an astronomic analogy, it is more akin to the change from the geocentric to the heliocentric view of the solar system at the time of Galileo, which changed our whole concept of the universe, than to the mere discovery of a new planet.[3] Perhaps because it is all about integration and exchange, the development of these new ideas and methods in the United States has so far avoided much of the polarisation into hostile factions or isolated non-communicating schools which has so sadly characterised the developments of other types of treatment, psychotherapy included. There is rivalry, conflict and argument to be sure, but this takes place in a context of ongoing open and self-critical discussion which renders disagreement stimulating and productive rather than the reverse. In this country we possess the advantage of having available from the start the solid foundations that our American colleagues have already laid, on which to build for ourselves.

Family Therapy in Major Teaching Institutions

At the same time, this has given us certain advantages. I have the impression, confirmed by Americans I have spoken to, that family therapy there has grown up mainly outside the main centres, often with considerable resistance from more established and orthodox forms of therapy, including psychoanalysis and the 'stranger-group' therapy movement. Indeed, the current issue of the *International Journal of Group Psychotherapy* includes a symposium by Family Therapists and Group Therapists which shows the two sides to be still taking quite competitive and mutually exclusive positions.[4] Here we have had the advantage from an early stage that the family approach has taken firm root in the major teaching institutions – in the Maudsley Hospital, the Tavistock Clinic, the Hospitals for Sick Children in both London and Edinburgh and many other major centres. Moreover, though it has met and will continue to meet with some resistance, the integration of disciplines and institutions here seems already to have gone far beyond that so far achieved even in the United States. Not only is there fruitful cooperation and sharing between psychoanalytically-based practitioners and those using systems concepts (some of whom have tended to take up opposed positions in the United States), but those based more in learning theory and behaviour modification methods, who have continued to keep themselves rather isolated elsewhere, here also work side by side with both the above groups, for example in the introductory and advanced training courses at the Institute of Group Analysis, and in this Association. I say this not to diminish the debt we owe

73

our American colleagues, but rather to emphasise the progress we have already made, and to emphasise the fact that we can be proud of our achievements so far. I believe that this country, despite its present problems in so many areas, is going to be one of the leaders in this new field.

The Future of Family Therapy

But our first task is to build up the Association within Britain and to do all we can to support and facilitate the learning and practice of family methods in areas where this is not yet well provided for, in addition to improving and expanding the existing training programmes in the capital cities of London, Edinburgh and Cardiff and other more fortunate centres. I have regularly attended the meetings of the Steering Committee and can vouch for the fact that no issue has concerned its members more than the problem of ensuring that the Association becomes a truly national organisation, both in resources and representation. A major purpose of this Inaugural Meeting and the following Conference is to try to explore together how this aim can best be achieved. However, we are therapists and so we all understand that we have to begin with the reality principle. Reality, which is made up of processes which develop over time, inevitably involves some measure of delayed gratification, frustration and consequent pain and aggravation. Coping with all this constructively is the mark of maturity. We need to anticipate that our situation, for some time at least, is going to bear some relation to an ordinary family. In a family, some siblings are born before others, and ride bicycles and learn interesting things at school before those who arrive later. It all seems very unfair, and inevitably produces rivalry and resentment, but of course the older ones have more homework, and are expected to take more responsibility to help those less experienced, so that in the end things even out. At any family table someone must be served first and someone else served last when mother dishes out the pudding, but perhaps this can be accepted if everyone can be sure that they will get their helping. No matter where one sits, the marmalade always seems to be on the other side of the table, and the people nearest to it are always engaged in animated conversation and never hear one's request to pass it across.

Fortunately, as one grows older, the significance of the age gap lessens, relationships become more equal and reciprocal, one is increasingly free to find what one needs from sources outside the original family situation; and family members, though maintaining contact and offering mutual support, are able to start their own families in distant areas. Encountering all the same problems again, but this time from the other side, they perhaps begin to view the more senior members of their original family in a different light!

The Association for Family Therapy began in London at the initiative of the teachers I invited to join my wife and me in running the first Course in Family and Marital therapy at the Institute of Group Analysis. During our work together as staff on the Family and Marital Courses, we constantly found these family dynamics appearing in our own interaction, but by facing and studying these difficulties we discovered a rich source of understanding for our teaching, both by experiencing the actual dynamics that led problem families to come to us for help, and also by clarifying, in doing so, those principles which underlie the more healthy functioning of both families and organisations.

Conclusion: Future Prospects

Whatever the Association for Family Therapy becomes, I hope that some of the good things that grew out of that first coming together of family teachers will be maintained. I hope that the diversity of disciplines and institutions, as well as the respect for, and willingness to listen to and to learn from, each other, whatever one's gender, profession or special interest, will be retained, enabling us to share and cooperate in the common endeavour of putting the task and the criterion of professional excellence before personal, professional or institutional rivalries. And in the course of all that, it is important to have fun, for it is perhaps by our pleasure and enjoyment in our personal and professional activities, as well as in the acceptance of difficulty and effort, that we help families most through the model we provide for them. I personally look forward to being a part of this wider network that we are forming here this week, which will give me so many more colleagues with whom to share and with whom I can learn.

75

Applications to Larger Systems

Notes

1 This paper was presented to the Inaugural Meeting of the Association of Family Therapy, London 1976.
2 See Sue Walrond-Skinner's introduction to her edited collection, *Developments in Family Therapy*, 1981. (Ed.)
3 See my introduction to Skynner's *Explorations With Families* pp. xvii and xxv for further references to *paradigm change* in psychology and comparisons with the Copernican revolution. (Ed.)
4 Skynner is referring here to the Symposium that took place on Family Therapy and Group Therapy at the 33rd Annual Conference of the American Group Psychotherapy Association, Boston, Mass., 1976. Some of the conference papers were published in the *International Journal of Group Psychotherapy*, Vol. xxvi No. 3, including those by Henriette Glatzer, Mel Roman, Don Bloch and Bernard Riess.

6 An Open-Systems Approach to Teaching Family Therapy

Written with Prudence M. Skynner

(Paper Given to the 1978 Annual Conference of the American Association of Marital and Family Therapists)

The American Association of Marital and Family Therapists honoured Robin and Prudence Skynner with Distinguished Affiliate Membership when they were invited to be main speakers at their Annual Conference in 1978. This paper, prepared for an audience abroad, brings into relief distinctive features in the British field including the importance of National Health and Local Authority Services. It makes salutary reading today when these features are so threatened.

For the occasion the Skynners undertake a major review of cumulative developments in family therapy training, by now well established at the new Institute of Family Therapy. They provide a definitive account of their training orientation referred to as the open-systems approach. It incorporates the group-analytic principles we saw being worked out in earlier chapters, supplements them with action techniques, and sets all this to work amongst a community of practitioners on an extended training programme catering for some 150 students annually. The approach involves:

- the combined use of a reflective, analytic style together with active learning techniques drawn from action therapies like role-play and simulation
- training in groups which are encouraged to focus upon:
  - individuals' professional motivation
  - group relations, inter-professional and inter-agency dynamics
  - institutional dynamics of the total training organisation

77

- the combined use of large and small group methods. This stimulates the interplay between individual, group and institution and brings into the open the dynamics affecting a therapist's work that might arise from:
  - his family of origin
  - his marriage and family of procreation
  - his professional network

The primary objective of the course is the development of skill which is given the importance it merits. But the paper provides convincing evidence of how skills can be fostered most rapidly on a large scale by using coherent groups that also facilitate personal growth. The open-systems approach locates development at the interface of a number of dynamic systems, and the interaction of all these systems is drawn upon for growth and learning, guided by analytic, systemic and behavioural (modelling) principles. We shall see in the next chapter how working principles from these three methods are brought together.

In his account here Robin describes how the open-systems approach evolved in group analysis and was then applied to the challenge of training family therapists in larger numbers. In her account Prudence describes the group dynamics of the training experience itself, giving particular attention to the family patterns the course was designed to re-evoke amongst students and staff. The Skynners' availability as a couple in the early life of the Institute of Family Therapy, when they served it much as parents, illustrates the modelling principle by which they recognise their own relationship as, inevitably, an important part of the training system.

J.R.S.

Part One Training for Family Therapy: The Professional and Theoretical Context, 1964–1974 (Robin Skynner)

Introduction

In 1964 I established a multi-disciplinary course with S. H. Foulkes and others to provide a training in group techniques for mental health professionals.[1] The teachers who came together to run this course established the Institute of Group Analysis and the course became known as the Introductory General Course which led on – for those interested in continuing – to a three-year Qualifying Course established in 1972.[2] During these developments I had been working with families as a child psychiatrist and had changed the focus of the two clinics I directed towards a family-centred approach.[3] In 1970 the demand for teaching in family therapy exceeded what was available in the London area and I designed a one-year course similar in structure to the introductory course in group work, but with certain fundamental differences.

Together with my wife Prudence, I brought together practitioners from a range of different centres and with the full range of orientations in the field, to offer a one-year training on family therapy at the Institute of Group Analysis. This association of colleagues was formalised with the development of the Association for Family Therapy to which I gave the inaugural address in 1975. This is published in chapter 5 above. In due course these developments in family therapy training led to differentiation from the Institute of Group Analysis and the establishment of a separate Institute of Family Therapy. The original one-year course became the first stage in what is now a three-year professional training at the Institute of Family Therapy.

In this chapter Prudence and I provide an account of these developments in family therapy training. In Part One, I describe the professional and theoretical context we were working in when the requirements for the training of practitioners led to the establishment of the country's first course in family therapy. In Part Two Prudence describes the experience of conducting this training programme with me during its early years. Other aspects of these developments, particularly the division between the Institutes of Family Therapy and Group Analysis are discussed in the concluding chapter of this book.

The Professional Environment

The first thing you notice in looking at the history of family therapy in Britain is the strange delay in its development. Apart from some early experimentation by John Bowlby (1949) which he gave up to turn his energies towards his other interest of maternal deprivation, and a systematic development of a family approach from the early 1950s by John Howells in Ipswich (1978), a more serious exploration did not begin until the early 1960s and an explosion of general interest did not occur until the beginning of the 1970s, both about a decade later than similar developments in the United States.

The advantage is that we have had available from the beginning the wide range of theory and technique already developed in North America, and have perhaps been detached enough geographically and emotionally from the associated rivalries to search more easily for complementary and constructive relationships among them. We are tremendously indebted to all the North American contributions, as those of you who have seen my book *One Flesh: Separate Persons*, will appreciate, but it has perhaps been easier for us to stand back far enough to try to see them as a whole, and begin to integrate them. This feature of integration, without losing the value of diversity, so fundamental in English history and in the British parliamentary system, has also been facilitated by the fact that family therapy has had to find its place within unified and comprehensive medical and social services. The majority of doctors in Britain spend all their time, and the remainder most of their time, within the National Health Service. More than half of all psychoanalysts in Britain are employed part-time in the health or social services in some application of their basic training as well as in psychoanalysis proper. Private practice in medicine is very limited, and it is almost unheard of in social work, where a network of social service departments, administered and funded by government, covers the country. There are many disadvantages to this centralised approach, and we know the idea is much more unpopular in the United States but it has had the advantage that family therapists have at least not had to fight for money by competing for patients and students. On the contrary, we have had every reason to cooperate and learn from each other in order to cope more effectively with the demands that such free services create, and so reduce waiting lists.

One result has been the firm establishment of family therapy in most of the major psychiatric teaching centres in London, where much undergraduate and postgraduate medical training has been centred in Great Britain. It has made easier the development of communication and cooperation among a professional network of people primarily centred in these different institutions. Thus, while family therapy appears to have developed at first in peripheral centres in the US, in Britain it is firmly established in the most prestigious and influential teaching centres. Alan Cooklin (1978) of the Marlborough Hospital, who was the first chairman of our Association for Family Therapy, has already written about this in some detail.

Differences in the Status of Psychoanalysis and the Influence of Group-Dynamics Concepts in Britain and the United States

Cooklin has pointed out that the situation regarding psychoanalysis was also very different in Britain, since it never gained the position of power and influence it occupied in medical schools and in public esteem in the United States. It was thus less threatened by new developments like family therapy, both because it had less to lose, and also because a greater struggle for recognition, and for a role in the Health Service, had led to an evolution and diversification of psychoanalytic methods developed by Foulkes (1948, 1964, 1975), Foulkes and Anthony (1965), and Bion (1961); the therapeutic community approaches of Maxwell Jones (1952), and Tom Main (1957, 1964); the work with general practitioners by the Balints (Balint 1964; Balint and Norell 1973), the research on attachment theory and problems of separation by John Bowlby (1969, 1973), and the Robertsons (Robertson 1970; Robertson and Robertson 1971); and Winnicott's *Therapeutic Consultations with Children* (1971). Psychoanalysis struggled harder, but was healthier in consequence, and more open to new ideas; as a result it has been easier for psychoanalysts to become family therapists, searching for the relationship between the two paradigms rather than experiencing a sense of opposition between them.

In particular, the analytic approach to group dynamics has been strong in Britain, in a way that recognises and taps the tremendous powers of the group itself for good or ill. The central role of object relations theory in psychoanalysis in Britain, and above all the group-analytic concepts and methods of S. H. Foulkes, have been important factors in this (1957). Both Prudence and I underwent a group analysis with Foulkes at different stages of our lives, as well as learning from and later practising and teaching with him, and it is this above all that has affected the practice and teaching of family therapy as we carry it out, as well as the character of the training programmes we have initiated. To have this background means that one is constantly aware of the group and the feedback that it provides about one's own functioning and those aspects of other relationships which might otherwise operate quite unconsciously. Further, it means that one is constantly attentive to the group process, trying to recognise the phase the group has reached and the events which are therefore likely to appear next. It helps the therapist or teacher to put himself/herself into the equation, to learn and grow with the others, to avoid obstructing the process by undue interference. Above all, it taught us that if we could bear the confusion produced by allowing free-floating group associations to develop, new insights and understanding would come.

Foulkes did not excel in conveying his understanding of these matters through the printed page, or even by formal lectures; one had to experience him at work over a period of time to begin to grasp what he was trying to convey, and it came more through the experience of the kind of person he was – absolutely natural, human, open, yet at the same time highly professional and aware of deeper implications – than through his attempts to describe what he was doing. I have made an attempt in *One Flesh: Separate Persons*, to convey something of what I understood from him, though I came to realise how extraordinarily difficult it was to do so.[4]

Defensive Systems Characteristics of Mental Health Professionals

Although interest in family therapy was late to grow in Britain, the interest in the small 'artificially-constituted' group for therapy, supervision and training was very active indeed. Many American visitors have felt that this was in many ways far more developed in Britain, and the influence of the Tavistock/Leicester Conferences in stimulating similar group explorations in the US is well known. Even while I was in training in the late 1950s, I found myself involved with a group of senior colleagues, including John Bowlby, in the use of group supervision to aid health visitors (community nurses) in the psychotherapeutic aspects of their work. In the years that followed, I utilised group methods in the teaching and supervision of almost every discipline of mental health worker of widely different levels of training and experience, from house parents of children's homes and newly-trained marriage guidance counsellors, to senior psychiatrists and psychoanalysts. I became interested in certain similarities in the personalities and defensive patterns characteristic of each discipline, and also of mental health professions as a whole. In my first paper, given at the 6th International Congress of Psychotherapy in 1964, I concluded (on page 12 above), '. . . that people are initially attracted to what have been called the "helping professions" by the need to solve their own problems . . .'

This recognition that we are rather like our patients is of course part of public folklore and is a source of jokes about therapists. We take the joke badly insofar as we do not acknowledge the truth which carries the sting, but the conclusion also has a positive side. If we can swallow this truth, we become especially adept at the work we have chosen, like a teacher who is recently enough qualified to have the basic knowledge needed by the student at his fingertips, as compared with the professor who may be out of touch and more interested in the small print. Apart from technical knowledge and supervision, it became increasingly clear that all trainees could develop the most valuable personal insights when the *focus in the group was on the reason why they had taken up their particular discipline in the first place*,[5] though, of course, the degree to which different kinds of professionals can be safely encouraged to alter this defensive system must be carefully gauged by the trainer.

83

Development of Stranger-Group Training in Britain

By 1964 I had become aware of a great need for a multidisciplinary course in group techniques for professionals in the London area, for there was increasing demand and no provision beyond apprenticeship at such centres as the Maudsley Hospital and the Tavistock Clinic. The opportunity came with a request from the Association of Psychiatric Social Workers to the Group-Analytic Society, where I had just joined the Committee, and I agreed to design a pilot course. Leading experts in different fields of group technique gave lectures in the first part of the afternoon, and the second hour and a half were devoted to a small group experience, conducted in a way which left the situation almost as unstructured as a therapy group, but with the focus more on group process and on the personal motivation which had led to the choice of profession rather than on individual pathology. This course steadily expanded until we set the limit at 120 participants, and other colleagues, who like myself had set up with Foulkes in private group practice, joined me to provide sufficient staff to lead small groups of twelve. This made up the group experience in the second half of the afternoon. As the course developed, we added occasional plenary sessions in place of lectures to give opportunity for feedback and discussion. The problems the staff found in understanding and handling these plenaries, together with the fact that many participants were experiencing similar problems with large groups in the hospitals and therapeutic communities they work in, made us decide to study these large-group dynamics more systematically. Accordingly, the lectures in the final term were replaced with a series of about eight large groups, preceding the small group sessions (which continued as before). These large groups were completely unstructured except that three concentric circles of chairs were provided for the 120 participants and ten staff, and a time limit of one and a half hour's duration was maintained.

Defensive Dynamics of Staff Groups

I have given a detailed example of a sequence of the large groups in chapter 7 below. What is relevant here, in relation to the development of the later family trainings, was the remarkable development in confidence and maturity shown by many of the students in the large group sessions, and the obvious fact that this was related to the way in which the students reflected, in their interaction, the unconscious or at least unadmitted tensions within the staff group. Each year we found they would ultimately confront us openly with these staff tensions, if we did not defend ourselves by denial, by being impersonal or distant, or by some other method. If we could face our own conflicts it seemed to free them, and it also helped us in our relationships with each other. Frequently, though, staff would either suddenly find patients who desperately needed to be seen just at the time the large group occurred, or they would opt out altogether, or try to arrange a rigid hierarchy, or offer to run the large group single-handed!

The teachers who had come together to run this course had meanwhile formed the Institute of Group Analysis and set up a Qualifying Course to train group analysts. I began to notice the extraordinary difficulty we found in arranging meetings where the students could have an opportunity to give critical feedback to us. Staff–student meetings for this purpose would be arranged, but were then changed into staff meetings, or the time altered to one that many could not manage. At that time the trainings were mainly concerned with 'artificially-constituted' groups, and my colleagues in the Institute of Group Analysis, although all group therapists, were basically trained as individual analysts. I had rejected this, choosing a group analysis with Foulkes. And though I guessed, and now believe, that this was partly defensive, I began to see that there was indeed something fundamentally unhealthy in the orthodox psychoanalytic training. Since 1964 when John Elderkin Bell published a paper in a British journal, I had been working with families and had changed the focus of two London clinics I directed towards a family-centred approach. I had already remarked, as Murray Bowen (1978) has done in the US, that it was important for parents to be able to fight, and better for the children if the parents fought in front of them. I had also noticed that the most healthy children seemed to come from families where, although there was enough hierarchy to provide structure and safety, communication was two-way and the parents could listen to, and learn from, criticism by the children as well as the reverse. Yet here were my colleagues and I behaving like an unhealthy family, avoiding constructive conflict and the growth it might bring by hiding our disagreements from ourselves and by refusing to listen to the students. Indeed we refused to see that mental health workers, myself included, used our role defensively to keep an unacceptable, unmanageable, infantile part of ourselves projected into our patients, offering in return to accept the projection from the latter of parental, controlling aspects and taking over responsibility of their lives. It began to become only too clear why analyses were getting longer, sometimes lasting ten years or more.

The degree and defensive rigidity of the split also explains why different groups of mental health professionals adopt different theoretical positions which are not really amenable to argument or evidence – psychoanalysts and behaviourists, for example. Once we recognise that there are not only 'different strokes for different folks', but also 'different thinks for different shrinks', we can save a lot of useless discussion.

Modifications of Structure for the Family Therapy Teaching Programmes

All this seems very obvious now, particularly since Lewis, Beavers and Phillips at the Timberlawn Foundation in Dallas have produced objective evidence that healthy families do not show these characteristics and that the orthodox analytic model is indeed based on the mid-range, not the optimal family structure (Lewis et al. 1976; Beavers 1977). But at that time I felt personally isolated, with no support for these views; and I encountered tremendous resistance when I presented them at scientific meetings. At this point, in 1972, the demand in London for some kind of teaching in family therapy, for those who were not working in one of the few centres where it was practised, exceeded my ability to meet it through my own seminars at the Institute of Group Analysis. I accordingly designed a one-year course, occupying an afternoon a week like the existing 'stranger' or artificial-group course, and following its structure insofar as the first one and a half hours were spent with the whole course membership together, and the second half was divided into groups of twelve or so, each with a family therapist as its leader. However, some fundamental differences were built into the structure from the beginning, to try to apply the lessons learned from the failures already noted in the group-analytic training.

First, the idea that communication should be two-way, and learning and growth shared by staff and students alike, was thought to be fundamental. Though there was to be didactic teaching about spontaneity and open communication, and about the need for some hierarchy and structure, we also decided to present these concepts through the actual models of our own functioning. Action techniques, such as simulated families and 'family sculpting', had just become known in London through American-trained British colleagues and visiting Americans. These were made a feature of the small group sessions for the students.

At the first plenary, after introducing ourselves, the whole staff drew cards from envelopes assigning roles in a simulated family – father, mother, children, grandparents, as well as roles of male and female therapists, and managers to keep the boundaries. The 'family' would then go out for five minutes to decide on a problem, and come back and spontaneously role-play it while being 'treated' by the 'therapists' in front of the student audience, which numbered 120 by the second year. The sessions were very lively, highly amusing, and most effective in giving students the courage to expose themselves too. 'But you're revealing all your psychopathology!' protested one senior psychoanalyst attending the course the second year. And that is exactly what we intended, to have an opportunity for staff dynamics and tensions to be *deliberately* fed into the total system, and feedback received, in a controlled situation where much learning could go on 'between the lines' as well as explicitly. This 'model' of 'modelling' in the first session took different forms at other plenaries. Each year one staff member would sculpt his own family of origin during another session. The use of the genogram was taught through another staff member describing his own. Needless to say, the staff needed opportunities to discuss and work through the feedback received at these various sessions.

The composition of the staff was quite unique in its diversity of discipline and orientation. None of my senior colleagues in the Institute of Group Analysis shared my training as a child as well as adult psychiatrist, nor my interest in family therapy. I had to look outside the Institute and gather together the most competent people I knew within the London area. A long ambition was achieved when

Applications to Larger Systems

I brought together psychoanalysts from the Tavistock Clinic with behaviour therapists, trained by Isaac Marks (1968) from the Maudsley, and to these professionals added group analysts from the Institute of Group Analysis, and a family therapist from the Tavistock who had studied in America. She brought with her such 'action' methods as family sculpting. An American psychiatrist had recently settled in England, who had trained with Norman Paul (1967) and he introduced us to the study of our own families, and in particular to the importance of unresolved mourning. You can imagine how rich the possibilities were for mutual learning and integration of concepts with such a group, provided we could survive our differences and survive the conflicts they would inevitably generate.

The first course, on 'stranger-group' techniques, was not only heavily biased towards orthodox psychoanalysis, but the staff was almost all male and mainly medically trained. By contrast, the family course was deliberately composed of equal numbers of male and female teachers, and equal numbers of doctors and social workers, permitting the equal representation of the two genders and of two main professional disciplines. Everyone received the same pay for doing the same job. At the beginning, no psychologist adequately trained in family therapy was available, but later a psychologist joined the staff, adding his important skills and knowledge to our resources. My wife had been working as co-therapist with me, treating groups of couples for the previous two years, and had hoped that we would share the responsibility of leading the staff group, but we were obviously not yet ready for this. Prue relieved me of the main administrative burden, but did not join the staff group for the first year. There were consequent problems to begin with, reminiscent of the Freudian patriarchal family; the females were rivalrous *for* me, and the males rivalrous *with* me for the women, as leader. The following year, Prue joined the staff group as a full member, and it was striking how the earlier dynamic, which tended to accentuate the hierarchy and block development changed its nature in a more constructive and manageable direction, facilitating growth and differentiation.

Part Two The Experience of an Open-Systems Training (Prudence Skynner)

Monitoring of Dynamics of Course and Staff Group

As you can imagine, the policy that the staff should 'lead from the front' and set a model of openness and involvement in the initial role-play and 'own family' presentations, rather than 'encouraging others on from behind' in the model of the analytically-based group therapy course, put considerable stress on the leaders. To meet this, the half-hour staff meeting which intervened between the first and second halves of the afternoon in both the group and family therapy courses, was supplemented in the family course by regular monthly meetings for a whole evening, and occasionally by other opportunities to share and digest the experience. To this end, all staff meetings were tape-recorded, and these were listened to, summarised and fed back by a different staff member each year. The meetings were used partly to enable the whole staff to learn something of the specialised knowledge held by members of different orientations and backgrounds, in order that all could know enough about the subject which was to be presented the following week at the lecture or demonstration, and thus be able to keep ahead of the students and lead the small groups. In this way, special techniques such as genograms, family sculpting, direct study of one's own family, and behavioural techniques of sex therapy could be shared with and transmitted by the whole staff group. This also provided great opportunity for us all to increase our knowledge and skills.

But the *main* focus, following the group-analytic background that the majority shared (and those that lacked this experience had more difficulty in coping with unstructured or confusing situations), was to study the group process as it was manifested in the small groups, both in the themes which emerged in more active parts of the session (for example, when participants presented examples of their work) and in the more passive, reflective and analytic periods which, by design, alternated with the activity.

The preoccupations or themes during the discussion period following each lecture or demonstration, or the pattern of each open plenary, would also be fed in and studied. Most importantly, we constantly monitored and tried to be aware of the themes and group processes of our own staff interaction in order to recognise and detach ourselves from issues which would have blocked our progress had they remained unconscious. The main responsibility for this was carried by Robin, with his specialised knowledge of groups, but the presence of so many people who had taken the group therapy course, or had been trained in the study of group process, enabled this task to be shared and pressed forward beyond his blind spots and vulnerabilities, or those of any other individual member. One could see the themes reflected back and forth between these different situations, with the major anxieties and conflicts funnelling up from the 120 participants into the staff group, and from the staff group into ourselves, like a tidal wave in a narrowing river.

Introduction of 'Pairing' and the Fundamental Problems of Sharing

In the second year of the course, after I joined in fully, it was agreed by the staff that the small group leaders should be paired, male and female, and that they and their groups should meet together every month or two for a joint project. The object was to give the groups some experience of co-leaders of the opposite sex, and so to stimulate the awareness of issues and conflicts centring around marriage and sexuality; and also to put the leaders in the position where they were faced with all the problems of marriage where tasks such as communication, sharing of power and decisions regarding appropriate gender roles, have to be resolved. We thought it only fair to put ourselves on the spot too, and it was agreed that Robin and I would also attend these joint meetings. Though each group would meet with its pair about once every month or two, this meant that Robin and I would meet with a different pair each week. This experience was usually intensely uncomfortable for all concerned, but the discomfort seemed to act like a powerful force propelling us through tensions and conflicts we would otherwise have avoided.

An Open-Systems Approach to Teaching Family Therapy

The dynamic patterns which would funnel up and down the structure we had created tended to vary with the stage the course had reached, in a phasic pattern. Early on, the course participants tended to show paranoid fears, after that intense dependent longings, followed by rebelliousness and a struggle for control. Confronted with these, the group leaders would often reflect the pattern, in turn becoming dependent, passive and demanding, or rebellious and provocative, towards us. Later, sexual issues, oedipal rivalry and problems over sharing would become more prominent. Issues of sexuality and sharing became intensely magnified once the small group leaders and their groups began to have paired meetings. The anxieties were intense, the resistances appearing almost unbelievable, but at the same time the issues seemed to be faced and some resolution found in a way I do not recall ever occurring in the 'group-therapy' course, or indeed, even in the therapy group I attended for two years, conducted by Foulkes for senior members of the Institute of Group Analysis.

Sometimes the groups would both refuse to meet, or one would make advances and be rebuffed by the other. Or the leaders would forget to mention this aspect of the programme, or would fail to make any preparation, or would find some 'good' reason why it was better for their particular group to continue to meet separately. When the groups got together, every imaginable device would be used to prevent a 'marriage' of any kind from occurring – in one such joint session a simulated family was presented where the two parents and the children in alliance with them were so noisily oppositional that nothing could bring them together.

Sometimes the leaders would deal with the issue of sharing power by setting up a dominant/submissive relationship, planning everything in detail beforehand to avoid the danger of spontaneity; or they might take more equal but rigid and segregated roles. Often they would hand over power to us by taking family roles themselves. When this happened we would experience all the difficulties of sharing power ourselves. Whether the issue being funnelled up to us was dependency, control or sharing, it had certainly reached a very high voltage by the time it reached us and we often had blazing rows on the way home, which probably stopped short of physical violence only because one of us was driving the car!

Binding Forces Counteracting the Destructive Dynamics

However, because we were married and in continuous contact between the sessions, we would work through it, begin to see the shape of the dynamic we were picking up, and then make it clear to the staff group at the next meeting. They, in turn, would be able to use this understanding to handle more effectively the current issues and conflicts in the small groups. At our evening meetings we always consumed large amounts of food and wine; I enjoy preparing food while Robin makes excellent home-made wine, which may be a partial explanation, but we later realised that this shared enjoyment of bodily appetites was important in holding us together through painful conflicts and crises. There was a great deal of fun and laughter too, so that our meetings were always enjoyable despite the tension, and I never remember being bored.

As with a real family, the fact that we were a couple, that we had a good sexual relationship which helped to hold us together despite disruptive forces, and the fact that this was recognised to be the case by others even though the physical relationship was private to us, later seemed an important key to the feeling of security that our *joint* leadership appeared to provide. The growth towards more competent functioning of staff and students alike was remarkably rapid.

Robin has suggested that the most powerful force towards growth and differentiation in children is the combination of infantile sexuality, oedipal rivalry and the incest taboo. As long as the parents' sexual relationship with the children is secondary and kept within proper bounds, there is powerful motivation for the children to leave the family and find their own partners. This kind of input would be given to the course itself indirectly through Robin and myself sharing, for example, the lecture on interviewing in relation to sexual problems, or demonstrating such techniques by working with a simulated couples group before the audience. We also arranged a day in which films and group discussions were used to help us all feel more at ease during sexual discussions, along the lines of the 'Sexual Attitude Restructuring' described by Rosenberg and Chilgren (1973).

Everything imaginable occurred throughout the course to den

92

and block awareness of real or symbolic sexual relationships, whether between us, or between the paired group leaders. Alas, it was often unimaginable until some time after it had happened, as when all the staff decided to spend a full day over a weekend at our home to give more opportunity to 'sculpt' our families. Robin was allowed to sculpt his in the morning, but though there was some suggestion that I should sculpt mine in the afternoon, excellent reasons were put forward that it would be more interesting to study everyone's 'professional family' connections. The outcome was that almost everyone traced their lineage back to Robin while I was the excluded, or at least the 'youngest' and least professionally connected member! I still have not been able to sculpt my family, and had to come to the US to do my genogram!

Corrective Emotional Experiences Arising from the Open-Systems Structure

It was as if the small group leaders and the student groups were able to repeat, in relation to us, all their childhood fantasies about destroying their own parents' marriage. The fact that we survived, with not many more fights than usual, enabled people to work through these and overcome fears of success in the oedipal struggle. These changes were demonstrated in the way that the staff role-play, which began the course, developed from year to year. In the first year, when Robin was a bed-wetting naughty boy, he was frog-marched across the stage by his 'father' – one of his former students – shouting, 'if you don't behave yourself, Robin, you'll get a good thrashing!' There was no acknowledged *marital* problem. The next year the problem was of a teenage daughter rebelling against her parents' problems through her sexual behaviour and the parents this time *had* problems, but *not* sexual ones. A year later, I took on this role and this proved to be related in the simulated treatment session to the impotence of Robin and the frigidity of a female staff member in the role-play, who had drawn lots to be father and mother respectively. This opportunity to re-live and work through fears in the child that it may win the oedipal struggle and destroy its security, which is so often related to a general fear of success, may have been one reason for the astonishingly rapid development of confidence, responsibility and initiative in the staff group generally, leading each year to similarly rapid movement towards autonomy in the students. The *group-therapy* course had always been experienced by students as an exciting and growth-enhancing experience, but the analytic model on which it was based had led to an emphasis on regression and dependency, with brief rebellions which were not carried through to real independence, and only a limited possibility of real exchange with the leadership, except in the large group experience where the staff tended to resist any personal involvement. The group-therapy course members functioned like a *dependent* family, where the parents could never quite allow the children to grow up and leave. In the *family* course, in contrast, the structure was such that communication and criticism could be two-way; power and responsibility could be handed over and increasingly shared. Autonomy and differentiation were welcome.

Within two years, most of the staff group were eager to set up an Association for Family Therapy in Britain, and there was eventual agreement to launch it. Every effort was made to involve all family-oriented individuals and centres throughout Britain and this Association now has over 1,000 members and is a democratic, representative organisation which includes almost everyone seriously interested in family therapy in this country.

Although we had to create some necessary kinds of experience artificially, some were provided naturally. Stuart Lieberman, our American colleague, had brought with him the experience he gained in the United States with Norman Paul; he convinced us of the importance of dealing openly with issues of loss and death in families, and the last term in training always included a presentation concerned with this. However, in the fourth year, our most recently added staff member was suddenly admitted to hospital and operated upon for cancer. A week later, I was admitted and operated on with the same diagnosis. Fortunately, we both had reason to believe that our disorders were completely operable, follow-ups are satisfactory, and I have never felt as well as I do now. But we had to decide quickly what to tell the group. In this, as in everything else, we had to decide whether we would practise what we preached and handle the possibility of our deaths in the open way we believed healthy families do (which the Timberlawn Research had confirmed and shown to be the most vital component

94

of healthy family functioning (1976)). Consequently, the news was shared with course members each week at the plenary.

Both Robin and I come from families which tended to deny change, loss and growth, and the positive side of this experience was a tremendous feeling of support, of being a part of a real family for the first time, and a marvellously warm, supportive family at that.

Conclusion: Effects on Development of Students

One is struck particularly by the increased freedom and confidence students seem to develop in their professional roles, partly because their sense of personal identity is not experienced *through* these roles. They seem better able to integrate the 'child' in themselves, are less compelled to be 'parental', and can be more 'adult' in consequence, in Eric Berne's terms (1964). By losing their compulsive helpfulness they are able to set boundaries, and are less vulnerable to manipulation. They pay more attention to their *own* lives, spend more time at home with their spouse and children, but they do the work better and enjoy it more. They are able to separate out the personal and professional, but also to bring the two together, and to use their greater experience of themselves and their families more directly and openly in their work. They seem to relate more responsibly within their own professional hierarchy, becoming more able both to take authority and receive it. Above all, the course teaches us that marriage and the family, and indeed human relationships generally, are about *sharing*. We discover endlessly how difficult this is, but everyone continues to move a little further towards that possibility.

During our second year, Ian Falloon, the youngest member of our staff, then still a trainee in psychiatry, listened to all tapes of the staff meetings and tried to summarise the development of the course (Falloon 1976). He concludes with:

> The male and female roles that had appeared threateningly confused in the first term and clearly defined in the second were, in the third term, again seen to be confused, but this time the confusion was more stimulating, with obvious enjoyment and much less tension. A link could be drawn between the development of the group and that of a maturing child;

95

from the blurred sexual differentiation of childhood to the clear-cut, but tension-laden identity in adolescence, leading to the relaxed togetherness of adult sexual contact. The groups ended in confusion over their own family roles, their roles as therapists and the theoretical basis of family therapy, but with confidence that they could work with that confusion and perhaps even enjoy it.

The students appear to develop an ability to bear confusion and use it constructively, rather than taking refuge in a particular ideology or school of family therapy. And this is perhaps one key to the remarkable openness and relatedness, combining a high degree of cohesiveness and communication with great variety and differentiation, which characterises much of family therapy in Britain today. Yet, this is only another way of saying that we are learning to *share*, as couples and families have to learn to share.

Notes

1 This paper was presented at the 1978 Annual Conference of the American Association of Marital and Family Therapists. It was first published in the *Journal of Marital and Family Therapy*, 5, 3 1979, and republished in *Group Analysis*, 81 1980.
2 For a useful description of the context and the training objectives of this Qualifying Course, written during the period it was established, see Malcolm Pines's chapter 'Training In Dynamic Aspects of Psychotherapy', in V. Varma (ed.), *Psychotherapy Today*, 1974. Pines was one of the principal architects of the Qualifying Course and has remained deeply involved with its development. Interested readers will find here an early statement of aims describing how 'this training is intended as an equivalent in the field of group psychotherapy to the training in psychoanalysis' (p. 313).
3 See the Author's Introduction, page xlvii, note 3.
4 See also, *Explorations With Families* chapter 10, and below, this volume, chapter 12, in both of which Skynner gives a moving, personal account of his relationship with S. H. Foulkes.
5 See chapter 1 above, pp. 5 ff, and chapter 10 below pp. 157 ff.

7 The Psychotherapy Teacher: Getting Older – Narrowing Down or Opening Out?

(Paper given to the Third Conference on Teaching Dynamic Psychotherapy, Association for University Teachers of Psychiatry, Oxford 1986)

In 1986 Skynner addressed the Third Conference on Teaching Dynamic Psychotherapy, organised by the Association of University Teachers of Psychiatry. Speaking to an audience composed largely of psychiatrists responsible for psychotherapy training in the National Health Service, he delivered this personal account of his working life, later published in the Bulletin of the Royal College of Psychiatrists.

Illustrated by some memorable anecdotes, the paper gives a revealing account of how the group-analytic approach evolved, guided by an intuitive sense of direction, through chance and circumstance. As Skynner takes stock of the individuals, ideas and orientations that have been a major influence on his work, the inner logic of his exploration becomes clear. Describing psychotherapy as a two-way process between therapist and patient in which the beneficial effects require change on both sides, he draws particularly on two bodies of literature:

- the ideas of S. H. Foulkes about the subjective quality of the therapist's contribution, and the relativity of his position
- the ideas of Gregory Bateson about achieving change through understanding rather than through power or control.

Skynner's combination of these two pioneers' work – and of the group-analytic and systemic schools they represent – is vividly described, and in the personal material particularly, we can follow

97

the detail of his struggle to forge this integration. Amongst the most important developments is the new significance given to counter-transference. It is used here as a bridge to link the new epistemology – based upon the principles of uncertainty and relativity – with a revised clinical approach. From the new work in physics which includes the observer in the equation, it is a short step to the new work in psychology which includes the therapist in the equation of change. The concept of counter-transference is a stepping-stone between the two. If the therapist allows himself to be affected by what he does, his intellectual control is to some extent diminished in favour of a greater level of emotional understanding which can be reflected in spontaneous behaviour as a means to induce change. A different definition of the behavioural approach can then follow, based on modelling and guided by the active use of counter-transference.

The technical aspects of the reconciliation – between be-havioural, analytic and systemic methods – are described in *Explorations With Families*. This chapter conveys the personal implications of this synthesis – notably, how much yet also how little a therapist's capabilities are a function of skill and technique. His personality and the qualities of his personal relationships are of much greater importance. Skynner acknowledges the importance of his own personal relationships on his journeyings, with a warm and humorous tribute to his wife and to those with whom he has shared a training, a practice, religious associations and the authorship of a book.

J.R.S.

Introduction

I count myself most fortunate to have been living at this time, working in our profession, and to have chosen psychotherapy as a main interest, for it has been a period of quite extraordinary growth and constructive development.[1] Exposed as one has been to such an exciting series of new discoveries, each following so hard on the heels of the last that one scarcely had time to absorb each new understanding and regain some equilibrium before it was upset again by the next wave of new ideas, it seems it would have been far more difficult to narrow down than to stay open.

When I began my training at the Maudsley in 1953, the ideas that so many psychologically-oriented psychiatrists now share about the dynamics of the individual were already well developed. In particular, the great clarification offered by object-relations theory was well worked out, and not only offered an explanation of human behaviour that instantly made sense to me, but also provided a bridge between older psychoanalytic concepts and those of the neo-Freudians like Suttie and Hadfield in this country, and Sullivan, Horney and Fromm in the US.[2] They also offered linking concepts to learning theory and behavioural approaches, then rapidly gaining acceptance through the influence of Eysenck and his colleagues, as well as to group therapy and family therapy which were to gather momentum later.

So in those first few years, I had the good fortune to be learning individual therapy under Willi Hoffer, and studying group analysis and running my first group under the guidance of S. H. Foulkes; while in the library the first papers on the startling new techniques of family therapy by Lyman Wynne, Murray Bowen, Nathan Ackerman, Gregory Bateson[3] and other pioneers, were arriving in the American journals. I did not feel confident enough to try this

99

then-revolutionary idea myself until 1962, but work with groups of children and adolescents prepared the ground by forcing me to become more aware of the therapist's inevitable role, whether one wanted it or not, as an authority, educator and model, rather than a neutral conveyor of understanding alone.

Aubrey Lewis[4] who was always kinder to me than I am sure I deserved, made a last effort to stop me going completely overboard by sending me to the department of neurophysiology to assist Professor G. W. Harris in his research on hypothalmic/pituitary connections. 'I understand you want to be a scientist, Skynner?' he said, in the friendly tones of an army sergeant asking a squad if anyone knows how to play the piano, while actually seeking a 'volunteer' for the job of carrying it to the other side of the parade ground. As I had said something of the kind at the appointment interview, in order to get in, I could not very well refuse, and I had indeed arrived with the belief that the 'harder' sciences offered a greater objectivity and was hopeful about what I might learn by this experience.

While working in the Animal House, I continued treating two individual psychotherapy patients and running my group under Foulkes's guidance, so during this short time I had the simultaneous experience of these two kinds of exploration. Which of them was the more scientific, the more 'objective'? Well, I came to the conclusion that what was going on in Foulkes's seminars was much closer to the scientific paradigm as I had understood it from my readings in epistemology and the philosophy of science; and from discussions I had been fortunate to become involved in during my medical training with philosophers like Russell, Ayer, Hampshire and Popper, and scientists like Medawar, Penrose and J. Z. Young.[5] Why should this have been so? Because some attempt at least was made to 'include the observer in the equation', to allow for the fact, encountered everywhere in physics, the hardest science of all, that our theories inevitably affect our observations as well as our observations affecting our choice of theories, in a circular fashion which makes every theory to some extent a self-fulfilling prophecy. And I think it is this idea, the idea that the observer has to include the effects of his own nature in the equation if any investigation is to be objective, that has been the main factor helping me to remain open to new ideas and so to have been more likely to grow than to become rigid and closed, to the extent that this has been true of me at all.

Including the Observer in the Observation

At the start I understood this principle more in an abstract, intellectual sense, as it applied in physics with Heisenberg's uncertainty principle, the impossibility of simultaneously determining the position and the speed of an electron, or Einstein's principle of relativity, the impossibility of any absolute measure of velocity at all. But as I began to practise psychotherapy, and to learn about transference and counter-transference, I began to be aware that this principle affected every aspect of our lives, particularly in the way we distort our perceptions to try to keep our relationships in later life as similar as possible to those we experienced in our family of origin. The animal ethologists, and those like John Bowlby who have extended attachment theory to human behaviour, have shown us why. Change, difference, meeting the unexpected, are all disturbing, upsetting, stressful. Too much can make us mentally or physically ill. So we need attachment, sameness, stability, in order to get our bearings again and recover our equilibrium.

I think it was during the time I was training that the word 'counter-transference' changed its significance profoundly. At the time when I began learning psychotherapy it had an entirely negative meaning, namely, distorted perceptions of the patient by the therapist, indicating that self-understanding derived from the therapist's training analysis had been insufficient. By the time I finished training it had begun to mean something positive as well. The influence of object-relations theorists like Winnicott and Balint was bringing an increasing awareness that the therapist's emotional reactions to the patient, however 'irrational' these might appear at first, could be a rich source of information if attended to but not acted upon, or, at least, not acted upon without adequate delay for reflection about its meaning.[6] However, even my psychoanalyst colleagues tended then, as they still on the whole do now, to distance themselves from these emotional responses by basing themselves safely in the head, taking a fairly cognitive stance in dealing with counter-transference and using such feelings just as background information which is helpful for formulating an interpretation. But gradually I found myself using the emotional information my reactions provided in more raw, immediate, emotional form, which had a direct impact on the patient, group or family through an emotional channel. I found myself increasingly using interventions which were more behavioural than intellectual – interventions which would indeed probably still be regarded as 'acting out' by conventional analysts – though they appeared to convey the same understanding in a non-verbal way and to my surprise did so often with extremely rapid effect, so that changes were often seen in the course of a single session or at the next attendance.

The earliest example I can recall where I noticed this was with one of my first family interviews which, at first, I used to give as an example of one of my worse failures until I saw how it anticipated techniques that I did not develop and understand fully for twenty years.

One question people always ask about family therapy is: is it dangerous? Well, as those here who practise it will know, it is sometimes – but only for the therapist! I can put my hand on my heart and say that I have been trying to damage families for twenty years now, and I have never been successful! I have followed up cases where there were the most horrendous scenes, but as John Bowlby found before me in his early experiments with families soon after the War, not only was there never any permanent harm, but the most alarming interviews usually proved in the long run to have had a positive effect. But at the time I saw the case I am now going to describe, which was in 1963, about a year after I had begun experimenting with seeing families together, I thought of it as my greatest disaster. As you will see, it very nearly was a disaster for me!

A Case Illustration

Tim, nine years old, was referred by the GP because he was showing signs of strong anxiety and refusing to attend school. The parents were written to, offering an appointment and asking them to bring the whole family.

Entering the waiting room to collect them, I found Tim,

three elder sisters in early teenage, and mother – a heavy, grim-looking woman – but no father. I asked why he had not come as we had requested. The mother replied that he *had* come, had indeed driven them to the Clinic, but she had sent him shopping. This was a warning signal of storms ahead, if ever there was one! But I was not then wise enough to tell them that we would not be able to make progress without the father – fathers being important in children's management – and offering them another appointment so he could be there as well.

Once we were seated in my office, I learned that Tim's anxiety and fear of school had followed a visit to the dentist, at which the dentist had told him that if he did not stop sucking his thumb his teeth would fall out. Though obviously not the wisest dental management from a psychological point of view, I nevertheless found it difficult to get much more out of the boy to explain the severity of his reaction. However, what I did encounter rapidly as I tried to explore how the whole family dealt with emotions, was a powerful resistance by the mother to any mention by the children that they sometimes got angry.

Although they seemed eager to respond to my questions as to what kind of things made them cross, mother always cut in and answered for them. 'We *never* get angry in our family,' she said repeatedly, after each child had begun to describe some episode of angry feelings. I asked what would happen if someone did something to *her* which would make most *other* people angry. She replied that she would not get angry even then; she would just cry, and leave the room. She then turned the questioning on me and said surely I, as a doctor did not ever get angry?

By this time I was feeling very frustrated by her interruptions, and said that I certainly did; I added that I was in fact getting increasingly angry at the way she was trying to take over the interview and control my clinic, as well as her family. At this, true to her word, she burst into tears and, sobbing loudly, rose from her chair and strode majestically to the door. The children all fell in line behind her in single file, like little ducklings, and followed her out. I have never felt so disturbed in the whole of my career; indeed, there was something in the way she did it which made me feel like a brutal murderer or rapist. However, my horror was somewhat relieved when Tim, who as the youngest was at the end of the file and the last to leave the room, turned round in the doorway, spread his hands, shook his head as if to say, 'That's my mother,' and shrugged his shoulders in a commiserating way. I felt a bit better, but not much.

Half an hour later I was still shaking with the powerful emotion this incident had aroused, when my phone rang. My secretary was on the line: 'That family's back again,' she said, 'and there's a very angry man with them in the waiting room who wants to see you, right away.'

As I walked down the corridor, I could see him through the glass doors. Luckily, I had the presence of mind to stride quickly into the room smiling warmly, grasping him firmly by the right hand as I said how very glad I was he had come, since the father's involvement in therapy was so important, and, still clasping and pumping his hand vigorously with my own, pulled him quickly out through the door before his wife could have time to ask him what he was going to do about it.

Once in my office, the father and I got on well. He was glad to have the chance to talk to someone about his wife's problems, he said. She had phobias of different sorts, was very critical and controlling in the home so that even he did not dare to argue with her, and their sexual life was not good, indeed, it was non-existent. I was sympathetic, and we agreed women could sometimes go through difficult times and needed understanding. By the time I returned him to the waiting room we had made a good relationship, his wife had cooled off, and we made another appointment for them all to come again a month later.

Nevertheless, I felt upset and disturbed for the rest of the day, and feared I had made a terrible mess of things, perhaps even lost Tim a chance of solving his problem. The next day I had a phonecall from his head teacher, and I feared he had called to condemn my behaviour too. 'What did you do?' he began. My heart sank as I waited to hear the worst. 'It's a miracle,' he continued, 'he's back in school and he's fine.' I said modestly that these new methods of family therapy were very powerful, and did often get very quick results, even though we didn't yet understand completely how they worked. A month later, all the family came again and confirmed there had been no further problem since the first interview. There was no mention of what had happened in that first session, and the whole family were friendly and appreciative of the result. Mother looked particularly positive, and the glint in her eye explained to me the trap I had fallen into.

Later on I was able to develop a theory to account for this, at first combining psychoanalytic and behavioural ideas and more recently the systemic, so-called 'paradoxical' methods as well. Foulkes had taught us to trust the emotions and fantasies we experienced while leading groups, assuring us that they were best considered as group-associations, as much a part of the group process as the spontaneous thoughts and feelings of patients and often best fed into the pool with the rest. My experience convinced me that he was right, for early on I found I would often arrive at a group to find to my surprise that patients were echoing themes that had preoccupied me throughout the previous week, which I had believed to be personal to me.

Psychotherapy as a Two-Way Process

Foulkes defined group analysis as 'psychotherapy of the group, by the group, including the therapist'.[7] This can be understood as meaning that not only the therapist, but the whole group, is the therapeutic agent. Some treat it like that. But I soon discovered that it could also mean that it is not only the group, but also the therapist as part of the group, who undergoes the treatment. As time went on I came to see psychotherapy as a reciprocal, two-way process where the failure of either patient or therapist to change inevitably limited the beneficial effect on both. I do not mean that patient and therapist have similar or equal responsibilities, of course, any more than mother and baby are doing the same job just because the baby is cueing the mother's responses as well as vice versa, or because the mother must enjoy the baby to produce a contented child.

This ultimately led me to the powerful method of family therapy I have called the group-analytic approach. In this method:

> The therapist discloses his counter-transference response to the family and shares it with them not by attributing it to them but as a strange response in himself which he cannot understand. He thus provides a model of tolerance for a feeling which he thereby gives the family permission to own, if they are ready and willing to do so. The identified patient often protects the family by picking up the family secret and running with it to the mental hospital. Some therapists protect themselves by lobbing the 'bomb' back into the family as an interpretation. With the group-analytic approach the therapist, by defusing the bomb in front of the family, shows how it can be made safe or even that it may not be a bomb at all. (*Explorations With Families* p. 393–4)

Once one has succeeded in clarifying the mechanisms underlying some new and effective method one has developed intuitively – often indeed almost by accident, as in the example I have described – one not only feels more confidence, but the results become more predictable and one can explain and justify the method to others. But while you are learning and searching for the truth you not only do not get it right a lot of the time; there is at that stage no right way to follow. You must be prepared to live a life of mistakes, rather than being able to follow a correct, approved body of knowledge where at least one knows one is in step with everyone else, even if you are all going round in a circle or marching over the edge of a cliff.

A Shared Journey: Colleagues on the Way

However, although in the final analysis one is always alone and at times must be prepared to find oneself absolutely out on a limb, one needs companions on a journey of this kind. Best of all, one needs a group of like-minded individuals who are all similarly dissatisfied with existing knowledge and searching for something better. This need not be a permanent association of a formal kind, but ideally is more a temporary alliance of individuals who can share a common cause and be useful to each other's development for the moment. Once a more permanent group is formed, one has the beginnings of an institution, where those who are ready to consolidate will stop and settle down, while others who need to continue to change will move on.

My first such support group was the one gathered around Foulkes at the Maudsley. When I left there it was replaced by a peer-group which grew out of that first association – indeed, all my subsequent support-groups grew out of it – and which met once a month to discuss a case-presentation given by members in rotation. There were about twelve or fifteen of us altogether, including Bob Gosling, later Chairman at the Tavistock; Clifford Yorke; and several Maudsley contemporaries who have since become professors or leaders back in their countries of origin. We all took turns at chairing the meeting, and it worked well for two or three years, finally fading out when Malcolm Pines and I, who had taken on the role of unofficial organisers, no longer performed that task as we moved on to other things.

My next support-group – one which is still current and now the main source of my livelihood – was the Group-Analytic Practice, where Foulkes became a peer, even though a respected elder peer. Out of this developed the Institute of Group Analysis, from an Introductory Group-Work Course I took the initiative of forming in 1964, and after that the Institute of Family Therapy from another course I started within the former Institute in 1973, both of which remained important support-groups for me for some years.

On reflection, I realise that each group ceased to be useful to me in a personal sense at the point when other members no longer wanted the therapist included in the equation to the degree which I considered necessary, and when this point was reached I was obliged to move on and find new companions for the next part of the search.

More recently, running out altogether of professional colleagues to share the exploration with me, I have had to go outside our own field of work to find companions who wanted to keep boundaries open to the same degree. One form of support has comprised groups of Church of England bishops that my wife and I were asked to lead in an exploration of personal, marital, family and vocational issues, but which we treated to some extent like the peer-group of colleagues mentioned earlier, leading by sharing our own personal experience rather than conducting the group from a position of detachment. And the other main collaboration, as most of you will know who have seen the book *Families and How To Survive Them*, was with John Cleese, a former patient.

A New Partnership: Writing *Families and How to Survive Them*

As I tried to work out the structure of the book under the impact of John's persistent questioning, and our shared search for the clearest, simplest language in which to express the basic principles on which our profession bases its work, I found that areas of knowledge that had previously seemed disconnected or incompatible – psychoanalysis, biological psychiatry, systems theory, behaviourism – were beginning unexpectedly to mesh together and form a coherent whole, each appearing to follow logically from the same simple principles that our use of 'everyday' language was forcing us to uncover.

Although we tried as far as possible to approximate a consensus of established views, or to acknowledge major conflicts of opinion, we also examined ourselves closely for minor, 'everyday' examples of each type of emotional disorder and found this 'self-analysis' the richest source of integrative ideas. But one unexpected consequence was that we found ourselves 'living' each chapter as we wrote it and at times feeling profoundly affected by emotional patterns we thought we had outgrown.

Having already had more extensive psychotherapy than John, this process affected me more deeply, and the intense experience of unexpected residues of schizophrenic and autistic functioning threw vital light on the real meaning of these disorders. John did not experience these very primitive levels, but recalls how he found himself writing painfully slowly about depression, then racing through the section on mania! An unexpected consequence of this emotional involvement with our subject was a great deal of beneficial change not only in ourselves but also in our marriages and other relationships, often occurring to both of us about the same time. Though I learned different things from my earlier therapy during training and from writing the book, the results were similar and equally valuable to me.

108

The fact that John is a former patient obviously posed a problem for some colleagues, notably at the Tavistock Clinic where we spent an evening talking about the book at a crowded meeting to help raise money for their house journal. John was asked how he could be absolutely sure he had not written the book just to get some more therapy. The question was put in a somewhat anxious, critical tone which he did not understand, and, wanting to be honest and still believing that we psychotherapists are all terribly nice people who just want to be helpful to others – I had warned him that it would be more like a swim in a tankful of piranhas – he said that yes, of course, that was the whole idea – could you ever have too much self-knowledge and what was the problem, surely all of them would be glad of a bit more? I added that it had certainly been one of my main ideas too, and why not, so that was the end of that discussion.

Of course, if one tries to operate according to these open-systems principles, one can no longer maintain the sharp divisions we often try to establish between different aspects of our lives. If everything is connected, to a greater or lesser extent, it is probably just not possible to be a really first-class therapist if one is at the same time a third-rate husband or wife. And one will at some point experience limitations in treating couples for sexual difficulties if one has not achieved a reasonably comfortable sexual relationship oneself, or at least faced up to one's inadequacies in this and other spheres.

The Therapist in the Patient's Way: Won't You Walk a Little Faster

I have certainly noticed how my own limitations obstruct the progress of patients at a certain point. This is particularly noticeable in doing group therapy. To start with, provided patients do not come with an identical problem to one's own, there is plenty of work for them to do in areas where one is reasonably well-adjusted and comfortable oneself. But as the ground begins to be made up and the gap is closed between the patients' level of adjustment and that of the therapist, there is an increasing sense that a kind of 'lobster quadrille' is beginning: '"Won't you walk a little faster," said the whiting to the snail, "there's a porpoise close behind me and it's treading on my tail."' At this point I experience myself as under

109

pressure, and as standing in their way until I can gain some greater understanding and move on myself in my own development.

Usually the group themes help me at this point to grasp some issue I have not been able to grapple with effectively before, and though I do not normally bring my own problems into the group in an explicit way (unless I have become completely stuck and there is no alternative – in which case I do), I am very aware of how much I am helped myself, when I am practising as a group therapist, towards dealing with my own problems more effectively. Indeed, this is a major reason why I particularly like to work with stranger-groups, since they force one to become aware of, and to struggle with, one's own unresolved problems in a way that I have never experienced either with individual therapy or family therapy. I have suggested some reasons why stranger-groups are more effective in this regard in chapter 12 below, and in *Explorations With Families*, chapters 10 and 14.

However, I have found that this process also spins off into one's life outside the therapy room. The opening up of new areas of exploration in oneself, provoked by exploration of these issues in the therapy situation, often continues in relationships with intimates, particularly in the most intimate of all, the marital or couple relationship. This does not necessarily, or usually, involve an explicit discussion of the issues, or even at first any awareness that something of this kind is happening. Often it is only on later reflection that one realises that one has begun to reveal some new aspect of oneself to one's partner, or is able to perceive and cope with some aspect of one's partner's personality which has previously been avoided and denied. But it can lead to a deeper, more fruitful interaction between the couple, or among family members as a whole, from which new understanding ultimately spins off back into the therapy group situation, leading to progress of all the patients there – again, without any of this being made explicit.

An Old Partnership: Working With My Wife

If one works with one's spouse professionally, as my wife and I have done for the past thirteen or fourteen years now, the whole process is accelerated, though it still tends to take place in a natural way through the interaction of the couple rather than through conscious and deliberate discussion. In both my previous books, I gave an example where my wife and I reproduced unconsciously, over supper after a session of leading our most destructive set of couples (which we had taken to calling our *Who's Afraid of Virginia Woolf* group), the typical quarrels that each of these couples had described in turn in previous sessions.[8] However, the next morning insight dawned, and we were later able to feed this information back into the group with beneficial consequences for all concerned.

Of course, one has to feel considerable confidence about being able to weather emotional storms before one dares to work with couples' groups at all. My wife and I began quite late in life, round about the age of fifty, when we felt we were ready. How did we know we were ready? I can remember very vividly the family incident which made us reasonably confident that we could begin to expose ourselves to the marital tensions of others, and you may be amused to know what it was.

> When our children were about eight and ten, which would make it about fourteen years ago, I had been prevailed upon to accompany them, and my wife, to a Saturday afternoon at the movies. It was one of the worst Walt Disney whimsies, which I particularly dislike. I had agreed to go to show what a good father I was, since my occupation at that time as a Consultant Child Psychiatrist made it difficult to deny that good fathers should take part in family outings. However, I went with a bad grace, and as soon as it was over, which certainly could not have been soon enough for me, we piled into the car to return home.
>
> Driving home, the children in the back seat asked for an ice-cream. I was looking forward to a stiff whisky as soon as we got inside the door, but before I could even have a chance to show I was a good father again, my wife told me the children wanted an ice-cream and could I stop. With a screech of brakes we drew up at the ice-cream shop, my wife got out, leaned back into the car and said, 'That's three cornets then?' I said, 'Why can't *I* have a cornet? I've driven you all to the pictures; why am I the only one who doesn't get an ice-cream?'
>
> My wife behaved with admirable restraint, and refused to be provoked. She just said 'All right, *four* cornets then,' and

111

went off to get them. When she returned, she handed two cornets to the children in the back seat, gave one to me, got back in the car holding hers, and shut her door ready for us to drive off again. Just as I was about to let in the clutch to do so, my ice-cream fell off the top of my cone on to the floor.

Now if you have, or have had, children, you will know that at this stage of life the floors of cars are covered with sand and grass. My wife said: 'Your cornet has fallen on the floor,' helpless with amusement. 'I know my cornet is on the floor,' I replied; 'pick it up and put it back on my cone.' The whole family were now convulsed with laughter. 'But it's got grass and sand all over it,' she said. 'I know it's got grass and sand all over it,' I replied, 'I'm not blind. Please pick it up, scrape the grass off, and put it back again.'

'But I've only got one hand. I'm holding my own cornet,' she replied. '*I'll* hold your cornet, now pick up *my* ice-cream and give it back to me,' I repeated. I took her cornet in one hand, and held out my empty cone with the other, waiting for her to replace my refurbished but shrunken ice-cream on the top.

Eventually, she had it reasonably clean, took the empty cone from my hand, and began to press it firmly down. But she took her time over it and laughed once too often. It was a fine summer evening, so the car windows were down, and I flung *her* ice-cream out of the window on my side. She said, 'Oh! All right,' and threw *my* ice-cream out of *her* window. I let in the clutch and we sped home, both now convulsed with laughter and in the most marvellous spirits, my bad mood completely gone, having achieved the first really 'good clean row' of our relationship, which we later realised had signalled our readiness to begin working together as co-therapists with couples' groups.

There was silence from the back seat for a few moments, and then my heart sank, and my enjoyment was temporarily subdued, as I heard my son say, 'Daddy!' in a reproving, anguished tone. I suddenly became aware of how this episode might appear to those looking on. We were in NW3, psychoanalyst country; suppose there has been one passing by, or a member of the Royal College of Psychiatrists or the

Association of Child Psychology or Psychiatry, speculating on the damage I was doing to our hapless children. Perhaps we had even hit this astonished bystander with one of the ice-creams. However, I was quickly reassured as our son added: 'Daddy! Don't you *realise* those ice-creams cost a *shilling each*!?'

Conclusion: The Alternatives of Using Power and Understanding

I have tried, as in the book *Families and How To Survive Them*, *to convey something emotionally, by personal anecdote, as well as by the more formal, intellectual channel. But the issue was put most clearly of all by Gregory Bateson, in everything he said and did. He never ceased to remind us that any attempt to change ourselves, or others, through the use of power rather than through understanding inevitably becomes a form of manipulation that diminishes them and – what I believe is more important – diminishes us as well.* I give greater importance here to the effect on ourselves only because there are many professional safeguards against this harmful effect of therapy on our patients, but we get little aid to make us aware of the importance, if our work is to be of the best and of increasing quality, of ensuring that we gain personal benefit from it too. *It is not a zero-sum equation where the less I gain the more there is for others. The more I gain the more there is for them, and vice-versa. Similarly, we . . . are a system, and part of a wider system. The more each of us gains the more there is for everyone, for all of us as a group, and then the more there is for each individual here, including me. Can we together find something valuable for us all in the discussion that follows?*

Notes

1 This paper was given to the Third Conference on Teaching Dynamic Psychotherapy, Association for University Teachers of Psychiatry, Oxford 1986. It was first published in *The Bulletin of the Royal College of Psychiatrists*, Vol. 10, December 1986.
2 The most accessible single set of references to the writers Skynner

draws from here is to be found in *One Flesh: Separate Persons*, Appendix A.

3 For an overview of the pioneering work of these contributors, see A. Gurman and D. Kniskern, (eds) *Handbook of Family Therapy*, notably the foreword by Lyman Wynne and *The History of Professional Marriage and Family Therapy* by B. Broderick and S. Schrader. (Ed.)

4 Aubrey Lewis was the first professor of the Institute of Psychiatry, established after the Second World War as the country's major post-graduate training and research centre. Amongst the most important of his contributions was his commitment to maintaining under one roof different perspectives, including those drawn from descriptive psychiatry, psychodynamics and behaviourism. (Ed.)

5 See the Author's Biography, p. xxi ff above, for an account of Skynner's early association with these scientists and philosophers in the Metalogical Society. (Ed.)

6 See Kohon's introduction to his edited collection, *The British School of Psychoanalysis: The Independent Tradition*, notably the section on counter-transference, pp. 51–73, for an account of how the influences to which Skynner is referring here – notably the celebrated papers of Paula Heimann (1950, 1960) – were assimilated by British practitioners. (Ed.)

7 See *Explorations With Families*, chapter 7, p. 154.

8 S. H. Foulkes, *Group-Analytic Psychotherapy: Method and Principles*.

8 Marriage and Personal Change

(Paper given to the Fortieth Anniversary Meeting of The Institute of Marital Studies, London 1988)

This section is concluded with the most recently written paper in the collection, given in 1988 to mark the Fortieth Anniversary Meeting of the Institute of Marital Studies. The IMS was established after the War as the Family Discussion Bureau by the Balints and Lily Pincus, amongst others, to train practitioners in Probation and Social Services to work therapeutically with marital problems. Although the approach adopted there is confined to one therapeutic method, the IMS is the foremost marital agency in the country. At their anniversary meeting Skynner shared a platform with others to present papers on marriage and social change examined from different perspectives.

Today the strain on durable relationships is unprecedented, with approximately one in three marriages ending in divorce. But we have only a limited understanding of the pressures responsible for this. Amongst these pressures, change in the social position of women, with inevitable consequences for gender role and marriage, has been a crucial factor. In the quarter of a century between the first of the papers in this collection and this one, these changes have led to such improvements in the balance between men and women as those in legislation to allow conflict-free divorce, protect equal opportunities, prohibit sexual discrimination at work and allow women independent financial status within marriage. The paper is written discursively around these changes, as they are reported in marital therapy. Elsewhere in Skynner's writing, change in gender role is a primary interest. *One Flesh: Separate Persons* and *Explorations With Families* contain extended discussion and detailed references on the subject. Those familiar with the material in those texts will find Skynner updating himself yet again here, revealing a constant readiness to put his own position under review.

115

Applications to Larger Systems

Describing a 'new order' of relationships emerging from the disorders of the old, he brings his subject full circle – back to ideas about the group-as-a-whole with which this collection begins. He points to important links between organic and holistic concerns of different kinds, and to developments in psychotherapy as it moves in this direction. The map he traces of the intellectual and professional changes he has witnessed and been responsible for over this period describes how the social context and its ecology has given a new emphasis to the understanding of psychological problems. Therapy influenced by these changes, guided by such models as object relations theory, attachment and systems theories, is now interactional. Though interaction is conceptualised in subtly different ways in each of these models, they share a theoretical paradigm that gives relationships primacy. Marital therapy is an important example of the interactional approach, and in the middle portion of *Explorations With Families* some of these different models are applied to marital work and evaluated.

J.R.S.

Introduction

It is a great privilege and pleasure to be asked to speak on this happy occasion of the Fortieth Anniversary of the IMS.[1] I have benefited greatly myself from its pioneering research – its work forms an essential base for my own work and writings, including the popular book, *Families and How To Survive Them*, that John Cleese and I wrote together – and I know of no other centre which opens its doors in the same way, not only to share its discoveries with other colleagues working in the field, but to invite their criticism and give opportunities for them to exchange with each other. It is typical that they should use this celebration of their anniversary to encourage an exchange among us in which we can all benefit from the experience and wisdom brought together in this distinguished gathering, and perhaps share some thoughts about what we have to do next.

There were various ways I could have used this limited time, but it seemed most useful to focus on the main theme – Marriage, Disillusion and Hope – and ask whether something hopeful might be emerging in a personal sense from a time when marriage and the family have seemed very threatened. In particular, I have responded to the invitation, first, 'to speak informally from my experience' rather than presenting a scientific paper, and second, 'to make some comment about why it might be that there has been a change in conceptual emphasis in regard to marriage and the family', a question I found more interesting the more I thought about it.

Breakdown of the Old Order

There is increasing concern at the effect on marriage and the family of what has appeared, at least on the surface, to be a progressive breakdown in the structure of society. In the western world over the past forty years our values have become increasingly individual, rather than group-centred, swinging the balance away from social cohesion towards personal freedom, often regardless of its social consequences. We have been losing the concept of duty, role, place in society, and of authority and order, including the former influential role of the father, the extended family and the community. There has been a decline in the influence of religion, in the force of social expectation, and in respect for law.

One consequence of this lack of structure is that couples are no longer held and supported through periods of difficulty. We have been losing the idea that creating a marriage is work – even if that work is normally made worthwhile by much pleasure – and that it takes effort and struggle, self-denial, patience, tolerance, kindness and generosity, mixed of course with plenty of humour and fun, to build an enduring relationship. Where before couples might have matured and become strengthened through struggling to overcome their difficulties – 'cooked', as it were, by the heat of conflict, they can now more easily jump out of the frying-pan of one relationship, into the fire of another similar one, just when the stress they are escaping from may be signalling that beneficial developmental changes were about to take place.

Emergence of New Forms of Relationship

However, at the same time as these degenerative changes in society have been occurring overtly, the seeds of new integrations have been forming in the background and growing in influence. In preparing this talk I became much more clearly aware than before of how we have been going through the painful transition between an old type of order and a new, emerging one. The old type of order is more hierarchical, paternalistic, with authority centred on the leader, and draws mainly on left-brain thinking. The new order is more organic and holistic, drawing on the intelligence of the whole system, including the resources and managerial qualities of both men and women and with a better balance of right- as well as left-brain functioning. The idea that governments know and people do not, that management know and the work-force do not, that teachers know and pupils do not, that men know and women do not, is giving way to an understanding that the group-as-a-whole has an intelligence far beyond that of any of its members, including the leader(s), and that it is the leaders' main task not to dictate and direct, except in times of crisis, urgent action and otherwise unresolvable conflict, but mainly to nurture and facilitate the group process and resources.

This change towards a new way of thinking is represented in forms of medicine, traditional and alternative, which consider the whole person, treating bodily, mental and spiritual needs together and in a social context; in increasing concern for the environment and awareness of ecological consequences; and in a greater feeling of responsibility for world conditions, evidenced at one extreme by vast spontaneous movements of young people sharing a common goal of helping others in dire need, as for instance the extraordinary phenomenon of 'Band Aid' in 1986. And at the other, there is increasing coordination of financial policy through summit meetings of world leaders and financial institutions, thereby avoiding many disasters that would have happened in the past, however partial and limited in scope such cooperation at present may seem.

New Ways of Thinking about Relationships

This widening of our field of awareness has been reflected in our understanding of personal relationships, including those within marriage and the family. In our own professional work I would see three developments as particularly relevant to our changed understanding. These are: object-relations theory; attachment theory; and general systems theory.

Object Relations Theory

The early development of both psychoanalysis and learning theory was based on individual-centred thinking, looking at and treating each person separately, one at a time, in isolation. Object-relations theory placed the human individual back into a social context, as part of a network of relationships which influences and sustains us throughout life. Once the group was established in our model of the inner world, it inevitably led some practitioners to take the next step and experiment with the living group itself. Foulkes, Bion, Balint and other psychoanalysts began to explore the actual interaction of

119

groups, watching the intermeshing of the member's projected inner worlds and discovering powerful new forms of treatment in the process.[2] Others, including Bowlby, Dicks, and many members of the Institute of Marital Studies, brought together marital partners and other family members to learn about the structure of their inner worlds not just by questioning or listening to the free associations of patients about their family relationships, but by watching the interaction at first-hand.[3]

Attachment theory

Attachment theory, as developed by Bowlby and his colleagues from its origins in animal ethology, has gone far towards providing an objective, scientific base for this different way of thinking, by systematic and detailed studies of the interaction of parent and child from birth. This research has made us much more aware of the fundamental role of the family and of other social support-systems throughout life.[4] It long ago completely transformed the care of young children needing hospitalisation and threatened by separation from parental care, all over the world, and I was pleased to be able to help implement some of its recommendations about mothers visiting and living-in with their children twenty years ago at the Queen Elizabeth Hospital for children. I have also now recently experienced the beneficial effects of attachment theory first-hand, on the receiving end, as it has been so marvellously applied at the other end of life in the hospice movement, and I cannot find words to describe what a difference its application makes to the happiness and quality of life of both the dying person, and the partner. In these and in other ways, attachment theory has created a new climate of opinion in making us more aware of the social context of all our behaviour.

Systems theory

System theory, which had its origins in the late 1940s from such sources as Weiner's 'Cybernetics' (1948), the 'Information Theory' of Shannon and Weaver (1949), and the 'Games Theory' of von Neumann and Morgenstern (1947), has developed its tremendous influence over the four decades we are considering. Initially it had a greater influence in the United States and has reached us, or at least reached the mental health professions in this country, indirectly through the American family therapy movement. But in Britain we understood and were applying much of it already – the first paper I know of on family therapy was published here, by John Bowlby, in 1949, and when I used to tell my teacher, S. H. Foulkes, about these new American developments he would usually dismiss them and say, 'But that's group analysis'. He was indeed doing it already, from an intuitive understanding, but systems theory provided a new language, and a clearer framework of thought, which illuminated what we were doing and enabled us to see new connections so that we could understand and do it better. Where the knowledge has been applied, it has transformed the outlook for the treatment of psychological disorder.[5]

Responsibility in Relationships

Despite the costs of increased marital break-up, many people have been released by the more relaxed divorce laws and attitudes from what might in the past have been a lifetime of bitter conflict and misery. For many others seeking a more fulfilling marriage this possibility of choice has made life richer and more interesting, opening the way to new levels of growth and relationship. In days when many marriages were more like a business contract – a pay-packet and security exchanged for cooking, sex and house-work – divorce could be seen as a failure of the business, or a wrong choice of business partner.

But today the agenda is often based more on mutual growth. A lifelong commitment is probably the most growth-facilitating situation of all, provided there is an equal commitment to change. Divorce often indicates that one partner has grown, or wants to grow, more or differently than the other, and that this difference is irreconcilable. Some marriages are like a stage of a journey, where each partner is travelling to a different destination and they move on to other relationships when they have helped each other grow through the appropriate stage. Though I cannot help feeling a warm romantic glow when some couples I see end by walking off into the sunset hand-in-hand, some of those which end in amicable divorce and loving cooperation over care of the children can appear almost equally positive when seen from this point of view.

121

I have not found in my work that people are in general becoming less responsible about their relationships, as I understand the word 'responsibility'. The more one's behaviour towards others is regulated by rules, by law and social expectation, the more irresponsible one's behaviour is likely to be when there is no one around and one is distant from one's own doorstep. By contrast, a relaxation in external controls *can* lead to worse behaviour in some, but also to better behaviour in others. Since the social changes of the 1960s, I never cease to be impressed by the extraordinary responsibility and care young people in intimate relationships show towards one another, compared with the attitude common at the time of my own youth and young adulthood, and in many older people I see who were brought up in that time.

My colleague Margaret Robinson, who pioneered our conciliation service at the Institute of Family Therapy, pointed out to me that there is now far more negotiation during courtship or cohabitation and before a final commitment, about issues that in the past would have led to problems at a later stage. For example, couples work out mutually satisfactory agreements about separate friendships with the same or opposite sex early on, instead of entering into marriage with idealised notions of meeting all each other's needs, and then suffering a violent breakdown of this pattern when at mid-life one spouse has an affair. There is less illusion built into the relationships, and so the disillusion is less, or it occurs in time to call the relationship off at an early stage. Step-families in particular are leading the way in this process of negotiation at an early stage, and exploring such issues in a way that will ultimately benefit us all.

The Sexual Relationship

Another major change affecting personal relationships in marriage has been the enormous increase in knowledge of the range of human sexual behaviour, and in discovering ways to help couples to improve the quality of their love-making. Kinsey published *Sexual Behaviour in the Human Male* in the year the IMS was founded, 1948, and his *Sexual Behaviour in the Human Female* followed five years later. I remember the profoundly liberating effect it had on all those I knew who read it at the time, as well as upon myself.

Whatever the limitations of that research, it opened up this taboo area to more open discussion and scientific study. About half-way through this period Masters and Johnson's publication of *Human Sexual Response*, in 1966, and *Human Sexual Inadequacy* in 1970, was another milestone towards a scientific understanding of human behaviour, opening the way to modern rapid treatments of sexual dysfunctions. The skills are widely distributed among professionals in clinics and hospitals, and throughout the country the former Marriage Guidance Councils – or Relate as they have since been renamed – now have 101 such clinics operating.

These studies attracted great public interest and were widely publicised in the media. The relaxation of taboos on the publication of sexual material made this information available to all, in best-selling books like *The Joy of Sex* (Comfort, 1972), giving permission for couples to discuss their sexual difficulties, and enough help for some to overcome them without need of professional help. Although this greater freedom of communication was inevitably abused by some, and although it produced new anxieties where couples feared they might not be 'keeping up with the Jones's' in their orgasm tally, it is my impression that this increased openness and relaxation on the topic of sexuality has been of great benefit towards improving the quality of married life and of family happiness.

Changes in the Roles of Women and Men

These changes in sexual attitude are just one aspect of the tremendous change that has occurred over this period in the way women perceive their feminine role, whether or not they have belonged to the women's movement in any formal way or even support it consciously. In the couples I have seen during this time the women have shown a steadily greater confidence, a more solid sense of personal identity, an increasing demand for personal freedom, for equality, for a greater measure of independence and right to their own separate lives, for a more equal share in the partnership, if not an exactly equal deal, as regards child care and housework. Increasingly, it is the women in troubled couples I see who have been calling the shots, initiating divorce, having affairs.

The expansion in the self-image of women was potentially liberating for men, who were equally locked into restricted patterns of behaviour by social expectation. Men have benefited from engaging in the change too, and I am certainly grateful to feel so much more relaxed and free now than my father or my grandfather appeared to be, or than I did myself when I was young. But in general the male sex has been slow to follow the women's initiative, and men have tended either to dig in and resist the changes in women, or to follow their demands too slavishly (this second, too conciliatory reaction appearing to infuriate women even more than the first). What seems to be needed is for men to continue to be men, different and separate, but to engage in the process and learn from it.

This change can be observed regularly in the couples' groups I run, and which my wife and I worked with together for over sixteen years. To start with the women are intensely frustrated and attack the men in oblique ways, but at the same time they inhibit themselves as if fearful of destroying the male self-esteem, which they perceive as fragile and likely to collapse if not buttressed by their support. There seems to be no conditioning as powerful as that which inhibits a woman from criticising a man in ways that would really threaten his confidence in his male sexual role. However, if the woman is supported in sustaining her attacks, and the man in taking her criticisms on board, eventually he begins to engage in the dialogue in a more forthright, open and constructive way. Often he will seize the initiative and then take the lead for a time, but eventually they achieve a more equal relationship, embodying mutual respect for each other's strengths and becoming a match for each other. I believe this kind of struggle now has to be worked out at a social level.

Conclusion: Research on Exceptionally Healthy Families

Finally, the most hopeful development of all has been the research into exceptionally healthy families, which has been available for only the last of our four decades. When I first went to train at the Maudsley near the beginning of this period, in 1953, I searched the library there for references to papers about mental health – by which I mean optimal health in the sense that olympic athletes are exceptionally athletic. I found only three; two contained little of interest and the third was impressionistic, though it contained unexpected findings and whetted my appetite. It was another twenty years before information about really healthy individuals, couples and families – for instance that of the Timberlawn Research Foundation in Texas and Vaillant's report of the Grant Study on the health of Harvard Graduates over forty years, began to fill this gap.[6]

There are several very hopeful aspects of this research. Many of the qualities these families show are those that common sense would lead us to expect, like warmth, openness, trust, mutual respect, responsibility and neighbourliness. But some findings are rather unexpected; in some ways they seem able to have their cake and eat it, they can lead separate lives and do without each other, yet can also be unusually close and intimate, with the parents usually showing a pattern of long-term marital fidelity. Far from being dull, such families are unusually lively, spontaneous, playful and amusing.

All the ideas I have outlined earlier are helpful towards understanding why such families function well; for example, their strengths required a capacity to deal resiliently with change and loss, including the death of loved ones, and this in turn depended on powerful support-systems, including a sense of one's place and connection with the cosmos. This knowledge is helpful whatever one's own level of health, because it gives us a direction to aim for.

Notes

1 This paper was presented to the Fortieth Anniversary Meeting of the Institute of Marital Studies, London 1988.

2 For a useful introduction to the object relations approach, see *Object Relations in Psychoanalytic Theory*, J. Greenberg and S. Mitchell. (Ed.)

3 See *Marital Tensions* by H. Dicks. (Ed.)

4 In *A Secure Base: Clinical Applications of Attachment Theory*, Bowlby gives a recent account of the range of applications of attachment theory. (Ed.)

5 See Skynner's own account of systems theory and its applications in *Explorations With Families* chapter 12 (Ed.)

6 2 See J. Lewis et al., *No Single Thread: Psychological Health in Family Systems*, 1976; J. Lewis, *How's Your Family*, 1979; and W. R. Beavers, *Psychotherapy and Growth: A Family Systems Perspective*, 1977. (Ed.)

Three

PERSONAL GROWTH AND PROFESSIONAL DEVELOPMENT: Complementary Cycles

9 The Large Group in Training

This section is introduced by a major paper that, in its examination of large groups, contains a definitive account of the General Introductory Course at the Institute of Group Analysis, and of staff groups at the Maudsley Hospital. Through different editions of *The Large Group*, the book for which the paper was written as a chapter, the accounts contained here have had a wide influence. It is an earlier and more basic paper than many of those in the previous section but is located here because it introduces this section's theme – the interaction between personal growth and professional training.

Skynner established the training structure of this course for the Group-Analytic Society in 1964. Some eight members of the Association of Psychiatric Social Workers, the organisation for which it was at first designed, gathered at the Group-Analytic Practice in the first year and, by the time this paper was written six years later, the course had seven staff catering for seventy participants who were now drawn from various professions. Soon afterwards, the number rose to twelve staff catering for 150 participants and, for the last four years, the course has been run to this capacity size on the Institute of Group Analysis's own premises.

The course was instrumental in bringing together those who established the Institute in 1973. It remains the most extended undertaking in the Intitute's training calendar, in terms of numbers, and its largest single source of revenue. The approach has had a formative influence on the Institute of Family Therapy's development through the course described in chapter 6. There are also General Introductory Courses modelled on this one at centres in Brighton, Cambridge, Exeter, Glasgow, Manchester, Northampton and Oxford. Completion of one of these courses is a requirement for entry to the Institute's Qualifying Course. It has also provided a model for extending group-analytic training to centres abroad and, from the first overseas training programme offered by Institute members in Denmark in the mid 1970s, to the most recent one established in Dublin in 1987, some 31 training centres in 14 countries have drawn upon this course in one respect or another for many of their structures and principles.

Many of the qualities that have made the course so successful are conveyed in this paper, but it is a partial account which, for its descriptive content, focuses entirely on the course's large-group process. It is a curious reflection on developments as extensive as those described above that this remains the most extended account and, indeed, the only published critical study of the General Course. It is to be hoped that its re-publication might stimulate such work.

The hospital-based large group for staff described in the second section of the paper was, at the time, a major innovation. Many of those who followed it and applied large-group principles in hospital and therapeutic community settings, had their training on the General Course and in this way the two developments described in this paper stimulated one another. They were also factors that led to the formation of the Association for Therapeutic Communities, many of whose original members underwent their basic training on the General Course whilst working in settings like the Day Unit described here. A further development is the Large Group which, for many years, has met at the Institute of Group Analysis. It was convened until recently by de Maré who partnered Skynner in the foundation of the General Course and was mainly responsible for including a large group in its structure. The Large Group provides direct access to the kind of experience described in this paper and is used as a training resource by professionals of different kinds.

J.R.S.

Introduction

There is already a well-developed use of small groups, usually comprising six to twelve but occasionally up to sixteen members, for sensitising mental-health professionals to psychological factors.[1] Three main British approaches may be distinguished. The first, associated particularly with the Department of Children and Parents at the Tavistock Clinic (Irvine, 1959) avoids interpretation of the participants' counter-transference or group-interaction, focusing instead on case-discussion and relying on identification processes to provide insight for those who can accept it, in the manner of Caplan (Caplan, 1964, 1970). The second, associated particularly with the Adult Department at the Tavistock Clinic (Gosling et al., 1967) also begins from case-discussion but utilises the group interaction to illuminate counter-transference involvement and it aims, in the words of its main originator, Balint (1957), at a 'limited, though considerable, change in personality'.

Both the above techniques lean more heavily on the psychoanalytic model and on the group theories of Bion (1961), and Ezriel (1950). The third method, derived from the group-analytic principles of S. H. Foulkes (1948, 1964, 1975), operates closer to the depth of a therapy group. It avoids more personal interpretation than is absolutely necessary, and the developing themes and interaction in the group-as-a-whole are interpreted with the aim of facilitating a maturational process in the participants. In my own application of this method, described in chapters 1 to 3 above, there is a particular focus on the shared motivation of the participants in choosing and performing their professional work. This usually proves to be rooted in pathology similar to that typical of their chosen patients or clients, and because of this the insight gained not only replaces this pathological interest by more mature and realistic

131

motivation, but also enables the participants to become especially sensitive to the area in which their typical clients or patients find personal difficulties.

All three techniques are appropriate to different situations. The first is more suited to professionals with little previous sensitisation to psychological issues in themselves or others; the second to an intermediate group such as some general practitioners; and the third to some more sophisticated mental health professionals who are able to tolerate the temporary disturbance brought about by increased personal insight and questioning of their basic professional motives.

The use of large groups for training is by contrast relatively new. The yearly Tavistock/Leicester Group Relations Conferences have included a large group exercise for some years Rice (1965) and Rioch (1970) has described the introductions of a similar method into the US through collaboration between the Tavistock and the Washington School of Psychiatry. Rioch's clear and interesting account indicates that their large groups, like the Tavistock small-group training situations, are usually structured around a clear aim or task (at present the study of leadership), with particular valuation of intellect and rationality in the tradition of Bion. It is to be hoped that more detailed accounts of this approach, which would be especially appropriate to situations requiring a greater degree of structure, will become available in due course.

In what follows, I shall present some examples of large groups conducted in the group-analytic tradition. In this approach neither intellect nor emotion is seen as paramount, both being viewed as possessing creative potentials which, if harnessed through reciprocal exchange of thought and feeling, initiate a developmental process in the group as a whole from which new forms of understanding and new ways of relating emerge without prior imposition of a doctrine. Two large groups, each different in many respects, will be presented. Both were composed mainly of psychiatrists, psychologists, nurses, social workers and other professions involved in mental health. The first was much larger, was 'artificial' in the sense that the participants did not normally work together, and it met for only seven weekly sessions with multiple leadership. The second was much smaller, comprising the staff of an institution which was meeting and working together between the weekly sessions described, and it is reported over eighteen months, with a single group conductor.

A Larger, Unstructured Group

For several years, the Institute of Group Analysis has run an introductory course in group work for psychiatric staff of different disciplines and levels of experience, in which the membership is deliberately widened through including professionals from related fields, such as sociologists, priests, etc. This course runs for an academic year, taking up one afternoon a week, of which the first hour and a half is devoted to a lecture/discussion concerned with theory, the second hour and a half being used for sensitivity groups of twelve members each led by a group analyst. It had been the practice in the past to hold plenary sessions at the end of each term mainly to provide some possibility of communication between the course members and the staff as a whole. In 1970–1, the year described in this paper, there were seventy-two students and seven staff members. Because the staff had become increasingly aware both of the need for more understanding of large-group dynamics among the students, especially those working in therapeutic communities, day hospitals, etc., as well as of the limitations of their own knowledge in this field (even though half the staff in fact worked in therapeutic community situations), it was decided in planning the course for 1970–1 to have no lectures during the third term, but to meet as a large unstructured group comprising all students and staff, as in the plenaries, for the first half of the afternoon. It was clearly explained to the students that this would be a learning experience for the staff as well as for them. A series of seven meetings of this kind were then held in the third term, there being no programme or structure other than a seating plan of three concentric circles (as in the previous lectures), and a time limit of one and a half hours. The experience which followed made a profound impression on many of us, and demonstrated a potential in the large group that seemed to surprise even those with much experience of such situations.

Session 1

The first session was fairly tense and uncomfortable throughout. The inner ring was almost empty, and members seemed to be crowding towards the back away from the experience. The discussion was mostly concerned with structure – seating, timing, lateness and so on – and it demonstrated anxieties over losing control or fear of chaos and destructive conflict. Interventions by the leaders were welcomed since they structured and polarised the group temporarily, like a magnet giving a pattern to scattered iron filings.

Session 2

At the second session the inner ring was full and this time the group seemed to be crowding to the front rather than trying to escape. Splitting and projection in the Kleinian sense were prominent. A tape-recorder introduced by staff without prior discussion was the object of hostile feelings, while a pop group playing loudly in the room below received projections of primitive violence and orgiastic sexual fantasies. A crucial interchange took place between two group leaders; one, a follower of classical psychoanalytic ideas and techniques, appearing to represent reason, intellectual control, and a necessity for verbal, personal communication, to allay the anxiety stimulated by the large group; the other, interested in family therapy, encounter techniques, and mystical and religious experience, advocating by contrast an abandoning of previous expectations, and self-exposure to the uncertainties of the new situation. The latter expressed enjoyment at a sense of non-verbal contact and communion with the group as a whole, which was enjoyable and fulfilling, but which fear of envy by others made him reluctant to acknowledge. Following this, other members, staff and students alike, began to report similar enjoyment and the 'space in the centre' of the circles became increasingly significant in the contributions. One member said, 'That space is like God – everything is there, yet nothing is there!'

Session 3

At the third session a new polarisation and splitting appeared between the outer rings (representing reason, ideas, the large group, and perhaps parental authority), led by one staff member who repeatedly expressed preferences for large groups in a polemical way, and the inner ring (representing feeling, experience, the small groups, and maternal intimacy), led by another staff member fiercely defending the small-group experience. A violent altercation between these leaders, which continued for some time, was finally interpreted by the staff member interested in family therapy, firstly as a manifestation of depression in 'father' and 'mother' because the 'children' were becoming independent and leaving home, leading to the defence of splitting and projection between the parents, and secondly as parental intercourse (there were many associations suggesting this as well). This staff member was in turn dethroned by the course members who discussed his role in the family and it was decided, amid laughter, that he was the 'lodger'. Another staff member who had chaired the lectures, and was until this point regarded as the main leader, was next addressed without his medical title, while a non-medical course member was addressed as 'Doctor'. The irritation of the former at his loss of status caused much amusement, but he was able to point out how the group was using the leaders in a new way, as experts and advisers rather than as parental figures.

Session 4

By the fourth session this maturation of the group was already striking. Many members had become aware of the formation of the group through periods of deeply meaningful silence, and there was increasing acceptance of being, existing, living in the moment, and finding this complete in itself; with a lessening need to do, to achieve, or know and 'understand' intellectually. The staff member who had previously seemed to support reason and verbal communication at the second session this time took the lead in reporting his experience and challenging the escapes of his colleagues into activity. Following this, a course member, referring back to the staff member who had endorsed uncertainty and abandonment to the group experience two sessions before, declared himself as 'enjoying being lost', arousing mingled admiration and envious attacks from others by his evident enjoyment of his experience, which was expressed in terms of the phantasy of being on a picnic. Another course member attempted to join him, but playing, as someone later expressed it, 'Cain' to his 'Abel'. Eventually, fantasies of sexual orgies appeared in the associations and disappointment was expressed that although the staff member/parents had had exciting intercourse the week before, and the student/children were able to

135

indulge themselves on this occasion, there could be no total orgiastic fulfilment in the group as a whole, because of the incest taboo. Themes of the crucifixion, the resurrection and hopes for a saviour appeared several times during this interchange.

Session 5

At the fifth session, after expectations of a corpse on the floor in the open space, and an inquest regarding its significance, the first group dream was reported where the large group, in colour, was conducted by a long-haired stranger (was this Foulkes or Freud? we all wondered), while the small groups were supervised in the same room by the speaker's own small-group leader. Anxiety over the leaders' quarrel two sessions before, repressed in the previous session, reappeared and the leaders were asked if the quarrel was subsequently resolved in their staff meeting. Suspicions were voiced that the leaders used the large group to resolve conflicts they could not deal with in ordinary ways. The leaders evaded this latter question repeatedly, as if deaf, but finally confirmed that they did in fact use the large group to resolve staff conflicts and were indeed usually provoked to do so by the students. Several staff members continued to make bids to retain their special role and status, and the group dealt with them effectively. Two other leaders, champions of the small group, who set themselves apart by making interpretations from 'outside' or 'above' (i.e., 'you are anxious,' or 'the group is anxious,' rather than 'I feel anxious'), were also put in their place and it was suggested that their need to continue this interpretive function was an expression of their own anxiety. The associations revealed an increasing amount of anal material; words like 'shit' and 'crap' being repeatedly used in contexts suggesting a regressive defence against genital sexuality. The latter was expanded by the previous lecture chairman to the idea of loss of ego boundaries generally, including mystical experience and an oceanic feeling. Members commented on the absence of splitting and the remarkable cohesiveness of the group, one remarking that he arrived feeling 'in pieces' after many mishaps during the day, and that he felt he had been put together and made 'whole' by the session.

Session 6

In the sixth session, which began with lively, relaxed talk until silence eventually fell, the sense of maturity and responsibility in the group-as-a-whole continued to increase; some students spontaneously dealt with noise and interruptions outside, tasks normally performed by the staff. The main themes were of crypts, coffins, death, of eating the group as in the communion service, and of the course as a seed-pod bursting and scattering its seed/members broadcast to reproduce their own groups. Those who had tended to remain silent before began to contribute, and some splitting and conflict over the issues of talking or remaining silent occurred. Towards the end, restlessness and a desire to smash the group, to 'get it over', appeared and concern was expressed whether the experience could be preserved despite the imminent ending.

Concluding session

At the last session, a knocking overhead (where repair work was in progress in the room above) gave rise to fantasies about Shakespeare's *Macbeth*, of murder, of guilt, and of being 'untimely ripp'd'. Two course members established a bid for dominance which also demonstrated new-found though still uncertain independence, polarising the course into conflict which was used temporarily to escape the pain of separation. However, splitting was once again averted, and the painful affect was contained and shared. Increasing individualisation was demonstrated despite loss of ego boundaries and the obstacle to this combination of a simultaneous sense of personal identity yet communion with others, was seen as the fear of freedom and the fear of becoming responsible for living one's own life. Themes of violence once again intruded, followed by the balanced dual image of ambivalence, leading on to the recognition that the integrity of the group had been preserved to the end. Valuation of the experience was expressed and the staff member who chaired the lectures finally remarked, 'We survived!'. The leadership struggle continued to the end and would clearly continue after the end, yet this seemed more a measure of the leaders' own growth than a disruptive power struggle.

A Smaller, Task-Oriented Group

The second example is taken from a staff group at the Day Hospital at the Maudsley which increased in numbers during the first nine months in which I met with it from sixteen to over twenty-five members, demonstrating in the process some of the main issues which become more prominent in the large as compared with the small group. This Day Hospital, which is part of the postgraduate training complex of the Bethlem Royal and Maudsley Hospitals and the Institute of Psychiatry, plays a significant part in the treatment and rehabilitation of psychiatric patients, many of them long-term and seriously disabled, from the local district for which these hospitals have assumed a responsibility. It admits patients who can manage without full-time admission, but are too incapacitated for out-patient treatment alone. The daily life of the unit is structured around paid industrial work, supervised by occupational therapists, which stimulates the expectations and rewards of everyday life. In this context, the head of the unit has encouraged the use of a form of social therapy combining 'therapeutic community' techniques which help patients to cope with their emotional difficulties, with those principles of 'milieu therapy' which increase patients' ability to hold their own in everyday life. The staff is divided into three therapeutic teams, each of which meets four mornings a week with its own 'small group' of patients; the whole community comes together once a week in a large staff/patient group of about fifty-five people altogether. In addition there are behaviour therapy programmes supervised by the psychologists, social work provision for patients and their families, and the usual range of physical and other medical treatments.

Three years earlier, a consultant from the Psychotherapy Department had been invited to meet weekly with the staff group. The original purpose had been to provide some supervision of the group and individual psychotherapy, but this session with an outsider present had often permitted the beneficial ventilation of staff tensions. These seminars became highly valued and when this consultant retired I was asked by the Psychotherapy Department to continue in his place. I think the pleasure and interest I have found in doing so will show through in my account, but it is only fair to add that the situation is exceptional and it is difficult to know to what

138

extent the group development described could be repeated else-where. The trainees rotating through the Day Hospital and other units in this main postgraduate teaching institution are particularly lively, well-informed, and open to new ideas, while the whole staff has come to possess over the years high confidence, morale, and willingness to leave the security of familiar methods. I have felt particularly fortunate in collaborating with a consultant (I have called him below the 'senior psychiatrist', to avoid confusion with the Tavistock tendency to use the word 'consultant' for something closer to my own function here), who has always believed that the Day Hospital needed an organisation which would allow any member of the staff to act rapidly, confidently, and independently, and who considered that his staff could adjust and reorganise their work effectively only if they had opportunities in a group situation to master their accompanying anxiety and stress. Thus the group interactions reported here are a culmination of a long sequence of previous developments, and my own contribution has merely facili-tated a flexible and responsible mode of staff functioning envisaged many years before. (Bennett, 1969). I have been lucky also to work with a sister (senior nurse) whose memory of, and kindness to, me in my own days as a trainee could never be guessed from the support and respect she has shown towards my present role. It should be added that the senior psychiatrist had not attended the meetings with the previous visiting psychotherapist for fear of inhibiting the discussion, but after much argument among the staff it was generally agreed that the seminars could be far more fruitful if he joined them, which he did from the beginning of my own attendance.

What follows, then, is a description of these weekly meetings with the staff since I began to visit, and of the changes accompanying its development into the 'large group' category.

Phase I

The first two sessions and the beginning of the third were concerned with the structure of the meetings themselves. The first session was lively and spontaneous, but the main issue discussed: 'Should patients be allowed to read their notes?' (a patient had requested this) revealed an underlying preoccupation with our own bound-aries and limits. Though this issue was settled for us by a hospital rule forbidding such disclosure, the ensuing discussion revealed one sub-group favouring and another opposing the need for hierarchy, structure and clear boundaries generally. This polarisation was even more intense at the second meeting, the psychiatrists-in-training pressing for totally unstructured meetings, Maxwell Jones-type 'role-blurring' and 'flattening of the authority pyramid (1952, 1968)'; while others, particularly some of the more permanent staff, demonstrated increasing anxiety about such proposals and protected themselves by setting up their own boundaries, withdrawing into silence, or showing only guarded and limited participation. I perceived, by the end of this session, that more structure was temporarily necessary if the situation was to feel safe enough for all participants, and I opened the third session myself by expressing this view and imposing a rule that we would begin each time with a work problem, though there would be no restriction on the discussion which might arise from this. This proposal was strenuously opposed in principle but followed at once in practice by the young doctors, and my action appeared justified by the increased trust, spontaneity, and general participation that followed. (In fact, the rule about beginning with a work problem soon became unnecessary and was dropped.)

Phase II

The remainder of the third session, and the four sessions following it, took us quickly through the developmental phases we were to work out later in more detail, revealing in broad outline the unresolved family transferences normally operating in such professional groups. The case discussed at this session was a female patient whom all feared to criticise for fear of her self-destructive and perhaps suicidal tendencies, so that she was often allowed to dominate situations. Gradually it emerged that this patient was viewed as a favourite of the sister (who was absent from this session), the sister's disapproval being the real danger. Next it became apparent that the ambivalent feelings towards this patient were displaced from the sister herself and that these in turn were not realistic but were the result of transference of ambivalent, infantile attitudes towards mothers generally. 'Don't attack mother or she will die and there will be no one to care for us' was the eventual interpretation, leading to recognition that the sister was unfairly burdened by these transference feelings and that such maternal, nurturing functions should be shared by all the staff.

Next the senior psychiatrist came under disguised criticism, feelings being expressed that he should be more authoritative and firm, especially towards patients who were fit to be discharged but resisted leaving. These attitudes were in turn perceived as transference from early attitudes towards father, and such controlling, executive functions were also seen as responsibilities to be shared rather than left to the senior psychiatrist alone. At the following session a staff member asked to be excused attendance at the small groups with which each day began (in which everyone normally participated) because her personal psychoanalytic sessions obliged her to be late. No one actively rejected this request from a popular colleague, but there was obvious ambivalence about the 'special attention' she was receiving. I pointed out the feelings of envy and indulgence she was arousing, emotions normally experienced by elder siblings towards the baby in the family.

As might be expected, this progressive uncovering of unconscious, infantile components in the professional relationships aroused increasing resistance, and also a focusing of ambivalent transference elements in relationship to me. At the sixth session almost everyone was late, the atmosphere was tense and ambivalent and there was a good deal of teasing and banter towards me and towards psychoanalytic ideas generally. Analysis could not really be condemned, said one of the younger doctors, because it 'took place between consenting adults in private'; it might therefore be justified as enjoyable, even if of no practical use! Sexual themes, already coming near the surface in such comments as this, emerged clearly in session seven. Indeed, on entering the coffee room where I normally joined the staff for refreshments before we proceeded upstairs for the seminar, the subjects of conversation proved to be the stage show *Oh! Calcutta* and newspaper reports that day of nude girls helping to advertise cars at the motor show. The subsequent discussion revealed a high level of anxiety but feelings were open and amenable to examination and understanding. The staff had clearly been able to tolerate the emergence of sexual themes at the large staff/patient group the previous week, where one patient had spoken of wishing to marry another, and a third had affectionately stroked the hair of a psychiatric social worker (the staff had

141

complained previously of difficulty in helping patients to talk of sexual matters).

Phase III

What had been learned through interactions between the staff, and with me, now began more obviously to affect the management of patients. Session nine was taken up not only with discussion of professionals who clung to the partial viewpoint of their own speciality, failing to consider the needs of the total situation, but also with patients who sought special privileges in a similar way, particularly by playing off staff members who clung to attitudes characteristic of their speciality. The latter were seen increasingly as 'quarrelling parents' who could be manipulated by the 'children' because they valued their personal needs more than the welfare of the family as a whole.

By session ten, the more determined, challenging attitude developing in the staff was clearly evident. The large group that week had been stormy, a fight had broken out, and there had been much argument not only among the patients but between the staff as well. When I pointed out that this might be an inevitable, healthy phase, I was attacked too: it was easy for me to talk, they said – I didn't have to do the work!

Session eleven brought a temporary regression following on the successful suicide of a chronic patient. There were heavy silences and a depressive preoccupation with the dangers of aggression and sexuality. At times a further regression occurred as a result of paranoid-schizoid mechanisms, as a scapegoat was sought in the male patient who had been seeking this woman's favours. The reassurance of the senior psychiatrist, who had supported this woman through six years of suicidal threats and attempts, helped to relieve the guilt, but my use of the experience to illustrate depressive and paranoid group mechanisms stimulated a mixed reaction of anger at my 'callous' disruption of their mourning, together with relief at being called to resume a professional role. Practical matters were then planned to support those patients likely to be most affected when the news was broken.

By session twelve the staff had recovered, but the session was quiet, thoughtful and relaxed. They had been through a lot, had had enough for the moment, they said; they needed a rest and were

142

looking forward to Christmas. Looking back, we were surprised to see how much had changed over the three months of our meetings. A withdrawal by the staff of projections of dependent and aggressive feelings was taking place, leading to more confident, reality-based therapeutic interventions. There had been a further row as an occupational therapist had challenged the most manipulative patient over his cheating at work. And the hospital was reported almost empty, an unprecedented number of chronic patients having been discharged.

Phase IV

There was one further session (thirteen) before Christmas, and in this a new theme (or re-emergence of an old theme at a deeper level) commenced. The psychologist announced the integration of his students into the therapeutic teams and pressed for the inclusion of all students working in the Day Hospital and the Rehabilitation Unit next door. Next there was a general demand that the senior psychiatrist, who was medically responsible for both units, should have a show-down and impose the Day Hospital's new philosophy on its neighbour. Interpretation of all this in terms of a displacement of an emerging internal conflict was confirmed at session fourteen by a report that the doctors (the most powerful speciality) had been confronted by the patients in that week's large group and told they were untrustworthy, likely to experiment on people etc. This was followed in our seminar by a confrontation of the senior psychiatrist by the trainee psychiatrists, both developments being regarded by him as signs of healthy independence and ability at last to cope with negative attitudes towards authority.

By session fifteen the confrontation had moved towards me. People were slow to arrive at the seminar, there was a long silence and an impression, voiced by some members, of unusual tension and resistance. The issue of enlarging the seminar to include the students, always near the surface, took a central place again. Some supported their joining, especially the psychologist (as the only speciality with only one member he was perhaps more in need than others of an ally) but many resisted fiercely, claiming the seminar was much too large already. As in Menzies's (1961) description of defence mechanisms in a nursing population, which I described to the seminar, the students were being used as receptacles for projection of the more irresponsible, childish, rebellious 'id' aspects of the members, just as the senior psychiatrist and I had been used to contain the more controlling super-ego aspects before. The students had in fact criticised the staff in that week's large group (which the students were already invited to attend) and the fact that one had done so from a position of lofty superiority, reversing the projection in an infuriating way, only made these fantasies about the students more transparent.

At session sixteen I arrived to find the students present. As expected, they proved less satisfactory receptacles for unacceptable projections when present than when absent, especially as they were models of good behaviour (one was a priest). The staff's difficulty in accepting these projections back was illustrated by even greater lateness (the students were on time while even the sister and the senior psychiatrist were late) and a long initial silence. The remainder of the session was taken up with confrontations and the defining of boundaries between specialities and other sub-divisions – nurses versus psychologists, full-timers versus part-timers, maternal versus paternal role stereotypes. Such discussion led in this and the following session (seventeen) to the increasing questioning of existing boundaries, with excitement at the prospect of blurring roles and sharing more functions, together with fears that such crossing of role boundaries and mutual examination would reveal formerly hidden inadequacies. In session eighteen my boundaries were crossed and my skills examined as well. 'Why do you always sit in the same chair?' queried a nurse, usually silent and overtly submissive. 'So you can take it away from me,' I answered. 'And what do you think you have got that anyone would want to take?' she replied. This opening was followed by increasing criticism of me. I was accused of being unwilling to discuss the small groups (I had been longing to do so); of not knowing where I was going and instilling uncertainty, yet also of making them self-conscious and fearful of revealing themselves by the way in which I interpreted their behaviour in family terms, causing them to feel like children. Would they go on behaving like children then, and allowing me to do it? I asked. No! they cried.

Phase V

There followed five sessions in which the seminar worked through a depression occasioned mainly by the loss of the previous situation which, though it had been a 'large small-group' of sixteen now seemed in retrospect intimate and cosy; and by the difficulties of relationship and communication in the present situation which had become a 'small large-group' of around twenty-five. How could one hope to coordinate so many people? said the senior psychiatrist, a view echoed by the sister, a senior registrar and a student. There was laughter and some lightening of the atmosphere when I pointed out that, despite the evident fears of chaos, the despair was at least being expressed in hierarchical order. The increase in size also heightened the other source of anxiety and depression which had been expressed before and which indeed had influenced the decision to include the students: namely, an increasing awareness that the existing sharp definition of professional roles was largely defensive; that we needed to develop towards a greater sharing of skills and responsibilities; and that this process would be painful since a weakening of professional identities would inevitably place greater stress on personal resources and social skills.

This period brought the main crisis in the group's development, with resurgence of previous defences and new ones in addition. Splitting and projection occurred more intensely with attempts to make scapegoats of the students and, when that failed, the psychologist (the newest, least firmly established discipline in the team). The senior psychiatrist and I were both attacked more strongly and increasing demands were made on us to impose arbitrary solutions. A psychology student opted out altogether at this point and the psychologist himself said he might have to come less often, though in fact he remained and was, throughout, a vital member. Escapes into intellectualisation included demands for more structured discussions; rallying around a common task or premature definition of aims, as if round a flag; or retreat into more strictly defined professional roles. All of these were utilised one after another. But by the twenty-second session the corner was turned. The senior psychiatrist said that he had realised that he could never coordinate and control the situation himself – it was just too big – and that he would have to trust others in a way he had never needed to do before. He was the first (except for myself) to come through the depression but his healthy 'loss of false hope', like the despair, was clearly being passed down the line.

Phase VI

A further enlargement of the group was now proposed, the sister and nurses suggesting the inclusion of a male senior nursing officer. He was actually a member of the central administrative nursing staff but was responsible for liaison with the Day Hospital and was often called upon in crises, especially when the doctors were off duty. Conflicting views were expressed, many resisting a further expansion of the group so soon after the students had arrived, while the senior nurse was also clearly used as a receptacle for projection of 'super-ego' components just as the students had been used for projection of 'id' components earlier. The 'Young Turks' among the trainee psychiatrists, in particular, foresaw all their good work being undone and there were sexual associations to a fantasised 'undressing' which would no longer be possible. A 'unilateral declaration of independence' from the parent hospital was proposed by some, while others saw the value such a link could have in securing administrative sanction and support for the changes occurring in the Day Hospital's functioning, and indeed in enabling successful aspects to receive, in time, a wider application. By the end of the session everyone saw the need to seek partial changes only in the context of a greater whole and at the succeeding session (twenty-three) the decision to invite the senior nursing officer had been taken.

The next session (number twenty-four) is headed in my notes 'Psychiatric Social Workers' Lib.' It was reported that the psychiatric social workers had been attacked by some patients in the large group that week for not being sufficiently indulgent (their colleagues at a neighbouring hospital, who were said to give two-hour interviews to find people houses and to give them money, were held up as paragons) and for demanding, instead, that patients make an effort and learn to help themselves. The senior psychiatrist expressed concern over this ordeal the psychiatric social workers had suffered but was attacked by them for demonstrating that he was not as familiar with the details of their speciality as they would have liked, and was told they did not need his protection. Others

146

watched with ambivalent interest this 'blooding' of the psychiatric social workers, now strong enough to be attacked and to attack in turn.

The staff had for some time been studying and planning the use of conjoint family techniques for diagnosis and treatment (I had been appointed specifically to teach conjoint family and marital approaches in the hospitals) but until this point little systematic use had been made of them in the Day Hospital. However, in session twenty-five a visit from an American family therapist, Savaldor Minuchin, acted as a catalyst. A turnover of staff at this time, an important factor throughout, was also relevant. I returned from two weeks' holiday following it not only to find the senior nursing officer present at the seminar (his attendance proved as valuable as many of us hoped) but a lively, cheerful and welcoming group. The senior psychiatrist confirmed the impression of high morale by saying that they were 'over the hump' and the others informed me that the whole admission procedure was changed; initial interviews were now routinely being carried out with whole families rather than the referred patient alone, and this was being done not by the doctor as formerly, but by a staff team of three disciplines which might include a doctor or might not!

Over the next six sessions, until session thirty-two, I was used more as a resource person to supervise the new family work than as a group analyst facilitating the seminar. The usual swings of attitude occurred and needed clarifying, of course. After the very positive session described above, for example, there was the usual 'backlash' and I sat alone for five minutes waiting for anyone to arrive at the next session. The session continued with an aggressive attack on the neighbouring unit and then the successful provocation of the senior registrar to become more active and 'take over' again. However, these regressions were soon seen by the seminar as a result of fears of increasing shared responsibility and loss of the former safe professional boundaries. Subsequent progress in the new conjoint techniques was in fact striking and swift.

Later phases

The record will not be pursued further in detail, since this period of nine months covered the main difficulties presented by conversion of the seminar from a 'large small' to a 'small large' group as well as the general principles along which these problems were resolved. A further six months has elapsed at the time of writing this account, and while the sessions have been even more interesting they have mainly been concerned with working out the issues already outlined at deeper levels and in more subtle, detailed ways. In addition to further withdrawal from patients of projected aspects of the staff's psychology, the central theme has continued to be the search for new forms of interdisciplinary cooperation, with real sharing of responsibility and group communication, to replace the traditional hierarchical, one-way communication and control. These were changes which brought increasing demands for mutual adaptation (often painful and at first resisted) but which have also led to greater opportunities to develop and employ personal and professional skills and to engage in more real and satisfying team work. The earlier attempt to escape from safe but stereotyped professional roles has led on naturally to a similar questioning of sexual stereotypes, with some evidence already that benefits can accrue by greater sharing of so-called 'masculine' and 'feminine' roles without any loss of what is most valuable in real differences of sexual identity. The 'territorial' concept of gender, like that of speciality ('I am what you are not, I exist where you do not') is giving way to one of mutual exchange and responsibility ('I am increased because we share and exchange with one another, yet are different').

Perhaps it is not too much to hope that experiment such as this may lead, in time, to a true marriage of skills and disciplines in which the parts relate harmoniously through their perception of the need to serve the whole, rather than through an externally imposed order alone. Like the senior psychiatrist, I have become aware that a group of this size is beyond my ability to control, consciously or unconsciously, so that, like the others, I am constantly exposed to new attitudes and concepts that contradict or extend those I brought to the situation.

Discussion

Other writers in this field have provided detailed accounts of the development and present state of theories regarding large group functioning, particularly those aspects most clearly illuminated by Kleinian theory.[2] I shall therefore do no more than summarise the main principles briefly, particularly as they apply to training. I do, however, give some emphasis to those concepts about which my own experience has led me to conclusions which differ from those expressed by other investigators.

1. Energy available is proportional to the size of the group

In common with most students of large-group phenomena, I am impressed with their power, for good or ill. Though as yet we do not have even the rudiments of a truly scientific explanation, *it is as if some form of energy is generated when a number of people interact, proportional in some way to the numbers involved and available, like any other form of energy, for constructive or destructive purposes.*

2. The destructive potential of large groups

If uncontrolled, the forces concerned tend towards primitive, disintegrative types of interaction with breakup of the group itself into warring fragments leading to scapegoating and exclusion of parts; or to the creation of an external enemy or 'bad object' in order to avoid this internal conflict and maintain unity. On the level we are concerned with here, this results in patients and staff members being scapegoated and leaving, only to be followed by others; or there is a running battle with the Hospital Management Committee or other external authority. While this often happens in spite of the best intentions of the leadership, we are only too familiar, in larger, more chaotic social situations, with the way in which unscrupulous leaders can encourage and actively exploit such splitting and projective processes. One has only to experience an experimental large-group situation to understand all too easily the phenomenon of a lynch mob, or of the Nazi persecutions.

3. Creative depression in large groups

However, if something more akin to Klein's 'depressive position', can be maintained, with containment of painful affect, acceptance of ambivalence and sharing of experience between similar but unique and separate individuals (rather than the splitting and projection characteristic of the 'paranoid/schizoid' position already described), *it is as if energy becomes harnessed to other purposes, with increased consciousness of self and others, awareness of relatedness and interdependence, a sense of wholeness in the individual, in the*

149

group and in what is beyond the immediate situation as well. There can be a remarkable creativity in a group-as-a-whole which does not emanate from a leader or sub-group alone. One can see a connection here with the religious use of groups for constructive ends.

4. Constructive functioning and personal involvement

This achievement of constructive functioning seems to depend particularly on a certain form of involvement by a sufficient part of the membership. The following aspects seem to be important:

a: The tolerance of silence

A capacity to tolerate silence is crucial. Even more than in the small group, the most important events of the large group seem to occur in the long periods of profound silence. These are often experienced initially as uncomfortable and indeed painful, almost unendurable, but if survived without escape into defensive manoeuvres, particularly intellectualisation, they can become extremely pleasurable periods in which members experience direct connection and communion with each other, deeper and more sustaining than anything achieved through words. However, this requires a capacity of the individual to lose his ordinary boundaries without losing himself; or to put it another way, a willingness to abandon feelings of identity based on professional and social roles, on 'doing things' or 'getting somewhere,' and to trust to a deeper identity based on 'being' what one essentially 'is'. *This 'oceanic' feeling is indeed like floating in the sea, which also requires a cessation of activity as well as a trust in one's own essential buoyancy and in the support that will be provided by one's surroundings.* Many cannot bear this letting go, this loss of familiar ego boundaries, but cling to their familiar roles, and distance themselves from the experience by intellectualising, by making interpretations, by making light of what is happening, or protesting that 'nothing can be going on', instead of letting it go on.

b: Individuality and destructive envy

Involvement requires the willingness of the individual to maintain his separate identity and personal values despite the destructive envy that this arouses in others, which is experienced as greater and more terrifying as the size of the group increases.

c: Lowering defences and resolving ambivalence

Whoever can demonstrate to the group that it is possible and desirable both to lower defences and become one with the group, while at the same time maintaining individuality and standing against it (or rather for oneself despite it), is a true leader who enables the group to 'bind' its ambivalence and move towards more creative functioning. If the designated leaders fail in this, then at best there is defensive functioning where they lead an orderly retreat into limited problem-solving within restricted boundaries which are usually intellectually focused. At worst they abdicate and allow 'mad leaders' in the group to push it to more destructive ends. Harrington (1970), Stauble (1971) and Christ (1964) have pointed out the dangers of confused, fearful or indecisive leadership. It seems essential therefore, that those who will be concerned with large groups professionally should themselves receive some experience of a large training group, in order that they may develop confidence in facing such situations and in their management.

8. Leadership and dependence

One special aspect of the projective processes characteristic of large groups is the manner in which positive qualities of the participants become projected into the leaders at certain stages, just as negative qualities may be projected into scapegoats (or into the leaders also, of course, at other times). *For this reason the leaders seem to be, and indeed are made by the group, immensely powerful at certain points, while the participants appear to lose their capacity for independent thought and criticism.* The ability to contain and utilise these ego functions, despite the influence of the group, develops with experience in a large-group training situation and is one of its main objectives.

151

9. Sub-groups and spokesmen

Several authors have commented on the tendency for large-group interaction to take place between sub-groups, represented by 'spokesmen', rather than between individuals as in the small analytic group. Though this is sometimes seen as a handicap limiting its therapeutic value, others perceive it as one basis of the large group's often astonishing effectiveness. Curry (1967) has provided an excellent review of the literature on this topic, and I will only add my own view that *the greater feeling of anonymity in a large group, with the possibility this gives of developing insight and gaining confidence by vicarious means, does enable the leader to make interpretations at far deeper levels and to facilitate potentially disturbing insights at a far quicker pace than would be appropriate if the less insightful and more vulnerable participants were in a small-group situation.* The main burden of self-revelation is borne at first by those most able to tolerate it, who become spokesmen for sub-groups, but the other members are able to follow at their own pace, both by identifying with the spokesmen and often by subsequent increased participation. At the start they can retain their defences or 'hide silently in the crowd' until they are ready. The small group, on the other hand, involves more personal confrontation and a greater demand that all members shall 'keep together' in the therapeutic movement. In training, this feature of the large group is an enormous advantage when staff of widely differing status, skills, insight and ego strength need to be worked with together, as in the examples described above.

10. Phase-specific and active leadership

However, for this advantage to be secured, the leader(s) must recognise the need for more active, directive and controlling interventions than are usually necessary in small groups, especially in the early stages and when individuals threaten to become scapegoats, or at any time when anxiety rises beyond an optimal level. This crucial requirement is discussed particularly well by Schiff and Glassman (1969) and also by Christ (1964) in his critique of the position taken by Maxwell Jones (1965), which contains serious inner contradictions regarding issues of authority. Though these authors are speaking of staff/patient groups, staff training situations also require a similar feeling of safety and control if participation is to be wide and 'drop out' problems avoided.

Though leadership needs on average to be more active than with small groups, it should ideally be 'phase-specific', with a fairly high degree of structure, support and acceptance of dependency and idealisation of the leadership in the early 'paranoid/schizoid' and 'dependent' phases, followed by more active, provocative intervention in the anal-resistant, passively rebellious phase that follows and then firm 'standing of ground' and acceptance of challenge in the later, more actively-attacking anal sub-phase. Eventually, as genital-level functioning develops with increasing individuation and sharing of leadership, an analytic model becomes appropriate and the leaders can take a more neutral, passive role.

The amount of structure and degree of intervention required at each stage will also depend on the overall level of ego-strength, insight and professional confidence in the group as a whole. I have described, in chapter 3 above, the utilisation of a large group in sensitising the staff of a comprehensive school to psychological issues, where a much greater degree of control and focus on case discussion was needed than with professionals experienced in the psychiatric and social-work fields.

11. Multiple leadership

As with all large groups, the situation is so complex for one person to grasp, and the emotional pressures so great, that multiple leadership is an advantage. This is especially valuable if it is truly multiple, with room for normal expression of disagreement among the leaders rather than avoidance of conflict by formation of a 'monolithic bloc' around a particular theoretical model. As illustrated in the first example above, honest and open disagreement among the leaders provides the most powerful stimulus of all towards individuation of other participants. The conflicts can be fierce and it seems that immediate or clear resolution of them is not necessary, provided the staff group as a whole, or different parts of it at different times, can contain and 'hold' the conflict sufficiently to maintain adequate structure and sense of safety, as well as to keep the discussion open. This naturally requires a good basic relationship among the leaders, with a willingness to put the training task before personal preferences or rivalries, a state of affairs that probably develops only over a sufficiently long period of collaboration to permit the development of mutual trust.

Conclusion: Transcending the Group

The impossibility of containing and controlling fully the large group's interaction is perhaps one of its greatest assets. Anxious leaders can certainly block or restrict its creativity but in my experience one cannot avoid being exposed to new and challenging ideas which put one's whole outlook in question. I have suggested elsewhere that small groups tend to become like neurotic families, preserving a cosy security by colluding with the leader and reinforcing his defences.[3] So far the large groups I have taken part in leading have opened up new and exciting perspectives, throwing seemingly secure conclusions back into the melting-pot. In the smaller hospital group reported here, an entirely new approach to marital and professional relationships appeared to be developing. In the larger group at the Institute of Group Analysis we seemed each year to be brought to face the most fundamental questions of man's existence, and found emerging themes which illuminate the great myths, legends and religious symbols in new and unexpected ways.

Notes

1 This paper was first published as a chapter in L. Kreeger, (ed.) *The Large Group: Dynamics and Therapy*, 1975.
2 A recently published account of the Kleinian approach towards groups, developed at centres such as the Tavistock Institute and Clinic, is to be found in *What Happens In Groups*, R. D. Hinshelwood, 1988.
3 See chapter 1 above, and also *Explorations With Families*, chapter 10.

10 Make Sure to Feed the Goose that Lays the Golden Eggs: A Discussion on the Myth of Altruism

Skynner here brings together many of the threads we have followed in earlier chapters, providing a summation of his views on how therapy and consultation bring about – or fail to bring about – change. The paper was written for a symposium on the nature of altruism stimulated by a study of American social workers in the *Journal of Psychohistory*. It has been amended and enlarged for this collection and draws on:

- The study of vicarious experience introduced in chapter 1
- the distinction between 'haves' and 'have nots' introduced in chapter 2
- the understanding, introduced in chapter 3, of how care-givers' own problems are institutionalised.
- broad experience in the range of settings described a chapters 4–9

Lawton, the author of the study, investigates social workers and looks beyond extrinsic rewards in their work – income, professional regard and advancement – to examine intrinsic rewards which, arising from qualities in the work itself, are directly related to people's motives for choosing it, many of which are unconscious. Instead of the 'altruistically' motivated people he had expected, he finds social workers to be needy practitioners whose working structures help them deal with unacknowledged problems of their own through clients.

This material stands at the centre of Skynner's field of interest and, using it as his point of departure, he builds up his *philosophy of plenty based on the recognition of scarcity and deprivation amongst those in all the caring professions, which their working structures normally help them to deny*. This is the 'have not' mode and for those operating in it work is like a drug that soothes their own otherwise implacable needs. But, like a drug, it helps only by inducing a dependence that is decreasingly rewarding. People are driven to do more but get less out of it, and the less they get the more they have to do. This spiral underlies the exhaustion found amongst many in these fields and may be the root of many forms of 'burn-out' and work-related stress.

The philosophy of plenty can shift people from the 'have not' to the 'have' mode by changing the *vicious cycle of deprivation* into what Skynner calls the *virtuous cycle of mutual nurture*. Successful agencies, like successful individuals, need to begin by giving more to themselves first. They then have to deal with the 'have nots' – with envy and criticism that stems both from within the individual and the agency, and from outside. To be successful in dealing with these prohibitions an agency needs to bring about, in its internal relations, the changes it seeks to offer to its clients. The well-being of staff is made a priority through realistic work-loads and training, supervision and consultation. In this process, by drawing on the methods described in earlier chapters, the affinity between practitioners and their clients can be explored and become a source of strength.

Viewed positively now as 'the goose that lays the golden eggs', this affinity and the work in which it brings clients and workers together can free both sides, first from their respective histories and then from their over-dependence on one another.

Skynner describes these ideas as the distillation of his experience, and the paper leads naturally to the next in which the search for autonomy and equilibrium is taken beyond the domain of psychology.

J.R.S.

Introduction[1]

In 1982 Henry Lawton published an account of social work practice in the US entitled 'The Myth of Altruism'.[2] His paper contains a scholarly account of the history of social work and well-researched investigation of the problems in the organisations of the agencies there, and of problems amongst the people who staff them. I was pleased to accept an invitation to comment on Lawton's paper in a symposium that followed its publication. For there is something about the patterns that Lawton describes which gives them a timeless, almost mythical quality, as if they have their roots in certain basic qualities of human nature, present universally today and no doubt observable despite changes of fashion at any time or place in the past.

His main thesis is concerned with the 'selfish' aspect of seemingly altruistic motives in the personal and professional lives of those who choose the 'helping professions'. What follows are my own views on this subject in a more extended discussion than the one I originally published in the symposium on Lawton's paper. First, I have provided some information about my own point of view so that the standpoint from which I am writing is quite clear. Second, I have set out what I believe to be Lawton's main thesis in five points, each of which I have discussed. Third, I have described the pattern which Lawton has identified but from my own point of view, based on my own experience of teaching, supervising and consulting with staff in the helping professions. And fourth, I have traced this pattern back to early family life – where I believe it arises – to describe why the cycle of deprivation is itself reproduced in the professions concerned with its remediation.[3] I conclude with a summary of my own thesis, in which I take a more positive view about this state of affairs than Lawton's. Professional 'helpers', be they social workers,

157

psychiatrists, or any other, may be the only people willing to perform a difficult and thankless task. Their willingness may arise precisely because they are also getting something from the process psychologically.

This is the goose that lays the golden eggs. Many of us 'sneak' into caring or therapeutic agencies by the staff door to get psychological help without acknowledging the need for it. Solutions to this kind of dilemma are not necessarily to be found in some new recruitment drive to attract different personnel to these professions. Altered organisational structures and better conditions of pay and service, and even more advanced training, will not necessarily provide a solution, or if they do they will only solve part of this problem. For the goose to lay its golden eggs it must be fed and this involves some acknowledgment amongst 'care-givers' of the motives that draw them to their work.

If practitioners can begin to experience their real needs directly, if they can seek to satisfy such needs without routing them through their clients and in doing so evoke appropriate responses in their colleagues, whose help might be enlisted in a mutual regenerative process, the vicious cycle of deprivation can become a virtuous cycle of mutual nurture. Such opportunities can be provided within social work and other agencies, in the form of case-discussion, supervision or sensitivity groups. They are an important part of the teaching programme in organisations offering specialised training in group and family therapy. They are a central feature, for example, of the training offered by the Institutes of Group Analysis and Family Therapy. Whilst our primary concern in developing these organisations was the professional development of the participants, the groups are run close to the model of therapy and focus on the professionals' (unconscious) motives in their career choice. In the conclusion of this paper three different models for such experiential groups are described in outline. For further details readers are recommended to chapter 6 above for an account of such developments in family therapy training, and to chapter 9 above for an account of these developments in group therapy training.

My Own Professional Context

The fact that I am a professional 'neighbour' to the social work family, or even a member of its 'extended family', may give me the advantage of allowing a little more distance and objectivity even at the expense of detailed knowledge. I have worked very closely with a wide range of practitioners of social work – house parents of children's homes, probation officers, child-care officers, psychiatric social workers, etc., including field workers, supervisors and senior officials from both voluntary and government-funded agencies. Such contact has been direct and continuous in the case of psychiatric social workers in child guidance clinics, but there have been many other forms of involvement. These have included individual consultations and the leading of case-discussion groups within a variety of agencies. I have been responsible over many years for the teaching of large numbers of social workers passing through training courses at both the Institute of Group Analysis and the Institute of Family Therapy, where participation in small 'experiential' groups almost always includes discussion of work problems, of difficulties in agency relationships, and of personal material about families and individual problems. And, most intensive of all, I have been engaged in the treatment of a considerable number of social workers undergoing twice-weekly group therapy over three or four years as part of their training as group analysts within the Institute of Group Analysis.

I have not, however, made the kind of systematic study of family backgrounds of a representative sample that Lawton has done, though I imagine that the kind of material I am privileged to have access to here would in many ways be more intimate, explicit and detailed and has also included material from other professionals, like psychiatrists, psychologists, general practitioners, nurses, clergy, teachers and so forth.

The Myth of Altruism: Lawton's Main Points

According to Lawton's account, public service agencies dealing with the most deprived and disadvantaged clients are themselves demoralised and defensive. They resist change, show high turnover in the senior administration, are unsupportive to their caseworkers, are secretive and restrict communication; are controlling in an infantilising way, are rigidly bureaucratic, value conformity but dislike opposition or criticism; they 'use' their social workers rather than respect them as persons, demand loyalty to the organisation at the expense of encouraging the search for adequate training, and they generate rage in the workers but force them to suppress it. In short and in Lawton's own terms: 'The agency is like a paradoxical bad/good mother, implacable in her power and appearing vindictively dedicated to hampering the effectiveness of her workers/children at every turn.'

Lawton leaves us with a picture of the social work agencies he is describing like a family where the parents pretend to be, and desire to be seen as, paragons of excellence but where they are actually making a mess of their child-rearing function. He ends on this despondent note but he includes the small consolation that caseworkers can be comforted by the realisation that their clients are even more miserably served than themselves and do in fact derive a little comfort, even from them.

According to my own observations this picture is correct, as far as it goes. At least it is correct for those agencies which, working with clients trapped in the cycle of deprivation, reproduce this cycle in their own patterns of work. Why does this come about?

Lawton offers five main points which explain this situation:

1. 'Helping others is not an altruistic, selfless act; rather it serves the needs of a helper.'
2. 'The need to control stems from the social worker's childhood and points to the fact that there is a fairly specific type of "professional" personality which contributes to the maintenance of the system.'
3. 'The agency serves as a fertile field for the expression of the social worker's needs, because its structure and processes broadly resemble the workers' family of origin where the needs were formed in the first place.'
4. 'The agency serves as a theatre, in which the social workers, especially those who remain longer than a year or two, are able to relive important aspects of their childhood.'
5. 'Why people choose the work in the first place, [is to be

found] in this psychological relationship and in the nature of the institution in which the job is carried out.'

I shall take each of these points separately:

1. 'Helping others is not an altruistic, selfless act; rather it serves the needs of a helper.'

The problem here is Lawton's use of the word 'rather', which implies an 'either/or' choice between two incompatible alternatives. The first alternative is that the client's needs are satisfied as fully as possible, while the professional's needs are deemed to be irrelevant to the best performance of that task and therefore properly ignored while 'on duty'. The second alternative, which he implies is nearer what actually happens in practice, is the reverse of this: the professional is seen as taking something for himself or herself which should properly have been given to the client, rather like an official entrusted with the distribution of foreign aid in a country stricken by famine who intercepts and sells the charitable donations for personal profit.

However, in addition to these two choices of either focusing exclusively on the client's needs ('honesty', 'good practice') or exclusively upon his own ('malpractice', 'stealing') there is in fact a third alternative. Both client and worker can perfectly well have *some* of their needs met in the course of their work together. The greater responsibility of the worker certainly requires that this exchange should not be exactly symmetrical. But there is no reason whatever why it should not be mutual, and even to some extent satisfying the *same* needs in both persons. Mothers who derive physical enjoyment from breast-feeding are likely to have more milk, and to produce healthier and more contented babies. And the more we learn about the emotional side of child development, the more clear it becomes that throughout childhood, including the earliest days and weeks of a child's life, the effective functioning of the mother/child relationship is as dependent on the child 'feeding' the mother with satisfactions (smiling, gazing, for example) that 'cue' her to perform the next step in an interactive 'dance', as it does to the mother's provision of supplies and satisfactions in response. In some respects the mother even has to put her own needs first, for the *sake* of the child, a fact beautifully exemplified, as someone pointed out to me recently, in the aircraft safety procedure about which cabin staff remind us before every flight. We are routinely told that in the event of cabin depressurisation oxygen masks will automatically drop from above in front of each passenger, and mothers must make sure to put their own masks on first, before fitting another to their babes in arms. If they attend to the babies first, both have less chance of survival.

The special pleasures with which a happy baby rewards its mother, when she is performing her nurturing task successfully, compensate her for the many sacrifices and deprivations inherent in the mothering role and so help to support her through its more stressful aspects. The fact that the satisfactions are mutual within this relationship therefore makes it more likely that it will be performed adequately. I believe the situation is the same with Lawton's social workers and other mental health professionals in their quasi-parental roles; they are often the only people willing and able to sustain a difficult and thankless task precisely because they need, and are getting, something from it psychologically which they are otherwise unable to obtain in the normal course of life.

2. **'The need to control stems from the social worker's childhood and points to the fact that there is a fairly specific type of "professional" personality which contributes to the maintenance of the system.'**

The unsatisfied needs which help to motivate these professionals in the performance of their working roles do indeed stem from unsatisfactory aspects of their own childhood. The way they perform their quasi-parental roles will therefore understandably reflect something of the structure of the problematic family situations in which their own deprivation occurred, insofar as they have not understood, and so cannot yet 'stand outside' and be unaffected by, their own past history. The rigid control which Lawton describes as characteristic of certain social workers, both as manifested by them towards their very deprived clients, and also by their seniors towards themselves, reflects a pattern in their families of origin, and though other mental health professionals may differ in the details of their early family patterns, my experience suggests that there are also certain broad similarities among them.

3. 'The agency serves as a fertile field for the expression of the social worker's needs, because its structure and processes broadly resemble the workers' family of origin where the needs were formed in the first place.'

If what I have said so far is correct, this observation of Lawton's is to be expected. As attachment theory explains, it is impossible to change everything at once, and very difficult and stressful to try to change too many things too quickly. So when we try to grow beyond the personality problems we have been left with because of the limitations of the family in which we grew up, we opt for a compromise. We automatically seek an environment, including a work-situation, which is an improvement on the family of origin, but nevertheless similar enough for the psychological attitudes and social skills we learned in that original family to be good enough to cope with it – or perhaps even be specially valued and therefore an advantage rather than a handicap. In other words, as in marriage and friendship we seek out something better and different, but not *too* different.

4. 'The agency serves as a theatre, in which the social workers, especially those who remain longer than a year or two, are able to relive important aspects of their childhood.'

5. 'Why people choose the work in the first place [is to be found] in this psychological relationship and in the nature of the institution in which the job is carried out.'

What Lawton observes in points 4 and 5 follows naturally from what I have said above. It indicates a good choice as far as the professional's needs are concerned, for it provides both the security and support essential to mental health, and also the opportunity to grow beyond their unresolved problems.

However, Lawton also distinguishes two kinds of worker in the child care agencies he describes. Those of the first kind tend to cling to the agency because they fear change and loss of support; these tend to repeat the pattern and keep things the same. Those of the second kind become dissatisfied and move elsewhere; by their nature they are more confident and desirous of change, but the fact that they leave also makes for lack of change in the agency itself.

I believe the main difference between these two types of worker

163

lies mainly in the severity of the original deprivation, the consequent different levels of pain and feelings of inadequacy which
facing that truth squarely would involve, and a corresponding
difference in the need to cling to support and to deny the distressing
truth by focusing all attention outside the self on to others, ideally in
an 'altruistic' way which will compensate for the understandably low
self-esteem. Unfortunately, the *denial* creates a variety of double-
binds and vicious cycles which have the opposite effect to the
genuine good intentions.

'Haves' and 'Have Nots'

My own experience supports Lawton's observations and has led me
independently to similar conclusions. But I think that an under-
valuing of this positive (if unconcious) motivation in the choice of
profession, which I have explained above, makes Lawton's remarks
sound unnecessarily pessimistic. The example I shall draw on from
my own consultative work is offered here in outline. For further
details readers are recommended to chapter 2 above.

In one case-discussion group composed of representatives of a
number of different agencies within an area of London with severe
social problems and a high level of deprived, multi-problem families, this was the pattern of the Children's Department, a state
agency equivalent in function to Lawton's. Because of its nature the
department attracted second-rate, poor trained staff, whose incompetence led to poor results despite endless work. Under pressure
from above by anxious administrators frightened of their political
masters, they were also under pressure from below by manipulative, demanding clients. They were so busy running in circles that
there was no time to come regularly to the group – the only form of
skilled support locally available to them – or they were late, or
complained that they were too busy doing things to have time to
think how to do them better. So there was demoralisation, high
turnover of staff, and the poor reputation of the department
attracted second-rate, poorly trained . . . but this is where we came
in.

I privately called these the 'have-nots'. But in the same group
there were also some 'haves'. Most, but not all of them were
working at voluntary agencies (mine was a public agency). These

were well looked after by their seniors who ensured they were given time for training, such as attending this group. Of course, the time required to attend was available *because* they attended it and made use of other similar situations designed to enhance their skills, ensuring more and more effective work. The reputation of *these* agencies for professional competence and for opportunities for learning attracted staff of high quality, making possible a group of high morale and efficiency . . . so this was another kind of cycle working a positive direction.

I subsequently found a similar difference of this kind between the 'haves' and the 'have-nots' in groups made up of other professions, *and eventually concluded that we were dealing with two dimensions. The first dimension is something that attracts an individual to a certain type of profession or clientele, based on a similarity between the professional's background and the most typical problems of the clientele (e.g. serious mental pathology in the case of mental health professionals, marital problems in the case of marriage guidance professionals, but in all such cases these problems are dealt with by denial). The second dimension is something that leads at one extreme to a cycle of deprivation and failure, and at the other to successful nurture and growth.*

Now, as I see it, the first of these dimensions is like a compass needle that points the would-be professional in the direction where he has the best *hope* of recapitulating his family experience and perhaps moving forwards from some developmental stage at which he became arrested in his childhood. But whether that hope will be *realised* depends on the second dimension. Those at the 'have not' end of the scale are trapped in the same vicious circle, the same 'catch 22', as their clients and – here is the point I believe Lawton does not make clearly enough – so were their parents and probably their grandparents, and who knows how far back it goes. I have traced it four generations and others have explored the pattern farther back still.

The Cycle of Deprivation

Let us look at the pattern I am speaking about in a family. We call it the typical 'deprived' family, but in my view it is not the deprivation which is the main problem. The main problem is the denial of the

165

deprivation, understandable though that denial may be in order to avoid the intolerable pain of loss or neglect that would otherwise be felt. The parents, themselves deprived, are unable to face the pain and deny – split off, repress – the feeling of need within themselves. *By projective identification, they perceive that feeling not as their own, but as if it is within their children. Instead of remedying their own deprivation (which will occur automatically, I believe, if we allow ourselves to experience the pain and with it the need) the parents decide 'to give their children what they didn't have themselves'. The motive is good, but the mechanism is flawed. The parents do not see their children but instead see 'themselves-in-their-children'. So the children are not 'fed' when* they *are hungry, physically or emotionally, but are fed when the* parents *are hungry and with what the parents need. The parents do not get what they need and so remain deprived. The children get what the parents need, when the parents need it, not what they need, when they need it, so they grow up deprived too.* The children, in their turn – perceiving their parents' deprivation, need and pain – seek to nurture them, but this is another 'catch 22'. The only way the *children* can nurture their *parents* without confronting the denial and exposing the parents to pain is by enhancing the parents' self-esteem through treating them as the paragons they pretend to be but are not, thus joining in the collusive denial and perpetuating the pattern.

Underneath, of course, there is inevitable rage in the children at the real deprivation they are suffering, and these real feelings get expressed in devious ways like disappointing the parents' expectations, by failing and thus making them fail too. The parents naturally experience themselves as giving everything away and keeping nothing for themselves, so they understandably feel *envious* and this makes them destroy – unwittingly, or if they become aware of it, to their horror – the effects of the good things they give. The inevitable consequence, it will easily be seen, is what is noted by Lawton in the public child welfare agencies he describes and in the British equivalent that I have mentioned. This pattern is self-perpetuating and there seems to be no escape, at least without help from outside the system.

Conclusion

Feeding the Goose: Why Don't People Change This Unsatisfactory System?

At first sight, the view I have presented may seem even more pessimistic than Lawton's. In his scheme, there is at least the implication that someone is doing something wrong, something bad, something that could and should be changed. And this, of course, is a view characteristic of these professionals, their families of origin, and their clients. In therapy, they all usually begin by seeing their parents as benevolent and themselves as bad (but changeable). Later, they see themselves as badly served, and their parents as bad (but changeable). It is only when they see that the situation is hopeless for everybody, see that no change is possible within this system of 'double-think' and face the pain of this loss of false-hope, that real hope and real change become possible. *What has to change first is the denial of the deprivation, of their inadequacy, of their inability (through no fault of their own) to be either the generous parent or the grateful child. If this pain can be borne, each person then begins to experience his or her real need, seeks to satisfy it, evokes appropriate responses in others, and swallows the emotional food received into their own stomachs, thereby growing, eventually maturing and becoming able to give to others in turn. The vicious cycle of deprivation becomes a virtuous circle of mutual nurture.* If this process can be induced in a group which works regularly together, like an agency, the common gain can increase in exponential fashion.

In agencies or individuals already *partially* functioning in the 'have' mode, this is easier to bring about. However, the greater the deprivation, the greater the pain that has to be denied and projected, and the more intense the denial. What self-esteem there is has to be carefully protected by the teacher or consultant, and a long period of highly supportive teaching aimed at enhancement of skills and of general feeling of self-worth, is needed before insight into the dynamics described above can be tolerated. Premature focus on an individual's personality or family background is dangerous and may lead to breaking of the contact. (All this is also true, of course, of the *clientele* usually served by social workers functioning at this level.)

167

Personal Growth and Professional Development

As a result of this understanding, three types of group leadership are recommended for different levels of deprivation and denial. For the least competent and confident professionals the leader focuses entirely on case-discussion, along the lines of Gerald Caplan's mode of case-consultation (1964, 1970) or, for groups, Slavson's child-centred group guidance of parents (1958). At an intermediate level, Balint's model for training general practitioners (1951) is used, again focusing on case-discussion but also using the professional's counter-transference as information about the case. At the most sophisticated level the group is run close to the model of therapy and focuses on the professional's motive in choosing the career, though acknowledging the central importance of the task.

Provided the right level of intervention is chosen, good results can be obtained right across the spectrum, in my experience. Naturally, the least defended gain the greatest benefit. In a report on a large British course teaching family and marital therapy run by staff led by my wife and myself, fully described in chapter 6, we wrote:

> One is struck particularly by the increased freedom and confidence students seem to develop in their professional roles, partly because their sense of personal identity is not experienced *through* those roles. They seem better able to integrate the 'child' in themselves, are less compelled to be 'parental', and can be more 'adult' in consequence, in Eric Berne's terms. By losing their compulsive helpfulness they are able to set boundaries, and are less vulnerable to manipulation. They pay more attention to their *own* lives, spend more time at home with their spouses and children, but they do the work better and enjoy it more. They are able to separate out the personal and professional, but also to bring the two together, and to use their greater experience of themselves and of their families more directly and openly in their work. (chapter 6 above, p. 95)

The shrewd reader will already have wanted to point out that, since I have chosen to join the helping professions myself, all of this ought to apply to me as well. How do I know that *my* blinkers are removed, and that my denial is not still distorting my view of the situation to a degree that makes what I have written here as suspect as everything else?

The answer I must give is that it does all apply very accurately to me. I certainly sneaked in by the staff door to get some help without acknowledging my need for it, though I did not realise this until I began to get what I had really come for and to see my motives more clearly. However, the helpful effects I have experienced from this acknowledgment of the 'selfish' aspect of my seemingly 'altruistic' motives, in my professional as in my personal life, and the similar benefits I have seen others derive from such exploration of their motives, give me some confidence that there is at least a limited truth in the view I have presented. But this is an exploration that we all have to make for ourselves, afresh, step by step; or not, as the case may be.

Notes

1 This paper was first published in the *Journal of Psychohistory*, Vol. 10 No. 3, pp. 389–395.
2 Lawton's paper, to which Skynner is here responding, was published in the *Journal of Psychohistory*, Vol. 9 No. 3, pp. 265–308.
3 At the time this paper was published concern had been focussed by Bowlby, Rutter and others, on cycles of disadvantage. See, for example, *Maternal Deprivation Reassessed* by M. Rutter.

11 Psychotherapy and Sacred Tradition

This paper was first prepared as one of a series of lectures on Eastern and Western approaches in religion and psychology, delivered in San Francisco in 1975. It was first published as part of that collection in 1976 under the title *On The Way To Self-Knowledge*, and republished in 1983 in another collection entitled *Awakening The Heart*. Though currently available, it is included here because, as Skynner's only sustained piece of writing on the subject, it illuminates a dimension which is present in all his work, though mentioned only in passing in his professional writing, which goes beyond the personal and social to draw upon that understanding and experience common to all the great religious and ethical systems.

There is an extensive literature on how two profound changes in our culture are related – the pattern of secularisation over the last hundred years or so, and the growth of psychological therapies. For some in psychology and the other human sciences, a scientific discipline has supplanted religion entirely, whilst for others – like Freud – religion ceased to have meaning as a belief system but remained a form of cultural identification. Both religion and psychology remained important for another group, but as entirely separate, unrelated experiences. There is a further group who sought alternative paths, finding orthodox practice less meaningful but seeing something vital in sacred tradition and religious experience. Jung is amongst this group and so is Skynner, but in a subtly different way. After an experience recounted briefly here when he participated in the early medical trials of LSD, he looked to Christian and Eastern mysticism. Through this he became increasingly aware of the defensive nature of all forms of rigid belief, whether in religious dogma or a particular psychotherapeutic school.

Here he describes how he came to see the essential function of religious practice, as of effective psychotherapy, in freeing us to experience ourselves and our lives to the full, constantly learning and changing through that experience, here and now, in the moment. He writes directly from personal experience in language that is more than anything else poetic, uncluttered by theory or references. Those interested in pursuing references are recommended to the work of Schumacher who, in *A Guide To The Perplexed*, quotes from sources that he and Skynner share.

The affinity between the work of these two men is also evident in Schumacher's better known book, *Small Is Beautiful*, where the title conveys the search for a human order of experience rather than a technical one. Schumacher's work arises out of a search for transcendent order in the course of which he applies what he finds to economics and politics. Skynner is on a different path, but the same journey, and he conveys an intimate sense of the struggle to reach for levels of experience that go beyond the personal. He finds a moving way of describing this search and, as he applies his findings to psychotherapy, he discovers, by looking beyond its limits, a clearer view of its assets.

J.R.S

Introduction[1]

I hope you will not mind if I speak rather personally. I am not a scholar – to my regret – but a craftsman of sorts, and I find even in the course of my professional teaching that I communicate best when I speak from my own experience. It soon became clear to me that this was the only position from which I could approach the question I am examining here, and that I could only seek to live with the question more intensely than before, bringing it into contact with as much of my daily experience as possible and remaining attentive and open to the information it brought me. I have been made aware once again that this questioning attitude, and the immediate, receptive and sensitive responsiveness to my life which it brings about, is perhaps the only useful answer to our question, if the idea of an 'answer' is even appropriate at all. I therefore bring this attitude here and hope that some of you will share it with me.

This being so, perhaps I should begin by giving you some information about the path that has led me here so that you can better judge how much or how little you can trust what I have to say. In the first lecture in this series, Professor Needleman[2] spoke of a Celtic fable in which two brothers pass each other on a mountain; one is being dragged down by a black dog to which he is attached by an iron chain, the other is being drawn up by a golden thread attached to a mysterious crane somewhere above. The story has enchanted and preoccupied me since, perhaps because I am a Celt myself and Celtic dogs of this particular breed are perhaps bigger, blacker and more difficult to manage than most.

Certainly I was attracted to the study of psychiatry by a need to find a way of dealing with my own problems. And my present interest in training mental-health professionals leads me to believe that this is not only the usual motivation for taking up such work,

173

consciously or unconsciously, but also the best one, provided it leads the professional to a real, direct and systematic study of himself rather than a vicarious one through the study of his patients.

Without doubt the knowledge I gained from my studies of psychotherapy provided some help in finding a different relationship with this unruly animal. Even before my own group analysis began, an attempt at self-analysis during my student days, based at first on the ideas of some of the 'neo-Freudians', particularly Horney, Fromm and Sullivan, led the dog to begin a strange series of changes that have continued ever since. I mention this because ideas that can produce such effects must have some validity, and I feel it is important to add that these consequences seemed connected with a perception of the truth of many of the basic Freudian conceptions, particularly infantile sexuality and the oedipus complex, which led to a simple acceptance and enjoyment of ordinary sexuality not only in bed but also as this subtle energy pervades all relationships. I remember too the wonderful recognition that a strain of violence that had permeated my family history could be welcomed rather than escaped from, like a fearsome, untamed animal that could be a source of energy if one could find the right relationship to it.

At this time I was agnostic, indeed, a quite militant atheist writing regularly for the *Rationalist Annual*. But while still undergoing psychiatric training, I took part with other students as a research subject in an investigation into the effects of LSD, which had just then become available in England. Some of my fellow students had fearful paranoid hallucinations that haunted them for some time afterwards, but my own experience was more fortunate – a perception of successive, ascending levels of reality and consciousness, and of the interconnectedness and meaningfulness of everything, all of which I retained as a certainty afterwards and which exactly coincided with descriptions of mystical experience and religious ecstasy I had previously brushed aside as fantasy. I saw that this was what I had been searching for all along. And although I realised that drugs could do no more than enable one to glimpse such possibilities, and therefore did not use this approach again, the experience led me to a deep and increasing interest in the relevance of sacred tradition.

My own analysis – a combination of group and individual – took place some time after this interest had developed, so that I had the

174

rather unusual experience of being under the influence of sacred tradition and psychotherapy simultaneously. And I have been working as a psychotherapist with individuals, groups, families, and institutions ever since, while also continuing this guided search for deeper, spiritual significance in my life.

Two Kinds of Inquiry: Spiritual and Psychological Questions

Now what does a psychotherapist do? Certainly I am constantly made aware, especially by acquaintances following one or another of the traditional paths, that though they accept that we might be able to relieve discomfort by drugs and soothing falsehoods, we could not possibly achieve much in the way of reliably facilitating change in those who come to see us. This is nonsense, of course, as untrue as the obverse assumption that we can change the world.

The kind of change that often happens in psychotherapy can be illustrated by a postcard I received from one former patient, a young married woman lacking any secure sense of identity and so unable to control her intense negative feelings that I had found it difficult to be in the same room with her and would not have taken her on for therapy myself had she not been so persistent in seeking it. As so often happens with such cases, she worked hard and did unusually well over her year of attendance. The card she sent me conveys what the psychotherapeutic process meant to her.

> I guess the most important thing to say is that what I gained from being with you all is extremely supportive during a period of enormous adjustment. I truly carry you all around with me, and am able to accept the ups and downs with much more equanimity and lack of self-doubt than before. It is possible now to be more open and honest, without being consumed and defeated by self-doubt. I think I will never lead a conventional life, but I am better able now to contain that reality and not be so frightened and disturbed by it [I think this is a reference to her bisexuality], even to enjoy its good side. I send you all much love and all best wishes for continued progress and support – the same which enabled me to take hold of my own life and not feel so helpless in doing so.

Personal Growth and Professional Development

The typical psychotherapy patient has failed to develop an adequate sense of identity (in Erikson's sense), having failed to internalise in their early family environments adequate 'models' of behaviour and relationship, which could subsequently serve as reliable guides to action. Change appeared to take place through increased awareness of the existing, inappropriate 'models', accompanied by learning of new ones from the therapist or other group members – a kind of second, corrective family experience. This is made very clear by the note from the patient mentioned above, when she says, 'I truly carry you all around with me . . .'

Now this patient did not display during her therapy any real interest in the deeper meaning of her life on this planet, orbiting our sun within its galaxy in this universe, at this time in its history. Usually I am given early on a clear indication from those patients who will later seek out a more spiritual path. They are in some way more open and vulnerable, more aware of themselves as part of mankind, part of the universe, 'leaves on a tree'. They are more troubled about and interested in the meaning of their existence as a whole rather than the meaning of what happened to them yesterday or in their childhood, or in the hopes and fears of what will happen to them tomorrow. They behave as if they have at some time been given a view from higher up the mountain, which they dimly remember and which leads them thereafter to seek again what they once glimpsed. Such patients are more widely interested and more interesting to treat, not least because they are more directly challenging both to me as a person and to my practice as a psychotherapist. To work with them is a shared endeavour in which I am more in question and receive more of myself in consequence.

At some point, often late in therapy, they usually express their impression that I am holding something back from them, that I have another kind of understanding, which is implicit in all I do and say but not directly communicated. (This never happens with the other patients.) At this point I may become more explicit, though always in the context of the therapy, which remains my central concern, and within the context also of what they already understand. Some, previously members of established churches, may eventually return again to their faith with a more mature relationship to it, often after an earlier period in therapy when they have rejected religion, or rather rejected the childish, magical attitude towards it with which they came. Others find their way to the Eastern teachings, which have emerged in England as here. For example, some without any suggestion from me went to a Tibetan Buddhist monastery in Scotland.

This is not to say that other patients, or at least those whose treatment is successful, do not develop a deeper sense of themselves as part of something larger. Such a loss of egocentricity is, as Alfred Adler insisted, an inevitable accompaniment of any improvement, perhaps the most fundamental change of all. But there has always been for me a clear distinction between these patients and those who cannot forget that they have once perceived this other meaning of life, who behave as if they are in some way 'children of God'.

Apparent Similarities

Now why is that these two kinds of inquiry are confused at all? Perhaps we could look first at features that *appear* similar between them, which might lead to some confusion.

First of all, there is in both psychotherapy and sacred tradition the idea that man's perception is clouded and distorted, that he does not see things as they are but as he wants to see them. In the spiritual teachings, there are the ideas of *samsara*, the false world of appearances, the shadows in Plato's cave; in psychotherapy we have the defences of denial, projection, idealisation and withdrawal into fantasy.

Second, in both man is seen as being divided. His problems and suffering are believed to stem from this fragmentation, this failure to become whole and to take responsibility for himself.

Third, self-knowledge, whereby he can find the lost parts of himself and become whole again, is seen as the key to the rediscovery of his integrity, so that he may become no longer divided into 'I' and 'not-I' – identifying himself with some parts of his being and rejecting others, which then become projected and perceived in negative fashion in those around him.

Fourth, this rediscovery and re-acceptance is in both processes expected to be painful but regarded as bitter medicine that can ultimately heal and lead to growth. In individual and group psychotherapy, in encounter techniques, and in the challenging confrontations of family and marital therapy, we find a systematic exposure of associations of thought, or of spontaneous emotional responses, or of actions, in a situation where, though it is supportive and containing, escape is prevented and the truth has sooner or later to be acknowledged. In the 'confession of sins', in the acceptance of whatever internal manifestations arise during the stillness of meditation, in the openness to this inner voice of conscience, which is sought during the concentration of prayer, similar processes appear to be occurring. The unconscious is made conscious, the self is expanded as denial and projection are reduced and dissociated parts return; the lost sheep is found, the prodigal returns and is welcomed. In both spiritual tradition and in psychotherapy, a clearer perception of the world and a greater capacity to understand, accept and relate to others can be seen to follow from this greater self-acceptance and objectivity.

Fifth, both see man as possessing hidden resources, which cannot become available without this greater self-knowledge and integration, even though the scale of this hidden potential is differently perceived in different schools of psychotherapy and, of course, even more so between psychotherapy generally and the spiritual traditions.

Sixth, a corollary, much of man's suffering and pain is in both regarded as unnecessary, a product of ignorance and blindness, of confusion and complexity resulting from the inner division and the deceit and subterfuge necessary to preserve some illusion of coherence. This is differently described as intellectualisation, fantasy, Jung's 'persona', the 'ego' in the ordinary sense, Horney's 'ideal image', and what Krishnamurti calls 'thought'. It is expected, therefore (and it is the case), that negative feelings, suffering, and pain (or at least those which serve no useful purpose) gradually diminish and disappear in the course both of competent psychotherapy and the following of a sacred tradition.

And finally, seventh, both require that the searcher shall be in personal, regular contact with a teacher, guide, guru, analyst or leader who has already been through the same experiences; who has seen, understood and accepted at least some aspects of himself; who has escaped from some of his own fragmentation, delusions and distorted perceptions; and so can, through being able to perceive the searcher more objectively, help him in turn to become more objective about himself.

178

Real Differences

There is, as we see, much *apparent* overlap, and I think we may be forgiven if we experience some confusion, at least initially, between these different kinds of exploration. My personal experience leads me to believe, however, that these two paths lie, if not in opposite directions, at least in quite different dimensions, and that we need to look for a much more subtle relationship between them. The fable of the two brothers, the golden thread, and the black dog, and the idea of the third brother arising from the relationship between them, hints at this. Having looked at some similarities between these two paths, let us now summarise some of the differences, which I believe are not only greater but incommensurately greater.

First, all sacred traditions begin from the idea of an ordered, intelligent universe, where the idea of *hierarchy* is central and where each level is related to others in reciprocal dependence. Man appears very low down on this scale of being, though he has a definite place and serves purposes beyond himself necessary to the total structure.

Second, in the sacred traditions, man is perceived as having a choice of two purposes he may serve in this grand design – God or Caesar; the ordinary world of appearances or a more real world behind it; his natural appetites and desires or an inner voice or conscience, which comes into conflict with these; the black dog, perhaps, or the golden thread. The traditions tell us that we all serve nature, in our ordinary state of development, as unconsciously as the grass feeds the cows and its manure in turn feeds the grass again; and that our illusion of power and freedom, and our fantasies about ourselves and mankind ensure that we do this, just as the beast of burden walking endlessly in a circle to drive the primitive pump is kept at its job by the pole attached to its back and the blindfold that prevents it from seeing its true plight. But the traditions tell us that it is also possible, in the scheme of things, for some men to awaken to this situation and to perceive another possibility, another task they can fulfil, another influence that, if they can submit to it, will free them in some measure from the blindness and slavery of their ordinary existence. Though they must still live on earth, a connection begins to be made with heaven. For the person who is awakened to this other realm, a higher energy, a more subtle intelligence becomes available and begins to change the whole purpose and meaning of ordinary life, though the latter continues as before and may show little change of a kind discernible to those still circling the treadmill and absorbed in their dreams. Caesar must still be served, but the service of God transforms this totally and causes life to become an endlessly rich source of knowledge and experience to feed the new life growing like a child within the person called to this new service.

Now this kind of idea is not part of ordinary psychology, whether 'scientific' or 'humanistic'. Though the latter might recognise and show more serious interest in some of the *experiences* previously called 'religious' or 'mystical', man is still perceived as being at the centre of things. His ordinary desires, ambitions, hopes and plans, whether selfish or altruistic, are taken at face value and used as a basis for action, for planning utopias and eupsychias. There is no concept of the second purpose to which man can give himself, and because of this, there is no real questioning whether the first could be illusory. Ordinary psychology then becomes another elaboration of the delusion itself, providing more blindfolds, another ring through the nose, more 'hope' to keep us turning the treadmill.

Third, and following on from this, the possibility of recognising and beginning to understand the significance of the sacred traditions begins from a disillusionment with ordinary life, with one's ordinary self, with ordinary knowledge. Only after the blindfold is removed and we see we are going in a circle all the time have we the hope of choosing another direction. We have to see that life is not going anywhere in the way we formerly imagined, that it never has and never will. Having faced this, we may realise that no escape is possible from the repetition of our ordinary level without help from another. Coming to disbelieve in our ordinary thought and emotion, and so becoming still enough and open enough to reach a deeper and more fundamental part of ourselves where another energy, a different possibility of consciousness exists, a connection may be made, since we are for a moment available for it. Thus we have to begin from the point of failure, to relinquish our valuation of our ordinary selves and to let this be replaced gradually by something which at first does not seem to be ourselves at all. Having awakened, we have to die in order to be reborn.

Now, does not ordinary psychology rather lead to an *increase* of the ordinary self – more efficient, more fruitful, more enjoyable and less conflicted perhaps, but still the same thing writ larger, the same ambitions fulfilled instead of unfulfilled, the same desires satisfied instead of frustrated? Ordinary psychology surely seeks to *improve* the self, according to the ideas *of* the ordinary self; it scarcely seeks to destroy it.

Fourth, sacred traditions are by definition, if they are anything at all, a manifestation of the higher level about which they tell us, a point at which the levels actually touch each other. And, perhaps because they can only touch *within* man himself, they have been transmitted by a chain of individuals who actually manifest, with part of their being (rather than simply knowing about), the possibility with which these traditions are concerned. From this follow two further differences between the paths. One is the idea that the traditions have always existed, from the beginning of recorded time, and are simply spread into the world from the human chain that transmits them, the influence widening or contracting from one period to another and the means of expression being adapted to the prevailing forms of thought and current ordinary knowledge, though always conveying the same essential truth. If anything, the understanding *deteriorates* as it spreads wider from the teachers, like ripples on a pond. This is totally different from ordinary psychology, where knowledge is seen as a progressive development, beginning perhaps from Mesmer and the nineteenth-century hypnotists, and leading through the pioneering work of Janet, Freud, Adler and Jung to the achievements of the present day. For ordinary psychology, the present time is one of unusual enlightenment and progress; for the sacred traditions, it is more likely to be seen as a dark age.

A fifth difference, which also follows from what was just said, concerns the relationship between teacher and pupil. The ordinary psychotherapist would certainly recognise a difference in authority between himself and his patient based on age, experience, knowledge and skill, but this would be expected to change in the course of treatment. As the patient matures, it is hoped that the 'transference' is dissipated, and, while some regard and gratitude may remain, persistent dependency and acceptance of the analyst's authority are taken correctly to indicate incomplete treatment. In the sacred traditions, by contrast, the teacher is in some part of his being an

181

actual manifestation of a higher level, and so a sharply hierarchical pupil/teacher relationship is not only appropriate but, since the human chain continues presumably all the way up the mountain, the authority of the guide, or of the next man above on the rope, may appropriately continue indefinitely. (I am less sure about this difference than about the others. Though essentially true, I think analogous developmental processes must nevertheless occur in both kinds of change.)

Different Conceptions of Consciousness

I will mention other differences more briefly. The most important is the differing view of consciousness in the sacred traditions from that found in Western psychology. Following what one might call an 'archeological' concept of consciousness, our ordinary Western psychology tends to assume that we already possess the light of consciousness but that some parts of ourselves have been buried and need to be found and brought into this light again, after which they will remain at least potentially accessible. The light is assumed to be burning already, at least while we are out of bed and moving about, and its brightness and continuity are not very much questioned. By contrast, the great sacred traditions maintain explicitly or implicitly the idea that man's consciousness is much more limited, fluctuating, and illusory than he usually realises, and that an extraordinary amount of persistent effort is needed even to maintain it more steadily, let alone increase it. For the sacred traditions, consciousness is more like the light powered by a dynamo which is driven by the wheel of a bicycle. We have to pedal constantly if it is to remain alight and pedal harder to make it brighter. In the ideas of Janet, the Frenchman who in so many ways anticipated Freud, there is of course the idea that attention and consciousness require effort and work, as well as the idea of finer levels of energy generated by the effort of more sustained attention, and the further idea that the two can lead automatically to the reintegration of dissociated psychic elements. But then Janet was a religious man, and his eclipse by Freud was no doubt another consequence of the attitudes current in this epoch.

If we are to accept these differences as valid, it seems to me that they lead us to a view of psychotherapy and of sacred tradition as different dimensions at right angles to each other, with fundamental aims that cannot in their nature coincide at all. Psychotherapy is about ordinary life, the development of man along the horizontal line of time from birth to death. Just as the physician is concerned with countering threats to life and obstacles to physical growth, and remedying deficiencies and deviations in the development of the body, so the function of the psychotherapist (which developed originally, and is still based most firmly, within the role of the physician) can be seen as averting threats to psychological stability, relieving obstacles and inhibitions in the process of growth from the dependency of the child to the relative responsibility and autonomy of the adult. To do so the psychotherapist seeks to supply those experiences that have been lacking in the patient's history, particularly those that were missing or distorted in the early family environment.

The sacred traditions begin from the horizontal line of time but are concerned with a quite different, vertical line of development. This is man's increasing awareness of, connection with and service to the chain of reciprocal transformation and exchange among levels of excellence, which the cosmic design appears to need some of mankind to fulfil. There is an analogy here with the physical sphere, where man is obliged to move about on the horizontal, two-dimensional surface of the earth if he is to survive at all. But he is not obliged to fly and exist in the three-dimensional atmosphere, though he can do so if he wishes, and if he does so he may find that this has consequences for his ordinary existence.

Confusion Between Two Endeavours

If these two endeavours are in fact quite distinct, then forms of psychotherapy that confuse them could be much more harmful to the possibility of spiritual development than those that do not recognise the traditions at all. Thus, I believe that the ideas offered by such people as Maslow, Fromm, Rogers and many leaders of the encounter movement may as easily hinder as help people towards a recognition of their actual position. It is true that these approaches may indeed stimulate a desire for the kind of understanding that only the sacred traditions can supply, and I am grateful for the way in which they have all personally assisted me. But because they mix the levels, they stand in danger of offering a half-truth sufficiently like the real thing to satisfy this deeper hunger without leading to anything more real, and even of simply increasing the attachment to the ordinary self. Jung, too, though so much admired by people of religious persuasion, in contrast to that 'terrible' Sigmund Freud, seems to me to offer a particularly subtle temptation, precisely because of the depth and quality of his personal understanding, together with his fundamental confusion of psychology and sacred traditions, psyche and spirit.

This is why, when I cannot find a good eclectic psychotherapist (in the sense of someone who seeks to integrate the best of the different schools), I tend to refer patients to competent Freudian analysts, provided that they are agnostic rather than militantly atheistic, and that they demonstrate by the quality of their lives that they are decent and responsible people. For I find that the better Freudians at least have their feet on the ground rather than their heads in the clouds, a good beginning if one wishes to travel reliably along the surface of the earth. Being concerned first and foremost with the development of ordinary competence in making a living, forming responsible relationships, enjoying sexuality and other natural appetites, raising a family and generally coping adequately with life, they help to establish a firm base from which an interest in deeper meaning can develop.

The Meeting Point of Two Dimensions

The differences now seem clear enough, and it is hard to see how we could ever confuse these two different kinds of development. At this point we can all feel satisfied. Followers of sacred traditions can reassure themselves that, after all, they did not really need to have that analysis which seemed so much to improve the life of their neighbour. The psychotherapists can also feel relieved, finally satisfied that people who follow a traditional path are not really living in the real world and are best left to their delusions. Had I been wiser, I would have arranged matters so that I could stop here and be well on my way home before the cracks appear and the whole edifice falls to pieces.

But if we go on, I fear that the simplicity disappears. Even though I believe that what I have said is correct as far as it goes, we begin to see that the important issue for us is the relationship that exists at the meeting point of these two dimensions: that cross, within each man, of the line of time and the line of eternity, level or scale. In approaching this, I find I have to reconcile a number of facts, or at least a number of observations that I can no longer doubt.

The first is that many who follow a sacred tradition change profoundly as regards their ordinary life adjustment, whereby many of the problems that might otherwise take them to a psychotherapist simply melt away – like ice in the sun, disappearing without any systematic attempt to change – under the influence of some subtler, finer influence that begins to permeate and alter the whole organism.

Second, I have noticed that others who follow such traditions appear to become more closed, narrow and intolerant both of others and of their own hidden aspects. Of those I see professionally, this group is the most intractable and untreatable of all, for the knowledge derived from a religious tradition has been put to the service of perceptual defences of complacency, of narcissistic self-satisfaction, of comfort and security.

Third, the difficulties of working with such individuals are only equalled by those encountered with people who have misused the ideas and techniques of psychotherapy in a similar fashion. Excepting only the group that I have just mentioned, no patients are as difficult to treat as psychoanalysts, particularly those who believe they have had a 'full analysis' (what a marvellous expression!) already.

And fourth, others in psychotherapy, particularly those in psychotherapy groups – and in encounter groups in the early stages, before they become a new game – can reach a point of simple openness, of awareness of themselves as part of mankind and of the universe, and of direct communion with others, more intensely than many following a traditional teaching, at least as far as one can judge from the statements and external behaviour of each. It does not last, of course, and cannot be pursued systematically, but in the psychotherapeutic experience it is often there, sometimes in an awe-inspiring fashion, and we have to make a place for this in our ideas.

Conclusion: For Love and Delight

For some time after writing this I was uncomfortable with it and could take it no further, till I saw that I had assumed, for want of any real question to myself, that I might belong to the first or fourth groups, and that the second and third were made up of other people. But a moment's reflection showed me that I was a member of all four, and that the principal obstacles to my own development were precisely those that stemmed from the misuse of such professional or religious understanding as I possessed, in order to preserve and enhance my ordinary image of myself. And this, I see, applies to us all; it is in the nature of things.

Whether in my ordinary life or in my search for its hidden significance, I am most alive, closest to the source and meaning of my existence, when I am open to my immediate experience, receptive to what it can teach me and vulnerable to its power to change my being. In this moment, when I am sure of nothing, I am yet most deeply confident of the possibility of understanding. My actions spring most truly from myself, yet I have no idea beforehand what I will manifest. Like water welling up from a spring, I am new every moment, appearing miraculously from some source hidden deep within the ground of my being.

The next instant I have lost this movement, this freedom, this life constantly renewed and am once again trying to be right, to be good, to know, to change, to be normal, to be successful – or alternatively to be bad, rebellious, a tragic failure, a pathetic victim – but one way or another always seeking to preserve some experience, like a butterfly gassed in a bottle and pinned to a board, losing in the process everything that made me wish to capture it in the first place. Seeking security, certainty and beliefs to buoy me up, I cling to my experience in order to preserve it but find myself holding only the dead residue of a living process that has already changed and moved elsewhere. Small wonder that I find my life colourless, dull, flat and boring, needing ever-increasing artificial stimulation to restore me to some feeling of alertness.

Perceiving this, I realise that I must live nearer the source of this inner spring, somehow maintaining myself at the point where this 'living water' gushes forth into the visible world. I may see that I am constantly carried by the current into the more superficial manifestations to which this energy gives rise as it flows away from the source. Once I see this, I may begin to swim against the current, struggling to remain closer to the source where my life is constantly renewed, no longer trying to hold on to things for fear of sinking, and realising that the formlessness and endless change from which I shrink is a condition of real life itself.

If I can only realise my true situation and thereby loosen my attachment to the forms my life energy takes as it moves further from its origin, I may find that I *remember* the source, and that this memory brings a desire to find it again. Now I find myself swimming against the current to regain it, from love and delight. I need only free myself from my hypnosis long enough to remember what I have lost.

Then I am in the middle, between the hidden source of my life and its manifestations in this world, and I must then struggle not to deny either. If I forget the source, I drift downstream towards increasing repetition; or if I forget the nature of the stream itself and its constant downward pull, then I begin to dream that I am already at the source, rather than to experience it and to swim towards it, and so I drift downstream again. Only when I realise my nature as a creature of two worlds do I discover the full potential of my life, which must be lived everlastingly between them.

Now, this immediate experience of my living energy can be brought about by many kinds of events. Vivid and profound emotional experience can produce it, such as death of a loved one, the birth of a child, sometimes sexual love, great beauty, pain, an event on a world scale. Drugs like LSD and mescaline can give a taste of such experience by their capacity to destroy defences and release emotion, and so can psychotherapy, particularly perhaps encounter techniques and the gestalt approaches that seek to release the most primitive and childlike emotions.

But without deeper knowledge, we drift downstream imagining we still live at this zenith, while the experience in fact becomes degraded, copied and repeated, fantasised. Then we need larger doses, stronger stimuli, bigger groups, new techniques to startle us out of our dreams again. If this is in fact the case, it would at least explain why those undergoing analysis appear for a time more real and open, only to become more closed than others sometimes, when the analytic process is over, particularly if there is a professional vested interest in demonstrating a good result. Many will recognise exactly the same process among followers of the sacred traditions – a marvellous openness and simplicity in younger people just beginning, deteriorating gradually toward complacency, rigidity and parroting of formulas in those who begin to 'know' and, in doing so, cease to live.

It is here, perhaps, that the place of the family and community as a 'middle zone', and the need for ordinary efforts and work, become vital factors. For our natural tendency to drift with the streaming of our life energy into increasingly dead and ritualised manifestation – or to put it another way, our predisposition to convert real experience into fantasy and then repeat it, so that our lives not only become B-movies but even the same old B-movie over and over again – is so great that we need the discipline of *effort* to convince us, through our constantly experienced inability to swim against *any* current, that we are always drifting. And for this we need also the discipline of a group of intimates who know us well and love us enough to make demands on us for ordinary effort, who remind us when we drift too far from our more real selves and begin to live in dreams and selfish fantasies, and who demand of us that we be not less than ordinary men and women, fulfilling our ordinary responsibilities. For if we are not at least this, how can we hope to be more? Here, I believe, psychotherapy has its proper place, above all in the facilitation of this function of the family and the outer discipline and support it provides, or the provision of substitute group experience where this is missing. Given this ground, the sacred traditions have some possibility to guide us back to the source of our lives.

Notes

1 This paper was presented at a Lecture Series held in San Francisco in 1975. It was first published in J. Needleman, (ed.) *On The Way To Self-Knowledge*, 1976, and republished in J. Welwood, (ed.) *Awakening The Heart: East West Approaches to Psychotherapy And The Healing Relationship*, 1983.
2 Prof. J. Needleman was the organiser of the lecture series at which this paper was presented, and editor of the first collection in which it appeared.

12 Institutes and How To Survive Them

(8th S. H. Foulkes Annual Lecture, London 1984)

Like all commemorative events, the annual Foulkes Lecture is important for its content and – equally – for its sense of occasion as an institutional ritual, a celebration in the presence of a collective, cherished memory, marking the passage of time. Foulkes's working life, honoured by the occasion, saw the publication of four major texts, the founding of a Society, a training Institute and a definitive approach towards groups that was in turn the foundation for further developments – therapeutic communities, open-door psychiatry, family therapy and group work in education and consultation. Beneath this creative activity was Foulkes's close involvement with a group of associates who, after his unexpected death in 1976, have given the successive Foulkes Lectures.

He was Skynner's analyst, teacher and then his colleague. At the lecture in 1984 Skynner addressed a capacity audience in the large hall of the Institute of Education, where – by speaking about the terms of his own original apprenticeship – he evoked many of the qualities for which Foulkes had been so appreciated. As Skynner examines what he has made of what he received from Foulkes, he makes warm references to his humour, openness and capacity for self-examination. On the day, these qualities were re-enacted in the hall between Skynner and his audience; there was humour and, as people were moved by the affection remembered and kindled, great strength of feeling.

Skynner's use of paradox is conveyed in a style which had emerged in the book *Families and How To Survive Them*, then recently completed with John Cleese. He helped the audience laugh at its own formality and 'de-institutionalised' the occasion by bringing Foulkes *the person* into people's experience. Subsequently, perhaps as a consequence, the format for the lectures changed, with

189

greater scope being given at succeeding lectures to dialogue between speaker and audience.

The substance of Skynner's lecture is an account of institutional growth, regeneration and division. It includes the history of events documented in the preceding chapters of this book and in the other collection of his papers, *Explorations With Families: Group Analysis and Family Therapy*. The two forms through which he has made his explorations, group analysis and family therapy, have functioned much like the principles of triangulation in navigation by which two references provide the location for a third point. The lecture conveys how he kept his bearings by constantly operating from within two worlds first as a child and adult psychiatrist, then as a psychotherapist and psychiatrist and now as a group analyst and family therapist.

He remains integrally involved with both the institutions he founded. He reports that his resources in each area continue to be enhanced by his association with the other and that, from the period of this lecture, his writing assumed a new interest, taking him to a third position – as author – now independent of both the organisations which had once been his offspring. Reflecting on how they had served him, he describes them as substitute families which provided developmental experiences for what had been missing in his own.

J.R.S.

Introduction

Once a year those of us who have been touched by S. H. Foulkes's liberating influence gather, on the occasion of this Annual Lecture, to honour his memory.[1] In his technique of group analysis we acknowledge an immensely creative way of learning that has enriched our professional work and continues to illuminate and enrich our lives. To remember Foulkes and thank him for this fine gift, one of us is privileged each year to share with others what we have made out of what we received from him, and I am happy that the honour has this year fallen upon me.

The Message in the Medium

However, what is not so widely known, but needs to be said at the start, is that the Foulkes Lecture serves another purpose, intended to further his work in a different way. The forces of light usually stimulate a reaction from the forces of darkness; and it is inevitable that a method of pursuing knowledge, health and happiness as powerful as the one Foulkes taught us should arouse in response powerful forces of resistance and opposition, certainly in society and perhaps even in the universe at large. Because of this the outward form of this event is designed as a kind of ritual, a magical ceremony designed to ward off the main dangers that we see threatening our group-analytic ethos. To lull these opposing forces into a false sense of victory, we set aside one evening each year during which, as a paradoxical prescription of the behaviour to be avoided, we do the exact opposite of everything we believe in. We thereby purge ourselves of any unhealthy desire to run away from the confusing yet creative open exchange of the group-analytic process towards a comfortable, slavish blind following of authority,

191

so that, following homoeopathic principles, our whole organism will revolt against any further back-sliding of this kind.

For one evening, we go to the opposite extreme. Seated in orderly rows in a crowded lecture theatre, all facing the same way, the audience listens silently to a long monologue following which even questions, let alone group-analytic discussion, are most strictly avoided; and the audience departs feeling understandably virtuous at patiently sitting through a painful ordeal so alien to anything they believe in or are used to, thankful that it is over for another year and resuming their normal group-analytic discussions as soon as they get beyond the doors.

However, provided we adhere to the totally non-group-analytic outward form, there is no rule against trying to say something of interest, so that we can all get through the ritual as painlessly as possible. I quickly saw that the only way I could hope to approach the task, if I was to say something interesting and meaningful to senior colleagues, to graduates and students with different levels of experience, and to those with no experience of Foulkes's work at all – and there are several here – would be to talk about its history as I have experienced it. So what I am going to say about group analysis and its development is seen from the point of view of a personal Odyssey, a search for meaning from where I was standing, that is, something about my personal history too.

Where Do I Stand? Self-Reflexiveness

Even as I scribbled those words down, in preparing this lecture, I noticed a sudden change in my posture, my attitude. I realised that one had to take a step back to see where one had been standing a moment before. The same principle applies in the mental sphere; and I found myself wondering whether, when I said this here tonight, I might evoke in some of you a similar shift of attitude. Did you notice, at that point where I spoke of the limitations of my own knowledge and my need to step back to see them, that you immediately felt a healthy doubt as well? Did you step back a pace from me, perhaps, and look at me a bit more carefully to see what I was like, how far you could trust what I was going to say? And did that doubt, that moment of healthy scepticism, automatically bring with it an increased alertness, a sense of heightened interest, a little flash of greater consciousness even, as if you had stepped back a pace too? (Don't say anything, for heaven's sake! Much as I want to engage you in the fruitful dialogue that would normally develop at this point, we would shatter the ritual and awaken the demons. We have to endure this ordeal for less than an hour now, so let me proceed to get it over as quickly as possible.).

I had sketched out the form of the lecture several times, roughly in the form I am presenting it tonight, but a central unifying principle, tying the whole thing together, seemed to be missing. I now saw what it was, and realised at the same time that it was precisely this central principle in Foulkes's ideas and methods which had attracted me to seek contact with him in the first place. In everything he did, he seemed to have this open, curious, questioning attitude, whereby he was always stepping back to examine the ground that he himself had just been standing on. By engaging in this constant search for truth himself, in a light, amusing and enjoyable way, he seemed to arouse in others, quite automatically, the same lively, high-spirited, searching attitude. And it was good fun, like a game. You were expected to catch the ball and throw it back, or throw it on. In teaching he expected to learn, and made you teach him what was wrong with what he had said. Thus a stimulating process of mutual learning would occur, a shared search for a new knowledge in which all could join, all could contribute and all could receive, including him. This simple principle was the most important thing he had taught me, I suddenly realised. And I saw that this, in essence, is the basis of the process we all call group analysis.

When a Change is Not Always as Good as a Rest

Now, if I do step back and consider what I was doing a moment before – assisted in this by others who provide feedback about what they have observed – I begin to see myself more clearly. I see what I am, and how I fit into the pattern of the group-as-a-whole, instead of just observing and understanding others as if I am outside it all. Like the modern physicist, I begin to include myself in the equation, to see that my past experience invariably affects my view of anything I study. I see that there is no possibility of objective knowledge of others unless I first become more objective to myself. However, our work teaches us, as John Cleese and I have tried to set out as simply as possible in *Families and How To Survive Them*, that most of us will have grown up in families where some aspects of human nature were feared and denied, so that we were encouraged to hide certain emotions from others and often ended hiding them from ourselves as well to avoid feelings of worthlessness and disloyalty. Where this is so, stepping back and seeing ourselves more clearly will involve change in our habitual view of what we are. And change is stressful, disturbing, disruptive of our ordinary routine, so that we experience it as uncomfortable, disturbing, even painful. No matter how confident and secure we are, there is a limit to the amount of change that we can cope with in a given time. More new insight than we can absorb and digest leads to distraction of our attention from other tasks, to a degree that interferes with ordinary life. We become muddled, confused, may even suffer a 'nervous breakdown' if the confusion is sufficiently extreme. So we need intervals of quietness, solitude or relaxation where we avoid introspection and we let our attention focus on something outside ourselves while we have time for tidying up and filing away of information in our inner world, until we regain our balance and feel at 'peace', 'in one piece' again. Then, having closed the boundaries while this integration of the new information was proceeding, we are ready to open them again to admit the next quota.

The discomfort of change is more readily faced and endured if there is something familiar and unchanging to hang on to, a source of support that provides a feeling of stability in the face of the upsetting, unfamiliar new experiences. This may be provided by a person who has proved reliable and trustworthy in the past, to whom we have previously made a secure attachment.

Networks as Safety Nets

Instead of a person, this function may be served by a group or an organisation, where the disturbing changes are shared with others to whom good attachments have been made. Or the support may come from good memories of either of these actual experiences, or from associated ideas, ceremonies or symbols that sustain them. In later life at least, our support to cope with change usually comes from a combination of all these together: we are members of a group, within an organisation with certain valued aims and traditions, with trusted leaders who have been through similar changes themselves and understand what we are going through.

Now, a group possesses one great advantage. Although all the members may be going along together in a similar direction, they are not necessarily undergoing the same changes simultaneously. The situation is usually more like that of climbers on a mountain, where each individual undertakes a difficult traverse one at a time, while the other climbers temporarily stop and make themselves secure in order to hold the rope and protect the one in danger against the consequences of losing balance. In marital therapy – and of course in ordinary married life as well – one partner tends to leap-frog over the other into a new adjustment, following which the one left behind is stimulated to catch up and leap-frog in turn. In group or family therapy the same principle applies, except that there are more possibilities. What we often call the 'resistant' members of a group or institution are the ones temporarily holding the rope, and without their apparent hesitation the seemingly 'bolder' members might feel less inclined to hurl themselves into 'inner space' and take the risks they seem to do.

How Can 'Helpers' Help Themselves

All these issues will apply to anyone who is engaged in the process of gaining self-knowledge, whether as a patient in psychotherapy, an analyst in training, someone undergoing a 'pilgrim's progress' of a religious path, or a person growing in self-knowledge through the ordinary knocks and home-truths of daily life. But there is an important difference in the situation of the 'helping professional'. Those of us in the mental health professions – psychiatrists, social workers, psychologists, psychoanalysts and so on – have an additional option to reduce the discomfort and stress that would accompany gains in self-knowledge; namely, we can keep our boundaries closed and maintain our attention firmly on our patients and clients, studying them instead. There are many pressures on us to do this. First of all, we are usually taught during our training that this is what we should be doing; that it is what our job consists of, what we pass exams and get promoted and rewarded for. Secondly, there are strong expectations in society that we should be unusually

195

altruistic, and even free of problems that beset everyone else. And third, I think these expectations society has of us are pressures to which we are particularly vulnerable because our families – I mean the families we professionals grew up in – often found it hard to accept a reasonable degree of separation, independence and self-assertion in family members, relying instead on appeals for self-sacrifice and 'living for others' as ways of dealing with relationships. At least, that is true of my own background, and I have heard the same story often enough now from colleagues and students to have confidence that I am by no means alone. Given these pressures, the natural human hunger for self-knowledge can come to feel like selfishness, self-indulgence, failure and weakness.

Discouraged from direct study of ourselves, we can nevertheless gratify our curiosity at one remove, by studying others and helping them to grow instead. Turning away from the lost parts of ourselves that would complete us if we could find them, we search for these outside, in our patients and clients. We are thereby drawn, automatically, to some branch of the 'helping services' where we will find people with similar problems to those in ourselves and our families, though with less ability to conceal and control them. In many ways this is good for the clients and good for the service we join; we are highly motivated, may have an unusual patience with people others might not tolerate, and a curiously acute interest in and perhaps insight into their problems. We may even be prepared to work overtime, for nothing!

So far the situation is the same, you will notice, as the one I claim is usually operating as part of marital choice. There both partners are also looking for lost parts of their own personality, and they choose someone very like themselves at a deep hidden level, no matter how different the surface appearances may be. Not only that, but as in marriage, where the partner is the ideal person with whom to learn more about oneself – if one can bear the discomfort of it – the mental health professional automatically selects the ideal clientele in which to study himself or herself vicariously and discover what the missing, denied aspects are, though the knowledge cannot benefit us personally – or even our patients as much as it could do – until we acknowledge the fact that our work, however useful, has also been an evasion of the truth about ourselves.

196

I'll Look After You, If You'll Look After the Bit of Me I Can't Look After

Thus, as in marriage, there are three main options available. One possibility is that the profession and the clientele we have chosen can be used to learn more about the self, to accept the missing parts, and grow. Alternatively, the work can be used to keep the missing, denied parts projected, in a basically benevolent if growth-inhibiting way, so that the therapist remains stuck in an altruistic parental role but never learns to be childish and spontaneous too; and the client stays stuck in a childish, irresponsible role and can never take on adult responsibility and power. I have described this as: 'Me Tarzan – clever, normal doctor, and You Jane – hopeless, crazy patient.' It is a formula for longer analyses, if the patient has the money, or endless attendance at hospital out-patients receiving one useless treatment after another, if the National Health Service has the money. The third possibility – projection of the denied parts with destructive malevolent attack, the mental health equivalent of the *Who's Afraid of Virginia Woolf?* type of marriage – is not often found in the helping professions unless the normal controls maintained to prevent abuses in some way fail. Such people are unlikely to want to help people weaker than themselves.

Are these three different types, three different groups of people? To some extent, and at any one time, I think this must be so. But the possibility that they can be three stages we can each pass through is more interesting. I am certainly still aware of the persecuting bully in myself who wants to attack any weakness close to his own, and of the person who came into psychiatry both fleeing from and searching for those weaknesses by studying them in others, though I hope and believe that a third way of functioning, in which I am more often aware of my own limitations in the immediate moment, is now more available to me.

One Flesh: Separate Persons

A further vital principle I need to add is that the autonomy of adulthood necessarily involves an acceptance of separateness, of being alone – 'all one'. Stepping back not only makes us more aware of ourselves: it also clarifies our relationship with others. Being

197

separate is a lonely experience in which at first one feels sad and lost. To cope with this we need permission from those we feel we are leaving behind, and the most effective permission is an example, a model provided by someone who experiences being separate already and is happy with that kind of relationship, someone who is therefore happy for us to have it too.

However, a moment's thought shows us at once that the model we need is not just someone who feels separate from us, though that is a minimum requirement. If we are not yet separated from that person ourselves we will not perceive that separateness for what it is; we may misperceive it as lack of love, as rejection, coldness or hostility. The model we need is of two other people being separate and independent of each other, yet also continuing to remain in contact, to communicate and to struggle and compromise to reach agreed solutions for the benefit of all. We have to see this combination of independence and cooperation demonstrated before our eyes, by people we love and respect, if we are to endure what at first seems nothing but painful loss and conflict.

Within the family this example is perhaps the most vital contribution the father and mother can make to their children's development. But even if our parents fail us, we can still get the same benefit from witnessing demonstrations of people feeling separate, yet cooperating, in group situations.

Role-Segregation in the Mental Health Profession: Psychotherapy and Anti-Psychotherapy

Those of you who are familiar with the Timberlawn research study on healthy families will remember that they found the married couples they studied varied in their ability to be separate and differentiated from each other, ranging from complete muddle and fusion at the most unhealthy extreme to a capacity, in the really healthy couples, to move freely to and fro between great intimacy at some times and great independence at others.[2] In between were the majority of marriages, the average marriage, where some degree of separation is achieved, but at a cost to the capacity for closeness. There is the role-segregated marriage in which, at best, the two parents maintain their separate identities by sharply demarcating and avoiding each other's territories: the house and children –

hers; the outside world – his. Or where at worst, the couple fight like cat and dog, with no compromise at all, over the children's management.

It had always puzzled me that so much of what happens in the mental health professions resembles this pattern of the role-stereotyped marriage, though it was suddenly blindingly obvious, in trying to think out this lecture, that if most of us are mid-range in our own mental health then that is exactly what one ought to expect! It is then entirely understandable that people tend to polarise strongly either towards the traditional stereotype of the mother's role, placing high value on unconditional acceptance, emotional warmth, understanding, nurture; or towards the traditional father-role stereotype, emphasising interventions that impose values, make demands for effort and action, with acceptance conditional upon adjusting to society's values and with the use of rewards and punishments, even if only approval and disapproval, to encourage this result. The first group tend to explain behaviour in psychoanalytic or at least broadly psychodynamic terms, without worrying too much about success in terms of loss of symptoms as long as everyone is happy; the second are interested mainly in changing behaviour, using either a behavioural or biological model, without going too deeply into explanations of how it came about. Each group tends to avoid communication with the other, publishing in different journals, each using a private jargon and ignoring each other's literature. When obliged to be in contact and to communicate, as they have to do to some extent at teaching institutions like the Institute of Psychiatry, they each listen to the other side only to rehearse well-worn arguments reinforcing their polarised, mutually rejecting positions. The Journal Club there, which I have attended off and on over a span of thirty years, is at times like a ritual dance designed to reassure these two groups that they have absolutely nothing in common, almost like groups of men and women fearful of changing sex.

Group Analysis: 'Mothering' and 'Fathering' Combined

Encountering Foulkes's group-analytic techniques, as I did at the Maudsley, against this strange background of what at first looked

199

like primitive tribal behaviour, probably highlighted the exciting fact that his methods seemed to have brought these two aspects of parenting – what people used to call 'motherly-love' and 'fatherly-love' – together. His way of conducting groups recognised the value of acceptance, support and understanding, but gave equal scope to the operation of group pressures, whereby the group-as-a-whole became a microcosm of society and its values, and aberrant patterns of conduct were confronted and challenged by other members.

Looking back over my life since that time, it is striking now how much of what was to follow – though I did not see it clearly at the time – was just an attempt to explore this issue more deeply, to take up this challenge from the point where Foulkes often seemed to get stuck, and pursue the question: 'What is "fathering?"' 'What is "mothering?"' 'How are these two parental roles, or these two functions in the same person, best combined?'

The confidence and sense of freedom he so readily induced in others soon had me questioning his own organisation in this way. Finding the Group-Analytic Society as run by Foulkes too much like an enmeshed family pattern, still biased, as I saw it, towards the maternal mode, with too little challenge and conflict either among the membership or by openness and confrontation with other ideas outside it, I seized the chance to design a more open and systematic course in group psychotherapy for the Association of Psychiatric Social Workers, whose request for this had until then been turned down by all organisations they had approached, including the Group-Analytic Society on a previous occasion before I joined the Committee. At first Foulkes was not really happy about my plan for a course that would include all the main schools of thought, though with his ideas at the centre, but eventually he agreed. I invited Pat de Maré to join me to chair the lectures while I conducted the experiential group, and after the successful pilot course, in 1964, it was expanded in subsequent years to a total of 130 participants from different mental health disciplines, while additional members of the Society were brought in to enlarge the staff. Other courses were later added, and this venture was eventually developed by all of us into the Institute of Group Analysis.[3]

Meanwhile, having trained in both adult and child psychiatry, I had begun experimenting with family therapy in 1962, stimulated by a paper by John Elderkin Bell in a British journal which was remarkably close to Foulkes's ideas. Ten years later, in 1972, the demand for family therapy teaching had grown to a point where there were more applicants for my family therapy seminars in the Institute of Group Analysis than for all the other 'advanced' seminars put together, so I designed another large systematic course, this time in family therapy, which was first run in 1973.

As my colleagues in the Institute of Group Analysis did not share my experience of child psychiatry and family therapy I had to find staff from outside it. Because of this I was able to fulfil a long ambition by bringing together, as the staff of the new course, teachers from both psychoanalytic and behavioural backgrounds, as well as group analysts and experts in techniques developed in the United States. By design, the staff was composed of equal numbers of men and women, and my wife and I shared the leadership as a couple.[4] Not only was the range of orientations presented in the lectures and demonstrations deliberately made even wider than on the stranger-group training (subsequently called the 'General' Course); the process of standing back and looking at our own group dynamic was built in more firmly from the beginning, and two-way communication, with criticism from the participants, was also ensured by the way the staff exposed their own dynamics in the presentations. For example, the course always began with the whole staff role-playing a simulated family on stage, after each of us had picked a family role out of a hat.

Almost all the people I brought in to staff the family course had strong past connections with the stranger-group courses at the Institute of Group Analysis; a majority had been through the existing introductory course and several had continued in my colleagues' advanced seminars, so that there was already a network of friendships between the existing and the new staff.

Also, since not everyone knows it nowadays, I should add that the new venture received the greatest possible support from my existing colleagues, particularly other members of the Training Committee. How complete this support was can be judged by the fact that one of them, Malcolm Pines, signed on for the new family course the second year it was run, and many others followed, including Elizabeth Foulkes.

'A Bridge Too Far'

However, despite the basically good personal relationships which had always existed and have in fact continued, tensions were nevertheless growing between the two sides. These were, I now believe, an inevitable consequence of my attempt to hold together and explore these two parental stereotypes, trying to discover what 'mothering' and 'fathering' involved and to find the right relationship between them.

Why should that produce tension? I believe the stereotyping of male and female roles, and the role-segregation that goes with it, has always been popular because it works – after a fashion. It is a way of avoiding the struggles that couples have to face once they accept a greater equality and begin to share and collaborate in the task of child-rearing. When couples in our marital groups are moving from the role-segregated relationship they usually begin from, towards the more open and collaborative relationship they hopefully end with, they usually have first to become more independent of each other, to differentiate and do some more growing up.

For this reason they often go through a period of painful separation which at first looks like a step towards divorce. We have to accept this risk and support them through this stressful stage because, unless the two individuals develop stronger, more separate identities first – a clearer sense of their own boundaries – there is a danger that more openness and sharing will lead not to growth but to regression, to an earlier state of fusion, and so also *con*fusion, and role *diff*usion: blurring of boundaries rather than true sharing of equally rich but different resources. So for a time they have to go their separate ways and build up their strengths as individuals.

At the time I am speaking of I had already begun to see this pattern in marriage: indeed, it is spelled out in the title of my first book: *One Flesh: Separate Persons*. But it did not occur to me then to expect the same pattern in the development of institutions, and the increasing drive towards separation of the family and stranger-group trainings at first felt like the painful breakup of my own family.

Institutes and How They Survive Us

'Make or Break' year was 1976. The London Workshop in January
that year, run by Jim Home, Malcolm Pines and myself and
attended by all the main leaders of both the stranger-group and
family-group courses in England, as well as many colleagues from
abroad, had a cross-over design where all moved back and forth
between analytic and action groups. Foulkes seemed to love it, and
as usual declared that family therapy and group therapy were two
inseparable aspects of group analysis. (Foulkes was assigned to my
wife's 'action' group, while she was at that time a member of one of
his therapy groups, and their ability to take that in their stride says a
lot about them both.)

But one participant from abroad spoke of the experience of what
he called 'psycho-shock', and though he did so very positively,
others complained of a 'terrifying erosion of boundaries', con-
firming the danger of fusion rather than creative exchange. Foulkes
died in the middle of that year; the staff of the family course made
their decision towards its end, and the separate Institute of Family
Therapy came into being the following spring, in May 1977.

At the time I experienced much anguish trying to hold the two
sides together, but I was surprised to feel enormous relief when the
final separation came, almost as if one's parents had finally divorced
and one could get on with one's own life. I have remained in both
institutes, serving as chairman of the Institute of Family Therapy
during its first two years, and enjoying the stimulation of both
groups. However, though the relationship between them is friendly,
each institute has tended to move away from the mid-position
where integration of ideas is more possible: the Institute of Group
Analysis moved back towards the psychoanalytic model, and the Institute of Family Therapy, following a worldwide trend in the field,
towards techniques where *change* is the main aim and the therapist
operates from a position of power. For me, both groups have moved
away from Foulkes's vision that the most effective therapy, whether
of families or strangers, is 'psychotherapy *by* the group, *of* the
group, including its conductor' – that is, where the therapist stands
back repeatedly to include his or her problems and errors in the
analysis of the total system, instead of a 'mother knows best' or
'father knows best' attempt to straighten out other people.

203

My central interest has continued to be the integration of these two paradigms, a task that members of the two institutions could hardly be expected to share once they had divorced or entered a temporary period of separate development, whichever it may prove to be. So I have had to go outside my own professional field altogether to find others to share in the exploration, finding unlikely – though most enjoyable – companions in the search: first, in a group of bishops and their wifes; and second, in John Cleese, my collaborator in *Families and How To Survive Them*. Our book makes a start at trying to put the two paradigms together, while a more professional formulation, bringing together psychoanalytic systems ideas, as applied to both group and family therapy, was put forward in April in my Keynote Lecture to the International Congress of Group Psychotherapy in Mexico City (published as the concluding chapter in the companion volume to this one, *Explorations With Families*).

Guidelines for a Creative Institution

Now if, arising from this experience, we try to express the ideal structure of a teaching institution – accepting that ideals are to be regarded as 'stars to mariners', as guides to steer by rather than to hope to reach – it seems that some simple principles noted in healthy families keep appearing here too.

First of all, it seems that the most fruitful relationship within a group of teachers forming the staff of an institute is akin to that in a good marriage. The members will all be separate individuals, perhaps with a variety of orientations, different styles and views of their own, all of which will provide a rich resource of knowledge and skill upon which the students can draw, and by which the staff can continue to learn from each other. We will expect strong tensions within these relationships, arising from these differences, but members will be prepared to continue to communicate, constantly negotiating compromises and resolving conflicts, each accepting that it is normal and healthy for us to want our own way, but also knowing that it is not usually good for us to get it all the time, since we can see ourselves more clearly through the reflections provided by others, and can therefore grow, learn and develop in skill only by accepting some measure of painful confrontation and challenge.

As in marriage there must be respect for difference and separateness for this to be possible. The different members must therefore feel an essential equality in their right to communicate and speak their minds in open discussion, even though they otherwise respect their different degrees of power by virtue of their roles within the organisational structure. And as in marriage again, they need to be prepared to tolerate a considerable measure of 'held tensions' between conflicting points of view, treating these as normal phenomena, a sign of life rather than a nuisance to be avoided.

Nevertheless, those responsible for the boundaries within and between organisations will need to ensure that these are not opened so rapidly or widely that the degree of change and stress threatens the integrity of the system itself, and especial care will need to be taken when other unifying factors are weakened or other disruptive influences are strong.

Not So Far to Go, After All?

If all this is true, then it seems to me that our institutes are in quite good shape, at least compared with many in other parts of the world. Though I have poked a little fun earlier at some of the things that go on at my Alma Mater – The Institute of Psychiatry and the Maudsley Hospital – the lively confrontation which has always been encouraged there between all the different schools of thought, leaving the trainees to make up their own minds, is a rare and precious freedom for which I, and so many others like me, have reason to be deeply grateful.

One striking feature of the Institute of Psychoanalysis is the way in which supporters of the classical Freudian ideas, and others prefering their Kleinian derivatives, have held together by choosing the more creative path of holding the 'controversial dialogues', and then making room for similarity and difference by formation of the A, B and independent groups within the same organisation, instead of through splitting and the formation of hostile schools. The consequent creativeness of the psychoanalytic movement in Britain has benefited those outside as much as those within.

Similarly, the wide range of orientations, ideas and techniques contained within the Group-Analytic Practice and the Institute of Group Analysis, which have always included people with Jungian,

Kleinian, Freudian and other forms of training, have lived together amicably and fruitfully, holding the tensions in creative dialogue for twenty or thirty years.

The Institute of Family Therapy and the Association for Family Therapy, both of which were initiated within the group-analytic movement, have successfully included a range of orientations, collaborating in creative endeavour, which as far as I know is unprecedented anywhere. I wanted more still, but then I'm greedy.

Small is Flexible: How the End of the Beginning Need Not Be the Beginning of the End

I realise that I have still left out the problem of size, and also time. I am happiest and most effective in the early stages of new organisations, so that when the numbers exceed about twelve to twenty, at the most, I begin to get restless and want to start again. That is one of my limitations, and I think I at least have enough sense to hand the baton on at that point to others with the qualities needed for the next stage. Yet organisations must grow, because they have to meet the requirements of the task, rather than just the needs of the members. And as organisations grow in size, an increasing specialisation of functions and roles is necessary, if they are to operate at all.

The same is true of individual, living organisms. The tiny, single-celled amoeba is small enough to move, breathe, eat, excrete and communicate using more or less the whole of itself as a kind of one-man-band – or 'one-amoeba-band'. But as animals get larger, food has to be taken in at one end and the residue pushed out at the other; distances become too great for the fuel thereby produced, or the oxygen to burn it, to diffuse fast enough from one place to another, so pumps and pipes are needed to transport it. Legs are needed to carry all this weight, nerves to carry the signals to coordinate them, and a brain to keep all the functions working in harmony.

Similarly, as organisations get larger, we cannot avoid committees, minutes of meetings, forms, rules and a hierarchy of command to coordinate the parts. As roles become more differentiated and defined, the hierarchy more established and communication more formal and restricted, it becomes increasingly difficult for the original creative brain-storming – the free exchange of group associations possible in small teams – to continue productively without disrupting the normal operation of a larger organisation. In particular, any attempt at group-process commentary, whereby a social structure openly investigates its own operation, automatically undermines arbitrary authority structure. As Yalom (1975) says: 'If an individual wishes to maintain a position of arbitrary authority, then it behoves him to inhibit the development of any rules permitting reciprocal process observation and commentary.' This is true even though such process-commentary may have strengthened the position of earlier leaders whose authority was more based on a level of understanding which the process-study merely made available to others too.

Thus the creative freedom of communication of the early stages, which were so striking in the group-analytic and British family therapy fields, must inevitably become reduced as these fields grow. Once again the situation reminds one of stages of family life, as the relaxed enjoyments of marriage are reduced when children appear, particularly when they reach latency and have to be got to school, encouraged to do homework, coached for exams. As the family comes under increasing pressures of this kind, some order and discipline ('Do as you're told . . .', 'Don't answer back . . .', 'Eat up your greens . . .', 'Mother knows best . . .') become essential to get through the day and make life tolerable for everybody.

The Need for a Place where 'Nothing' Can Happen

Is there no solution? Yes, I believe there is. And I think it is part of the genius of the group-analytic movement to have found it and embodied this solution in its structure.

At first the structure of this organisation seems strange, untidy, for it appears to duplicate committees, officers and meetings which would be better combined. In addition to the Institute of Group Analysis, which runs the training and other courses, provides a qualification, and prepares its students to take a professional role in the world by ensuring that they follow a certain course of learning, the Group-Analytic Society from which it sprang continues alongside it relatively unchanged, neither controlled by nor controlling the Institute, with considerable overlap in membership but not identical composition, and with rather vague, undefined functions other than continued exploration of what group analysis is and what the Society itself is for, if anything. In a younger, stupider, more brutish period of my life – indeed, until about a couple of years ago – I thought it a waste of time and money, which never seemed to achieve anything that could not be better performed by the Institute; wandering about in circles, getting nowhere, remaining perpetually chaotic.

Then it struck me, like a thunderbolt, that this was the whole point. The Group-Analytic Society provided time and space, sufficiently separated from the Institute and its functions and responsibilities for those who wished to keep alive the unstructured open discussion, with study of group process, which had been possible in the beginning. Because the committees, officers and hierarchy were different, there was no threat to the Institute hierarchy, so that teachers and students at all levels could exchange more freely without undermining Institute roles. I understood that if the Group-Analytic Society seemed chaotic, it was chaotic only in the sense that creation must always come from chaos, so that this chaos must be valued and preserved. The Society could retain infinite possibilities because it avoided taking on a definite form and growing towards some end.

Regeneration Requires Three Generations

Seeking some family analogy to complete my talk, at first I thought of the preservation of sex cells within the body, renewing themselves from one generation to another although each individual carrying them dies. But then I saw an even more obvious analogy. Have you guessed? It is going round to Granny's! For the first time, I grasped why families needed three generations.

As children, I am sure most of us looked forward to 'going round to Granny's'. I certainly did. There the family rules were a bit more relaxed. You were expected to eat a piece of bread-and-butter first, but then there were extra cakes and jellies, jam tarts and Cornish cream, and she was less worried if one was a bit greedy, behaved slightly badly, was not keeping up the family standards one's parents demanded. The conversation was more free, she did not mind if you got a bit excited, became a little cheeky, or wanted to get down from the table to play with the toys.

One's parents also changed at Granny's. They seemed to become more relaxed too, to be somehow younger, less forbidding, a bit more like ourselves. If the gap between our parents and ourselves seemed reduced, it was because Granny could remember when they were small, would tell us funny stories about them, scrapes they got into and embarrassing things they did when they were young, showing that their demands were not so unattainable because they were not such perfect figures as they sometimes made themselves out to be.

All this was possible because Granny was no longer a powerful figure in an executive sense, but was still respected as an elder, an authority by virtue of age and history, experience and the wisdom that only long experience can bring. So in her presence, and on her territory, the family hierarchy was temporarily levelled – but without destroying it, so that it could resume its necessary distance after we had left to go home. At Granny's, too, family myths are made conscious, information normally hidden is exchanged, cats are let out of the bag.

This process of temporary levelling, and revelation of truths usually concealed, happens even more strikingly in the presence of the extended family, who all respect Granny and like to visit her. They come on special occasions, and their presence too changes the family structure, making it even more open and relaxed, temporarily weakening the ordinary authority structure still more. The extended family are outside the local rivalries and squabbles, and make it feel safe for these to be dropped and relationships renegotiated.

Institutions share these features too, and it is no accident that the Foulkes Lecture, the Annual General Meeting of the Group-Analytic Society, one of the international gatherings, and an enjoyable party, all occur together at this time each year.

Of course, grandfathers can serve the same function, though not quite so reliably as grannies. My maternal grandfather, a Cornish fisherman who sang us sea shanties accompanied by his concertina, was more freeing to the conversation, though the other, the autocrat who dominated the family, at least reduced the parental hierarchy. But the females, the grannies, seemed to serve this function best, and it is no accident that Foulkes's widow, Elizabeth, and Jane Abercrombie, one of his earliest and most distinguished pupils, should have been such key figures in seeing the need for the Society and keeping it alive.

Conclusion: Life is too Serious to be Taken Seriously

Three weeks ago in Mexico City, in company with Elizabeth Foulkes, Jane Abercrombie and other friends in the Society, I had the pleasure of spending an evening at the house of Foulkes's daughter, who practises there as a family therapist, having trained at the Mexican Institute of Family Therapy. I told her I was struggling with this lecture, and asked her what she thought it was her father had communicated to us, that had made such a difference to so many relationships in our professions. She could not define it, but finally said: 'You know, when I was with him I *laughed* a lot.' We agreed that the laughter was never manic or cruel, and that he was not really witty; in fact, half the time he was worried that you might be laughing at his terrible English. I remember too that it was not so much open laughter that he engendered, as that you found yourself chuckling as you talked to him; you always enjoyed being with him.

At last I felt I was closer to recognising what he had given us. He had shown us how to take everything seriously, yet to take nothing too seriously. Simply by his presence, maybe without even being aware of it himself, he taught us something about enjoyment of life, enjoyment of learning, above all enjoyment of learning with each other. We all caught some understanding of that kind from him, and between us we seem to have passed a little of it on.

Can you feel something of that in the atmosphere here – even with nearly a thousand people in the kind of classroom situation he was never comfortable with – tonight . . . ?

Notes

1 This paper was given as the 8th S. H. Foulkes Annual Lecture, London 1984, and was first published in *Group Analysis* 15, 11/2, 1984.
2 See J. Lewis et al., *No Single Thread: Psychological Health in*

Family Systems, 1976; J. Lewis, *How's Your Family*, 1979; and
W. R. Beavers, *Psychotherapy and Growth: A Family Systems
Perspective*, 1977. (Ed.)
3 See chapter 9 above.
4 See chapter 6 above.

Appendix: Robin Skynner's Publications

Papers published in Explorations With Families *are marked by* *
Papers published in this collection are marked by †

1.   1957:   'The Relation of Muscle Tension to Awareness of Emotional State'. Dissertation for the Diploma of Psychological Medicine, University of London.
2. †1964:   'Group Analytic Themes In Training And Case Discussion Groups'. *Selected Lectures: VIth International Congress of Psychotherapy*, 1964.
3. †1967:   'Child Guidance From Within: Reactions To New Pressures'. Paper given at the 23rd Child Guidance Inter-Clinic Conference, N.A.M.H. Publications, London.
4. †1968:   'A Family of Family Casework Agencies'. *International Journal of Group Psychotherapy*, **18,** 352–360.
5. *1968:   'The Minimum Sufficient Network'. Paper read to the 2nd Athenian Symposium on Group Techniques, Athens, published in *Social Work Today*, **2,** 9, 28/7/71.
6. *1969:   'A Group-Analytic Approach to Conjoint Family Therapy'. *Journal of Child Psychology and Psychiatry* **16,** 81, October 1969. Reprinted in *Social Work Today*, 1970, and in S. Walrond-Skinner (ed.), *Developments in Family Therapy*, RKP, 1981.
7. *1969:   'Indications And Contraindications For Conjoint Family Therapy'. *International Journal of Social Psychiatry*, Vol. XV, **4.**
8.   1970:   'An Encounter With Esalen'. *Group Analysis*, International Panel and Correspondence, **3,** 180, 1970.
9.   1971:   'Group Psychotherapy With Adolescent Boys' in *Groups: Annual Review of Residential Child Care Association*, 1970–1.
10.   1972:   'Implications of Recent Work In Conjoint Family Therapy

213

for Group Analytic Theory. *Group Analysis*, **5,** 153.

11.   1973:   'Icelandic Saga'. *Group Analysis*, **6,** 39.

12. †1974:   'An Experiment In Group Consultation With the Staff of a Comprehensive School'. *Group Process*, **6,** 99.

13.   1974:   'Boundaries'. *Social Work Today*, **5,** 290–294.

14.   1974:   'Group Psychotherapy' in V. P. Varma, (ed.), *Psychotherapy Today*, Constable, London.

15. *1974:   'School Phobia: A Reappraisal'. *British Journal of Medical Psychology*, **47,** 1–15.

16.   1975:   'Development of Family Therapy' in W. Finn (ed.), *Family Therapy in Social Work*: FWA Conference Papers.

17.   1975:   'Family Therapy Techniques'. Proceedings of the Tenth Annual Congress, Association for the Psychiatric Study of Adolescents.

18. *1975:   'Marital Problems and Their Treatment'. Proceedings, Royal Society of Medicine, **68,** 405.

19.   1975:   'Some Consequences of Work With Natural Groups'. *Marriage Guidance*, **15,** 319.

20. †1975:   'The Large Group In Training' in L. Kreeger (ed.), *The Large Group: Dynamics and Therapy*, Constable, London.

21. *1976:   'Group Analysis And Family Therapy'. Paper presented to a Scientific Meeting of the Group Analytic Society. Published in M. Pines (ed.), *The Evolution of Group Analysis*, RKP, 1983.

22.   1976:   'Family Therapy'. Precirculated Papers: Conference on the Teaching of Psychotherapy, Association of University Teachers of Psychiatry.

23.   1976:   'Family Techniques in Social Work'. DHSS *Social Work Service*, **10,** 41.

24.   1976:   'Family and Marital Therapy'. Symposium on Psychotherapy, published in *British Journal of Hospital Medicine*, **15,** 224.

25.   1976:   *One Flesh, Separate Persons: Principles of Family and Marital Psychotherapy*, Constable, London.

26. †1976:   'On the Origins of Family Therapy and Developments In Its Practice'. Opening Speech to the Inaugural Meeting of The Association of Family Therapy, Imperial College, London (previously unpublished).

27. †1976:   'Psychotherapy and Spiritual Tradition' in J. Needleman (ed.), *On The Way to Self-Knowledge*, Knopf, NY. Reprinted in J. Welwood (ed.), *Awakening The Heart: East West Approaches to Psychotherapy And The Healing Relationship*, New Science Library, Boulder, and RKP, London, 1983.

28.   1976:   'Towards A Family Approach In A Psychiatric Day

Hospital'. *British Journal of Psychiatry*, **129**, 73 (written with Bennett, Fox and Jowell).

29. *1976: 'Sexual Counselling Techniques in General Practice'. Four papers. *British Journal of Sexual Medicine*, Vol. 3, **6**, 1976; Vol. 4, **1**, 1977; Vol. 4, **2**, 1977; Vol. 4, **3**, 1977.

30. *1978: 'The Physician As Family Therapist' in J. Lewis and G. Usdin (eds), *Psychiatry in General Medical Practice*, McGraw-Hill, NY.

31. †1979: 'An Open-Systems Approach To Teaching Family Therapy'. *Journal of Marital and Family Therapy*, 5, **3**. Reprinted in *Group Analysis*, 8, **1**, 1980.

32. 1979: Foreword to S. Walrond-Skinner (ed.), *Family and Marital Psychotherapy: A Critical Approach*, RKP, London.

33. *1979: 'Reflections on the Family Therapist as Family Scapegoat'. *Journal of Family Therapy*, **1**, 7.

34. *1980: 'Recent Developments In Marital Therapy'. *Journal of Family Therapy*, **2**, 271.

35. *1981: 'Referral For Psychotherapy'. *British Medical Journal*, Vol. 282, June.

36. *1981: *An Open Systems, Group-Analytic Approach to Family Therapy*, Gurman, A., and Kniskern, D. (eds.), Brunner/Mazel, NY.

37. 1982: 'Farewell'. Written for the Maudsley Gazette, Autumn 1982, on retirement from The Bethlem Royal and Maudsley Hospital.

38. 1982: Foreword to D. E. Scharff, *The Sexual Relationship*, RKP, London.

39. 1982: Foreword to R. Whiffen and J. Byng Hall (eds), *Family Therapy Supervision: Recent Developments in Practice*, Academic Press, London.

40. *1982: 'Frameworks for Viewing the Family as a System' in A. Bentovim, A. Cooklin and J. Gorrell Barnes (eds), *Family Therapy: Contemporary Frameworks of Theory and Practice*, Academic Press/Grune and Stratton, London and NY.

41. 1983: *Families And How To Survive Them*. Written with Cleese, J., Methuen, London.

42. †1983: 'Make Sure To Feed The Goose That Lays The Golden Eggs: A Discussion On The Myth Of Altruism'. *Journal of Psychohistory*, Vol. 10, **3**, pp. 389–395.

43. †1984: 'Institutes And How To Survive Them'. 8th S. H. Foulkes Annual Lecture given at the Institute of Education, London. Published in *Group Analysis* 15, 11/2, 1984.

44. *1984: 'What Is Effective In Group (and Family) Therapy?'. Keynote Lecture, 8th International Congress of Group

Psychotherapy, Mexico City. Published in *Group Analysis*, 19, 5–24, 1986.

45. 1985: 'Towards an Integration of Analytic, Behavioural and Systemic Approaches to Family Therapy'. Paper given at the 8th International Delphic Symposium on Family Therapy, Athens. Published in G. A. Vassilliou and V. G. Vassilliou (eds), *Family Therapy Evolving*, for the Athenian Institute of Anthropos.

46. †1986: 'The Psychotherapy Teacher – Getting Older: Narrowing Down Or Opening Out?'. Paper given at the 3rd Conference on Teaching Dynamic Psychotherapy, Oxford; Association of University Teachers of Psychiatry. Published in *The Bulletin of the Royal College of Psychiatrists*, Vol. 10, December 1986.

47. †1988: 'Marriage and Personal Change'. Paper given at the Fortieth Anniversary Meeting of The Institute of Marital Studies, Royal College of Medicine, London.

Bibliography

Abercrombie, M. L. J. *The Anatomy of Judgement*, Penguin, Harmondsworth, 1969.

Abercrombie, M. L. J. and Terry, P. M. *Aims and Techniques of Group Teaching*, Society for Research into Higher Education, London, 1971.
Talking to Learn, Society for Research into Higher Education, London, 1978.

Abse, W. 'Trigant Burrow and the Inauguration of Group Analysis in the USA', *Group Analysis*, 12, **3** (1979), 218–229.
Clinical Notes on Group-Analytic Psychotherapy, John Wright and Sons, Bristol, and Virginia Universities Press, Charlottesville, 1974.

Balint, E. and Norell, J. S. *Six Minutes for the Patient: Interactions in General Practice Consultation*, Tavistock, London, 1973.

Balint, M. *The Doctor, his Patient and the Illness*, Pitman Medical, London, 1964.

Barlow. *The Alexander Principle*, Gollancz, London, 1973.

Bateson, G. *Steps Towards an Ecology of Mind*, Chandler, New York, 1972.
Mind and Nature, Wildwood House, London, 1979.

Beavers, W. R. *Psychotherapy and Growth: A Family Systems Perspective*, Brunner/Mazel, New York, 1977.

Bell, J. E. 'Recent Advances in Family Group Therapy,' *Journal of Child Psychology and Psychiatry*, **3** (1964) (1) 21.

Bennett, D. 'The Day Hospital', in Petrilowitsch, N. and Flegel, H. (eds) *Social Psychiatry*, *Top. Probl. Psychiat. Neurol., Vol. 9*, pp. 4–18 Karger, Basle and New York, 1969.

Bentovim, A., Gorrell Barnes, G. and Cooklin, A. (eds) *Family Therapy: Complementary Frameworks of Theory and Practice*, Academic Press, London, 1982.

Berne, E. *Games People Play*, Grove Press, New York, 1964.

Bion, W. *Experiences in Groups*, Tavistock, London, 1964.

de Board, R. *The Psychoanalysis of Organisations*, Tavistock, London, 1978.

Bowen, M. *Family Therapy in Clinical Practice*, Jason Aronson, New York, 1978.

Bowlby, J. 'The Study and Reduction of Group Tensions in the Family', *Human Relations*, **2** (1949), 121–131.
Attachment and Loss. Vol. 1: Attachment, Hogarth Press, London, 1967.

Attachment and Loss. Vol. II: Separation, Anxiety and Anger, Hogarth Press, London, 1973.

Attachment and Loss. Vol. III: Sadness and Depression, Hogarth Press, London, 1980.

A Secure Base: Clinical Applications of Attachment Theory, Tavistock, London, 1988.

Broderick, C. B. and Schrader, S. 'The History of Professional Marriage and Family Therapy', in Gurman, A. and Kniskern, D. *The Handbook of Family Therapy*, Brunner/Mazel, New York, 1981.

Burnham, J. *Family Therapy: First Steps Towards A Systemic Approach*, Tavistock, London, 1986.

Campbell, D. and Draper, R. (eds) *Applications of Systemic Family Therapy: The Milan Approach*, Grune and Stratton, London, 1985.

Caplan, G. *Principles of Preventive Psychiatry*, Tavistock, London, 1964.

The Theory and Practice of Mental Health Consultation, Basic Books, New York, 1970.

Capra, F. *The Turning Point: Science, Society and The Rising Culture*, Wildwood, London, 1982.

Christ, J. 'Comment on "A Passing Glance at the Therapeutic Community in 1964" by Maxwell Jones', in *International Journal of Group Psychotherapy*, 5, **15** (1965).

Clark, D. H. *Social Therapy in Psychiatry*, Penguin, Harmondsworth, 1974.

Comfort, A. *The Joy of Sex*, Quartet, London, 1972.

Cooklin, A. 'Family Therapy in the British Context: Cultural Reflections in Practice,' *Family Process*, **17** (1978), 99–105.

Crawshay-Williams, R. *Russell Remembered*, Oxford University Press, 1970.

Curry, A. E. 'Large Therapeutic Groups: A Critique and Appraisal of Selected Literature' *International Journal of Group Psychotherapy*, 536, **17** (1967).

Dicks, H. V. *Marital Tensions*, Routledge and Kegan Paul, London, 1967.

Dowling, E. and Osborne, E. (eds) *The Family and the School: A Joint Systems Approach to Problems With Children*, Routledge, London, 1985.

Eliade, M. *Shamanism: Archaic Techniques of Ecstacy*, Princeton University Press, 1972.

Erikson, E. *Identity, Youth and Crisis*, Faber, London, 1968.

Ezriel, H. 'A Psychoanalytic Approach to Group Treatment', *British Journal of Medical Psychology*, 23, **59** (1950).

Falloon, I. 'The Small Group Experience in Family Therapy Training', *Group Analysis, 9* (1976), 36–38.

Foulkes, E. 'The Origins and Development of Group Analysis' in T. Lear (ed.) *Spheres of Group Analysis*, Institute of Group Analysis, 1984.

Foulkes, S. H. *Introduction to Group Analytic Psychotherapy*, Heinemann, London, 1948. Reissued by Karnac (Maresfield), 1983.

Therapeutic Group Analysis, Allen and Unwin, London, 1964. Reissued by Karnac (Maresfield), 1984.

Group-Analytic Psychotherapy: Method and Principles, Gordon and Breach, London, 1975. Reissued by Karnac (Maresfield), 1986.

Foulkes, S. H. and Anthony, E. J. *Group Psychotherapy: The Psychoanalytic Approach*, Penguin, Harmondsworth, 1957. Reissued by Karnac (Maresfield), 1984.

Freud, A. *The Ego and The Mechanisms of Defence*, Hogarth Press, London, 1976.

Fromm, E. *The Crisis of Psychoanalysis*, Penguin, Harmondsworth, 1970. Beyond the Chains of Illusion, Abacus, London, 1980.

Golembiewski, R. and Blumberg, A. *Sensitivity Training and The Laboratory Approach*, Peacock Publishers, Illinois, 1970.

Gorrell Barnes, G. *Working with Families*, Macmillan, London, 1984.

Gosling, R., Miller, D., Turquet, P. M. and Woodhouse, D. *The Use of Small Groups in Training*, Codicote, London, 1967.

Greenberg, J. and Mitchell, S. *Object Relations in Psychoanalytic Theory*, Harvard University Press, Cambridge Mass., and London, 1983.

Groesbeck, C. J. and Taylor, B. 'The Psychiatrist as Wounded Physician', *American Journal of Psychiatry*, **37** (1977), 131–139.

Gurman, A. S. and Kniskern, D. P. 'Behavioural Marriage Therapy: A Psychodynamic-Systems Analysis and Technique', *Family Process* 1978, **17**, 121–138.

(eds) *The Handbook of Family Therapy*, Brunner/Mazel, New York 1981.

Halifax, J. *Shaman: The Wounded Healer*, Thames and Hudson, London, 1982.

Harrington, J. 'Much Ado About Milieu', *Laval Medical*, 814, **41** (1970).

Heimann, P. 'On Counter-Transference', *International Journal of Psycho-Analysis*, **31** (1950), 81–84.

Hinshelwood, B. *What Happens In Groups*, Free Association Books, London, 1988.

Hinshelwood, R. D. and Manning, N. (eds), *Therapeutic Communities*, Routledge and Kegan Paul, London, 1979.

Howells, J. *Theory and Practice of Family Psychiatry*, Brunner/Mazel, New York, 1971.

Irvine, E. 'The Use of Small Group Discussions in the Teaching of Human Relations and Mental Health', *British Journal of Psychiatric Social Work*, **5** (1959).

Jaques, E. 'Social Systems as a Defence Against Persecutory and Depressive Anxiety', in *New Directions in Psycho-Analysis*, ed. Klein M. Heimann, P., and Money-Kirle, R., Tavistock, 1955. Reissued by Karnac (Maresfield), 1977.

Jay, M. *The Dialectical Imagination*, Heinemann, London, 1973.

Jones, M. *Social Psychiatry*, Tavistock, London, 1952.

Social Psychiatry in Practice, Penguin, Harmondsworth, 1968.

Maturation of the Therapeutic Community: An Organic Approach to Health and Mental Health, Human Sciences Press, New York, 1976.

The Process of Change, Routledge and Kegan Paul, London, 1982.

'A Passing Glance at the Therapeutic Community in 1964', *International Journal of Group Psychotherapy*, **5**, 15 (1965).

Jung, C. G. *The Practice of Psychotherapy*, Collected Works, *Vol. 16*, Routledge and Kegan Paul, London, 1954.

Kennard, D. *An Introduction To Therapeutic Communities*, Routledge and Kegan Paul, London, 1983.

Kets de Vries, M. F. R. *Organizational Paradoxes: Clinical Approaches To Management*, Tavistock, London, 1980.

Kets de Vries, M. R. F. and Miller, D. *The Neurotic Organisation*, Jossey Bass, San Francisco and London, 1987.

Kohon, G. *The British School of Psychoanalysis: The Independent Tradition*, Free Association Books, London, 1986.

Korzybski, A. *General Semantics*, Science Press, Lancaster Pennsylvania, 1933.

Kreeger, L. *The Large Group: Dynamics and Therapy*, Constable, London, 1975.

Lawton, H. 'The Myth of Altruism,' *Journal of Psychohistory*, *Vol. 10 No. 3* (1983) 389–395.

Lear, T. *Spheres of Group Analysis*, Institute of Group Analysis, London, 1984.

Lewis, J. M., Beavers, W. R., Gossett, J. T. and Phillips, V.A. *No Single Thread: Psychological Health in Family Systems*, Brunner/Mazel, New York, 1976.

Lewis, J. M. *How's Your Family*, Brunner/Mazel, New York, 1979.

Le Guin, U. *The Wizard of Earthsea*, Puffin Penguin, Harmondsworth, 1971.

Main, T. 'The Ailment', in Barnes, E. (ed.), *Psychosocial Nursing*, Tavistock, London, 1968.

'The Hospital as a Therapeutic Institution' in Barnes, E., ibid.

de Maré, P. 'Michael Foulkes and the Northfield Experiment' in Pines, M. (ed.) *The Evolution of Group Analysis*, Routledge and Kegan Paul, London, 1983.

Marks, I. 'Management of sexual disorders', in Leitenberg, H. (ed.), *Handbook of Behaviour Modification*, Appleton-Century-Crofts, New York, 1968.

Menninger, R. W. 'The Impact of Group Relations Conferences on Organisational Growth', in *International Journal of Group Psychotherapy*, 415, **221** (1972).

Menzies Lyth, I. E. P. 'The Functioning of Social Systems as a Defense Against Anxiety', Tavistock Pamphlet No. 3, 1961 and in *Selected Essays: Containing Anxiety In Institutions*, Free Association Books, London, 1988.

Miller, E. J. (ed.) *Task and Organisation*, John Wiley, Chichester, 1978.

Mitchell, T. R. *People In Organisations*, McGraw-Hill, Singapore, 1982.

Pines, M. 'Training In Dynamic Aspects Of Psychotherapy' in Varma, V. (ed.) *Psychotherapy Today*, Constable, London, 1974.

'Psychoanalysis and Group Analysis', *Group Analysis*, 11, 1 (1978) 8–20.

'Group-Analytic Psychotherapy of the Borderline Patient', *Group Analysis*, 11, 2 (1978).

(ed.) *The Evolution of Group Analysis*, Routledge and Kegan Paul, London, 1983.

Pines, M. and Rafaelson, L. *The Individual and The Group: Boundaries and Interrelations*, Plenum, London, 1982.

Paul, N. 'The role of Mourning and Empathy in Conjoint Marital Therapy' in Zuk, G. and Boszormenyi-Nagy, I. (eds), *Family Therapy and Disturbed Families*, Science and Behaviour Books, Palo Alto, 1967.

Rice, A. K. *Learning for Leadership*, Tavistock Press, London, 1965.

Rioch, M. J. 'Group Relations: Rationale and Techniques', *International Journal of Group Psychotherapy*, 340, 20 (1970).

Robertson, J. *Young Children in Hospital*, Tavistock, London, 1970.

Robertson, J. and Robertson, J. 'Young Children in Brief Separation: a Fresh Look' *Psychoanalytic Study of the Child*, 26 (1971), 264–315.

Rosenberg, P. and Chilgren, R. 'Sex Education Discussion Groups in a Medical Setting', *International Journal of Group Psychotherapy*, 23 (1973), 23–30.

Rutter, M. *Maternal Deprivation Reassessed*, Penguin, Harmondsworth, 1972.

Rutter, M. et. al. *Fifteen Thousand Hours: Secondary Schools and Their Effects on Children*, Open Books, London, 1979.

Schermer, V. 'Interactive Concepts in Psychoanalytic Developmental Psychology', in Pines, M. and Rafaelson, L. (eds), *The Individual and The Group: Boundaries and Interrelations, Vol. 1*.

Schiff, S. B. and Glassman, S. M. 'Large and Small Group Therapy in a State Mental Health Centre' in *International Journal of Group Psychotherapy*, 150, 19 (1969).

Schumacher. *Small Is Beautiful*, Blond and Briggs, London, 1973.

A Guide To The Perplexed, Abacus, London, 1978.

Shannon, C. E. and Weaver, W. *The Mathematical Theory of Communication*, University of Illinois Press, 1963.

Slavson, S. R. *Child Centred Group Guidance of Parents*, International University Press, New York, 1958.

Stauble, W. J. 'Evaluation of Psychiatric Services', *Journal of Canadian Psychiatric Association*, 197, 16 (1971).

Treacher, A. and Carpenter, J. (eds) *Using Family Therapy*, Blackwells, 1984.

Von Neumann, J. and Morganstern, D. *Theory of Games and Economic Behaviour*, Princeton University Press, 1953.

Wiener, N. *Cybernetics*, MIT Press and John Wiley, 1961.

Welwood, J. (ed.) *Awakening The Heart: East West Approaches to*

Psychotherapy And The Healing Relationship, New Science Library, Boulder, and Routledge and Kegan Paul, London, 1983.

Whiffen, R. and Byng-Hall, J. (eds) *Family Therapy Supervision: Recent Developments in Practice*, Academic Press, London, 1982.

Will, D. and Wrate, M. *Integrated Family Therapy: A Problem-Centred Psychodynamic Approach*, Tavistock, London, 1985.

Winnicott, D. W. *Therapeutic Consultations in Child Psychiatry*, Hogarth Press, London, 1971.

Wynne, L. 'Foreword', in Gurman A. and Kniskern, D. (eds) *The Handbook of Family Therapy*, Brunner/Mazel, New York, 1981.

Yalom, I. D. *The Theory and Practice of Group Psychotherapy*, Basic Books, New York, 1975.

AUTHOR AND
SUBJECT INDEXES

Author Index

Subject Index